Blueprint ONE

Teacher's Book

Brian Abbs
Ingrid Freebairn

With Liz Waters

R. P.

SPRING GROVE

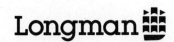

Longman Group UK Limited
Longman House, Burnt Mill, Harlow,
Essex CM20 2JE, England
and Associated Companies throughout the world.

First published 1990
Third impression 1990

Set in 10/10.5 point Times

Printed and bound in Great Britain
by Courier International Ltd, Tiptree, Essex

ISBN 0 582 06662 X

Contents

Introduction

The course   1

The needs of the students   1
1 The need to communicate effectively
2 The need to be familiar with the language systems
3 The need for challenge
4 The need to take on more responsibility for their own learning
5 The need for cross-cultural awareness

Description of the course   1
1 Students' Book
2 Class Cassettes
3 Workbook
4 Student Cassette
5 Teacher's Book

Special features of the Students' Book   2
1 Preview
2 Grammar and Communication Focus
3 Speechwork
4 Fluency
5 Check
6 Learning to learn
7 Language review

Methodology of Blueprint One   3
1 Speaking
2 Listening
3 Grammar
4 Vocabulary
5 Reading
6 Writing
7 Dialogues
8 Speechwork
9 Roleplay
10 Using the board
11 Repetition and choral practice
12 Questioning patterns
13 Pair work
14 Group work
15 Making mistakes
16 Correction of written work
17 Alternative ways of using the material

Abbreviations used in the Teacher's Book   7

Lesson notes   **8**

Grammar index   **114**

Vocabulary and expressions   **117**

Workbook tapescript   **122**

Workbook key   **131**

Introduction

The course

Blueprint One is the first book of a course for young adult and adult students of English as a foreign language. It provides approximately 100 to 120 hours of work. The course consists of a Students' Book, a Workbook, a Teacher's Book, a set of Class Cassettes and a separate Student Cassette, linked to the Workbook.

Blueprint One is suitable for beginners and for those who have a limited knowledge of English. Because of the influence of English as a major world language, the course assumes that few students will be complete beginners. Most beginners nowadays know quite a few words and expressions through advertising, pop music, films and TV, even though they may not have had any formal instruction.

The needs of the students

Students in the 1990s live in a world where political, economic and cultural barriers are rapidly disappearing. An ability to communicate in English with speakers of other languages is no longer a luxury but a necessity in life. When it comes to learning the language in a classroom with a teacher and a textbook, we believe there are certain needs which all beginner students share.

1 The need to communicate effectively

To be able to understand and use the language simply and effectively is the prime need of the beginner. Students need to know that the language they are going to learn will enable them to communicate their needs, ideas and opinions. Motivation at this early stage comes from knowing that language activities in the classroom are at all times meaningful and aimed at real-life communication.

2 The need to be familiar with the language systems

When starting to learn a new language, students need time to study and absorb new grammar. They need to be familiar with the basic grammatical systems of English before they feel that they can communicate successfully. This means that there has to be access not only to grammatical information and explanations on usage, but also to exercises which are specifically focussed on grammatical accuracy.

3 The need for challenge

For motivation to be sustained, students need to be continually challenged, either linguistically or intellectually, through texts, activities and tasks. Students easily lose concentration if they are allowed to be passive, or if the lessons are too easy or dull. Even at beginners' level, the subject matter must engage the students' minds and challenge them to think.

4 The need to take on more responsibility for their own learning

Learning can be more effective when learners take the initiative and have some control over their own learning. Students who are responsible for their own learning can continue to learn outside the classroom and apply their learning strategies to other subjects. However, as most students will be used to the teacher making decisions and controlling the learning, they will need training and help to get the confidence to become more independent in the classroom.

5 The need for cross-cultural awareness

With new possibilities of international access and the growth of global awareness, students today need more from their English course than a language syllabus and a vocabulary list. They need to extend their knowledge of other countries both within and without the English-speaking world. An awareness of how people in other parts of the world live and behave broadens intellectual horizons and enhances international understanding and cooperation.

Description of the course

1 Students' Book

A typical sequence of units in Blueprint One is as follows:
Preview Units 1–5, Unit 1, Unit 2, Unit 3, Unit 4, Unit 5, Fluency Units 1–5, Check Units 1–5, Learning to learn.

To give students a feeling of rapid progress, the Students' Book is divided into forty short teaching units. These units provide material for two 45 to 50-minute lessons. The focus of the units may be grammatical, communicative or lexical depending on the learning point. The forty units are grouped in eight sections of five units each. (The contents of the first section is listed above.)

1

Each of the sections is preceded by a 'Preview', which contextualises the language and gives the students a clear indication of the learning points to be covered in the following five units. The 'Fluency' section which follows the five units gives students an opportunity to practise the language of the preceding units in new contexts with a clear focus on communication. The 'Check' section enables students to test and monitor their progress in a more formal way. The cycle of five units ends with a short 'Learning to learn' section, which gives students advice and techniques on how to make the most of their learning situation.

At the end of the Students' Book there is a unit-by-unit Vocabulary list and a Language review which summarises the main grammatical systems covered in the course.

2 Class Cassettes

To help students understand spoken English, there is a set of class cassettes containing the recorded material from the Students' Book. These consist of the Preview dialogues (an extended version of the Preview dialogues printed in the Students' Book), the listening comprehension passages and the Speechwork exercises. The cassettes are an essential accompaniment to the course in that they provide exposure to a range of native and non-native speakers through dialogue, and both scripted and authentic listening passages.

3 Workbook

The Students' Book is accompanied by a Workbook to give students extra practice and to build their confidence. Each Workbook unit is linked to its corresponding unit in the Students' Book. It provides extra practice of important grammar, communication and vocabulary areas, as well as including simple reading texts and special exercises to develop the writing skill. All the exercises are clearly labelled in sections, e.g. Grammar, Vocabulary, Communication, Writing.

The Workbook also provides a regular Listening and Speechwork section after every five units. This contains the exercises which accompany the Student Cassette (see below).

4 Student Cassette

Speechwork is often neglected in the classroom for more 'important' work and is in many ways better suited to individual practice. The personal Student Cassette gives students a much-needed opportunity to concentrate on their own specific oral/aural problems, using the exercises in the Listening and speechwork sections of the workbook.

The cassette contains simple listening comprehension material, oral exercises and speechwork. The listening comprehension material is scripted and slightly easier than in the Students' Book, in order to encourage students to feel they can understand natural English. The oral exercises provide drills to practise structural and vocabulary items, and to improve intonation, whilst the speechwork exercises include the major features of word stress, sentence stress and pronunciation appropriate to the beginners' level.

Listening in the classroom can be difficult for some learners, so allowing them to work on their own and at their own pace can help them develop greater confidence.

5 Teacher's Book

The Teacher's Book contains an introduction to and description of the course, a guide to general teaching procedures and unit-by-unit lesson notes. The lesson notes include:
– detailed advice on how to handle the material
– tapescripts of the recorded material for the Students' Book
– keys to the Check sections
– suggestions for extra activities

At the end of the Teacher's Book are the tapescripts of the recorded material for the Workbook, plus a grammar index and an alphabetical vocabulary list with phonetic transcriptions.

Special features of the Students' Book

1 Preview

Regular Preview sections precede each segment of five units. The Preview sections introduce and prepare the students for the main grammatical, communicative or lexical areas which are to be developed and practised in the following units.

The Previews are presented in the form of a photo-story dialogue. They provide human interest by presenting people who live, work or study in contemporary Britain, but whose daily activities could take place anywhere in the world. The two main characters are Laura, a young American student on a short study visit to the University of York, and Adam, a young man who works in a travel agency.

The photographs are located in and around the city of York. They are designed to give background and authenticity to the language as well as to generate other types of language work, like vocabulary building and discussion of cultural differences.

Each photo-story is recorded in a slightly extended version to provide listening practice and is accompanied by comprehension questions.

At the end of each Preview section is a list of the learning objectives for the following five units. These are expressed in functional terms, e.g. 'In the next five units you will learn how to tell the time, talk about the weather ...'

2 Grammar and Communication Focus

In each unit, clearly labelled Focus boxes contain the main points of grammar or communication for that unit, with special notes highlighting particular aspects of usage. These Focus boxes are accompanied, where appropriate, by special inductive questions and tasks to help students discover the rules for themselves. The sections usually occur after initial presentation and practice of the language point but their positioning should be seen as flexible. Teachers may prefer to deal with the Focus box at the end of the lesson or even occasionally at the presentation stage.

3 Speechwork

Almost every unit has a clearly labelled speechwork exercise. These are specifically linked to the language point being practised and include simple exercises on word stress, sentence stress, elision and sound/spelling correspondence. In most cases students complete a task before listening to the cassette and repeating the words or phrases.

Speechwork also receives extensive coverage in the regular sections in the Workbook, which are accompanied by a Student Cassette. The syllabus includes combined language and intonation practice in the form of Oral Exercises, special practice of word and sentence stress, and pronunciation practice of key vowel and consonant sounds.

4 Fluency

The Fluency sections encourage freer use of language skills and draw together the language from the previous five units within a common theme. They place emphasis on producing fluent rather than accurate speech and are designed to give the students an opportunity to consolidate their learning and to reflect on the progress they have made.

5 Check

These sections provide students with a set of exercises to revise and test the most important grammatical and functional items from the preceding five units. Keys to the Check exercises are in the Teacher's Book, with an indication of the number of marks available for each exercise. Teachers and students will be able to use the Check section as useful feedback to monitor progress and provide guidance for remedial work.

6 Learning to learn

Regular Learning to learn sections are included after each Check section. They contain suggestions aimed at helping students to become good language learners. The types of areas covered include storing and learning vocabulary, learning grammar and making mistakes. Suggestions for handling these sections are included in the detailed teaching notes.

7 Language review

At the back of the Students' Book there is a short reference grammar which presents in tabular form the main grammatical systems contained in the Students' Book, with accompanying notes on usage. Students should feel free to refer to this at any stage during the course.

Methodology of Blueprint One

The teaching notes for each unit offer detailed advice on how to handle the material step by step. The following notes provide an outline of the overall methodological approach adopted in Blueprint One.

1 Speaking

Learning to speak a language is the most important aim of most language learners. As student talking time in class can be short, every opportunity should be taken to provide speaking practice. In Blueprint One, students are encouraged to communicate from the very first lesson. Initially the students follow models in controlled pair work exercises but they are later encouraged to use the language more freely in short group-work tasks and roleplays. As well as pair work and group work, *About you* questions (see Unit 17, Ex. 8) play an important part. These questions give students an opportunity to relate the content of the lesson to their own lives and experiences.

Students also get fluency practice in the Fluency sections, where several learning items are combined, and in the range of games and activities suggested in the Teacher's Book under the heading *Extra activities* at the end of each unit.

2 Listening

For many students, understanding the spoken language is a major source of difficulty. Listening practice which provides exposure to native speaker language is an important component in any language course. Students need to be given the competence to cope with material which is a little beyond their productive level and not be discouraged if they do not understand the meaning of every word.

In Blueprint One the listening passages are a mixture of scripted and authentic recordings. Students listen for a variety of purposes: for gist, for information, for stress and pronunciation models, and sometimes to recognise specific usage.

Many listening tasks lead on naturally from a spoken exercise (see Unit 7, Ex. 7) but others, which deal with separate topics, need special preparation. These are usually preceded by a *Before you listen* section (see Unit 29, Ex. 6). Otherwise, suggestions for preparation are given in the detailed teaching notes for each unit. This preparation might involve students predicting the content of the passage or raising questions which might be answered when they listen. Sometimes it is sensible to isolate difficult words and expressions and to check that students know what they mean before they listen.

3 Grammar

The understanding of grammar occupies an important position in the course. The word 'grammar' covers a wide range of learning points and it is unwise to suggest that there is a 'best way' of learning grammar. Different techniques are suggested for different types of grammar points. Some grammar points can be learnt in passing; others have to be learnt by heart (e.g. irregular past tense forms, preposition usage); while others (e.g. verb tenses) have to be studied and thoroughly practised before students can produce the language confidently and accurately in new contexts.

In Blueprint One, students first encounter new structures briefly when they are contextualised in the Preview section which precedes each five units. The structures are then reintroduced and fully practised in the following units. After controlled practice, students are given an opportunity to study the rules in a Grammar Focus box which contains paradigms and important notes on the structures. There is often a task or question attached to check if students have absorbed the rule (see Unit 1 Focus box). The final stage of the oral cycle of a lesson is an exercise which gets students to use the new language in a purposeful way – whether it be speaking or writing.

4 Vocabulary

Vocabulary occupies a central position in Blueprint One. The learning of new words is considered to be of equal importance to the learning of grammar. Problems in communication arise more frequently from errors in vocabulary than from errors in grammar.

Blueprint One introduces a core vocabulary of 1100 words. These words represent the most commonly used words and phrases in English and include closed sets (e.g. days of the week, seasons, colours); topic-related vocabulary (e.g. weather: *sunny, cloudy, foggy*); collocations (e.g. *bread and butter, fish and chips*); fixed phrases (e.g. greetings, leave-taking phrases); situational utterances (e.g. *Can I help you?*) and some compounds and multi-words (e.g. *telephone number, wash up, sit down*). At the back of the Students' Book there is a unit-by-unit list of active vocabulary and expressions which students can refer to when revising.

In the early stages the meaning of new words may be best presented by drawing, pointing, miming or giving examples. There is no 'right way'. The choice of technique will depend on the type of word, the context in which it occurs and whether you can use translation or not. When reading texts, students should get into the habit of guessing new words from the context before looking them up in a dictionary. At this stage, a good active study dictionary which gives information on usage as well as meaning is the most useful learning aid for the students.

To develop good study habits students should always be encouraged to keep a notebook for new words. These can be listed in several ways: as they occur in the lesson, in word fields, in grammatical categories (e.g nouns, verbs, adjectives), or alphabetically. In some cases, e.g. when prepositions are involved, students should add a sentence containing the new word in context.

It is essential that new vocabulary and expressions are continually recycled. One way of doing this is to use flashcards of individual words and expressions for quick checks at the beginning of lessons. These flashcards can also be used for games and for building dialogues.

5 Reading

Reading texts in the early stages of a language course can serve a number of useful purposes: they can present new language; they can consolidate; they can provide models for writing; they can inform and they can stimulate discussion and oral work. But an often neglected benefit is that they can motivate. Beginners find it very rewarding when they realise how much they can understand of a relatively challenging text. It is also important to remember that for many students, reading texts are often the only readily available source of language input.

The reading texts in Blueprint One are a mixture of specially written and authentic texts. Many texts are preceded by a *Before you read* section (see Unit 27, Ex. 4) which prepares students for the content and vocabulary in the text. Comprehension questions concentrate mainly on reading for important information. Students are encouraged to guess the meaning of new words before looking them up in the dictionary.

6 Writing

Writing is not only an aid to consolidating new language but is a meaningful activity in itself. The process of writing and of organising one's thoughts coherently is as important and valuable as the final piece of writing.

In Blueprint One writing for communication is encouraged from the very start. The course includes many suggestions for simple writing activities, ranging from controlled sentences (Units 1 and 6), letters (Unit 9), postcards (Unit 15), notes to other students (Unit 23), to narrative paragraphs (Unit 25) and simple biographies (Unit 40). All writing exercises are guided either by a full model or by a suggested framework. Special attention is given to conjunctions and linking devices (see Unit 12).

All the writing tasks should first be prepared orally to help students with the organisation of their writing, and special guidance is given in the teaching notes.

When planning lessons it is vital to allow adequate class time for this stage. Time should also be allowed for students to check their own work and identify any problems with which they would like help. (See Section 16 below.)

7 Dialogues

There are three main types of dialogue in Blueprint One: Preview dialogues, gapped dialogues and complete dialogues. The purpose of the dialogues in the Preview photo-story is to contextualise new language and to provide listening practice. The dialogues which occur in the body of the teaching material are either gapped (Unit 2, Unit 36) and students are asked to listen for key phrases, or complete and students are asked to listen to an almost identical dialogue (Unit 17) and note the differences. The dialogues are then used as models for roleplay. Students are not asked specifically to listen and repeat dialogues, so none of the dialogues are paused. However, many teachers find this useful speechwork practice and can pause the dialogues, themselves in the classroom.

8 Speechwork

The *Speechwork* sections in the Students' Book of Blueprint One are linked to the particular learning focus of the unit. The recorded exercises cover recognition and practice of pronunciation, word and sentence stress, weak stress, emphatic stress, sound to spelling correspondence and intonation.

In the classroom, guidance can be given to stress by beating out the rhythm of a sentence during choral repetition, and by underlining or using capital letters for stressed syllables, e.g. *BEAUtiful* or *beautiful* when writing new words on the board.

Intonation can be shown in sentences by using arrows, e.g.

Who's speaking?

When practising intonation, 'back-chaining' – where the sentence is built up in parts, starting from the end – can be an effective technique, e.g. *speaking? – who's speaking?*

A regular section on Speechwork, based on a syllabus of stress and pronunciation, is included in the Workbook. (See Workbook and Student Cassette page 2 above.)

9 Roleplay

Roleplay is an ideal way of providing useful fluency practice, provided that students are not confused by instructions which are too complicated, or frightened off by roles which are too unfamiliar. In Blueprint One, students are only asked to play roles with which they can readily identify.

Cues for the roleplay chains are expressed in simple language and should not need to be translated. Examples can be elicited from the students before starting.

For the freer roleplays, where rolecards are provided for Students A and B, students should be given time to read through the situation and instructions carefully, and to prepare their roles. Students who finish quickly can write down their conversations.

10 Using the board

Presentation of new language on the board is extremely important for the focus it gives to the lesson. It draws together students' attention and enables the teacher to control practice effectively. Line drawings can quickly explain a new word and substitution tables can show a grammatical pattern. Information should be arranged in sections, e.g. new vocabulary in one area and examples of key language structures in another. An additional area should be left free for spontaneous examples, drawings and game scores.

11 Repetition and choral practice

Repetition of new language can help to reinforce a sound or structural pattern, and repeating in chorus can help students to gain confidence before being asked to perform individually. The occasions when choral practice may be particularly useful are indicated throughout the teaching notes. The different patterns for this are:
a) whole class
b) half the class at a time
c) vertical or horizontal rows
d) groups
e) individuals

12 Question patterns

Many new structures involve a question and answer routine, e.g.

A: What are you going to do after class?
B: I'm going to have a cup of coffee.

When establishing a new structure, it is useful to work through a few examples of an exercise. At this point it is important to be able to draw on a variety of question and answer patterns, e.g.

a) Teacher to self (T–T)
b) Teacher to student (T–S)
c) Student to teacher (S–T)
d) Student to student (S–S)
e) Student 1 to Student 2 to Student 3, etc. in a chain (S1–S2–S3)

13 Pair work

Many of the exercises, activities and roleplays in Blueprint One require students to work in pairs. The advantages of pair work are now widely accepted. It increases the students' talking time dramatically and helps to release tension. It is neither possible nor necessary to correct each student. With plenty of practice, major mistakes tend to disappear. If there is an uneven number in the class, the teacher can either make up a pair or ask some students to work in threes. Pairs should be rearranged regularly to avoid boredom.

14 Group work

Group work, if used selectively, has several advantages: it offers students of mixed abilities a natural context for working together; shy students get a chance to talk informally; confident students get a chance to shine and develop their skills by acting as reporters and group secretaries; it offers a change of pace to a lesson; and, initially, it helps students to get to know each other. However, many students show resistance to group work. They feel that they are not learning English if their class mates are talking imperfect English. For this reason, group work in Blueprint One is suggested only for specifically group-oriented activities (see Unit 23, Ex. 7) and for certain types of games.

Groups can be formed either by the teacher or by the students themselves. Different ways of forming groups can be based on position in the classroom, alphabetical order of names, colour of clothes, etc.

When setting up group work, always give clear instructions and set a time limit for each task. The students should appoint a group reporter if the task requires it. When group work is in progress, it is best to monitor unobtrusively and contribute only when asked. Mistakes can be noted and pointed out when the activity is finished, or at a later date.

15 Making mistakes

Making mistakes is an important and positive part of learning a language. Only by experimenting with the language and receiving feedback can students begin to sort out how the language works. In general students like to be corrected, but it can be off-putting and demotivating to be stopped in free conversation whenever a mistake is made.

In controlled practice, where emphasis should be on accurate production, correction can be immediate. In roleplays and discussions, where emphasis is on communication and conversational fluency, students should not be interrupted. However, it is important to note any recurring or important mistakes for later comment and correction.

16 Correction of written work

Students' written work can be corrected in a variety of ways – not always by the teacher. Answers to exercises can be checked orally in a chain round the class, or students can correct their own or their partners' answers by using a key. For correcting written paragraphs, it is sometimes helpful to select a student's work (or parts of different students' work) and write it on the board (without naming the student) for the class to see and correct together.

Students need to be reminded to check their written work systematically, for meaning, grammar and spelling before handing it in. One way of doing this is for students to read their work aloud either to themselves or to their partners. Alternatively, students can be asked to underline or note in the margin any points or sentences they are unsure of, and where they would like the teacher to comment. In this way, the correction of their homework becomes a more personal dialogue between teacher and student.

For longer compositions, it is best to collect in and mark or comment on students' work individually. You may sometimes wish to write in corrections but it is generally better to get students to discover their own mistakes by using symbols (e.g. *vt = verb tense*) which both you and the students understand. In the Workbook for Blueprint One, there are several exercises which instruct students on the interpretation of symbols when correcting written work.

17 Alternative ways of using the material

It is important to experiment occasionally with the teaching sequence and methodology suggested in the Students' Book, not just for the sake of variety but also as a means of finding the best way of using the material in your own situation. For example, some teachers will want to use their own presentation of a language item before allowing students to look at the book.

Occasionally it may seem preferable to leave reference to the Grammar Focus boxes until the end of a lesson, while at other times it can be helpful to discuss the grammar point at the beginning of a lesson. Likewise, you can provide variety by starting a lesson with vocabulary work or a reading text and go on to structure practice later (see Unit 28). Exercises which are suggested as pair work can sometimes work just as well as individual or group work.

Abbreviations used in the Teacher's Book

T	TEAcher
S	Student
T–S	Teacher speaks to student
S–S	Student speaks to student
S1–S2	First student speaks to second student and so on
L1	Native language
OHP	Overhead projector
OHT	Overhead transparency
Ex.	Exercise
e.g.	for example
etc.	etcetera
i.e.	that is

Lesson notes

The first lesson

1 Preparation

AIDS
As well as a board and a cassette player, the following are also useful as general teaching aids:
1 some good bilingual dictionaries
2 maps of the world, the British Isles, the USA, and/or an atlas
3 a pin board display area for notices, students' work, and pictures which relate to the course book topics and themes.

AIMS
1 to break the ice
2 to develop confidence
3 to introduce the course book

2 Breaking the ice

With a newly-formed class, it is important to establish a relaxed and friendly working atmosphere. Many teachers will have their own favourite 'warm-up' activity to get the first lesson off to a good start. A simple idea is to ask each student to make a name tag for their partner.

3 Developing confidence

Ask the students to write down as many English words as they can in sixty seconds. Collect all the words on the board. Students will probably be pleased and surprised by the number of words and phrases they already know.

4 Introducing the course

It is important for students to be familiar with
1 the components of the course (the Students' Book, the Workbook and the Student Cassette)
2 the contents of the Students' Book, especially the resource material at the end of the book.

To encourage this, list the following sections on the board. As you write them, ask students to find the sections in the book.
1 Contents pages
2 Preview Units 6-10
3 Unit 10
4 Fluency Units 6-10
5 Check Units 6-10
6 Vocabulary and expressions index
7 Language review index
8 List of irregular verbs

Then ask students to find the names of the two main characters in the book. Write their names: *Adam* and *Laura*, on the board.

Notes

Some false beginners may be familiar with much of the language in Units 1 to 5. If so, work through Units 1 to 5 rapidly and use the first Fluency and Check units (on pages 13 to 16) to monitor gaps in the students' knowledge. You can also use some of the Extra activities which occur at the end of the teaching notes for each unit.

If you have a class of absolute beginners, you may wish to start with Unit 1 and come back to the Preview afterwards.

PREVIEW Units 1-5

The photographs and the dialogue

Ask students to look at the photographs and the speech bubbles. Ask:
What's his name? (Adam)
What's her name? (Laura)
What's her surname? (Martinelli)
What city does she want to go to? (Paris)
What is the present? (A pen from British Airways)

With false beginners, ask students to find the following in the photographs. Write the words on the board: *a computer, a telephone, a pen, a ticket, a desk, a chair.*

🔲 The tape

Play the tape for the first time and ask students to follow the conversation in their Students' Books. Explain that the conversation on the tape is a slightly expanded version of the printed dialogue. Play the tape again and ask students to 'shadow' the conversation, that is, to speak the words softly at the same time as the speaker on the tape.

TAPESCRIPT
Listen and follow the conversation in your Students' Book.
CHRIS: Good morning, Adam.
ADAM: Morning!
Hello! Can I help you?
LAURA: Yes, I'd like to go to Paris.
ADAM: Right. When would you like to go?
Right. Just a few details. What's your name, please?

LAURA: Martinelli. Laura Martinelli.
ADAM: Martinelli. That's an Italian name.
LAURA: Yes. My parents are Italian, but I'm American.
ADAM: How do you spell 'Martinelli'? With one 'L' or two?
LAURA: Two 'L's.
ADAM: And your address?
LAURA: It's 1, Hull Road, York.
ADAM: Here's your ticket.
LAURA: Thank you.
ADAM: And this is for you.
LAURA: What is it?
ADAM: It's a pen. It's a present from British Airways.
LAURA Oh, thanks. Bye!
ADAM: Bye!

The learning objectives box

Point out the objectives in the box in the bottom right-hand corner of page 2. In a monolingual class, explain the objectives in the students' own language. Then see if students can give examples of each objective in English (see below). In a multilingual class, read out the objectives in English and give the examples yourself.

Introduce yourself and others: *I'm Laura./This is Laura.*
Greet people: *Good morning.*
Talk about nationality: *Are you Italian?*
Identify objects: *It's a pen.*
Give personal information: *I'm nineteen.*
Days of the week: *Monday*, etc.
The alphabet : *A, B, C*, etc.
Colours: *Red, blue, green*, etc.
Numbers: *one, two, three*, etc.

UNIT 1 Names

Suggested lesson break: after the Grammar Focus

> BACKGROUND NOTES
> *The photograph*: This shows a street of medieval houses in York called 'The Shambles'. Originally a street of butchers' shops, the houses were built close together on a narrow street to protect the meat from the sun.
> *Hi!*: An American English expression which is now commonly used in British English as an informal greeting, particularly among young people.

PRESENTATION

Introduce yourself by saying: *Hello! My name's .../ Hello! I'm ...* Ask a student: *What's your name?* Elicit: *My name's/I'm (Anna).*

Exercise 1

Students need a piece of paper and a pen. Ask them to collect and write down the names of approximately ten other students, e.g.
S1: What's your name?
S2: My name's Carlos.
S1: And what's your name?
S3: I'm Natalie.

Exercise 2

Ask students the name of another student.
T: What's his/her name?
S: His/Her name's Carlos/Natalie.

Hold up the main Students' Book photograph in front of the class. Point to Laura and Adam separately and ask: *What's her/his name?* Write the following questions and answers on the board and practise them chorally and individually:

What's your name? My name's (John).
What's his name?   His name's Adam.
What's her name?   Her name's Laura.

Now write on the board:
Names beginning with:
C   S

Names ending with:
A   E   O

Ask students to look at the names on their lists from Exercise 1 and to select names that fit each group.
T: What names begin with C?
S1: Carlos.
S2: Christian.

To establish which are the most common names ask: *Who has the same name?* Then revise *his* and *her* by going round the class asking each student to say his/her partner's name.
T: What's your partner's name?
S1: Her name's Maria.
S2: His name's Jose.

Exercise 3

Ask a student: *What's your mother's name?* Elicit: *Her name's ...* Ask: *What's your father's name?* Elicit: *His name's ...* Draw a stick figure of a boy on the board and write under it: *His name's Antonio.* Then draw a woman and write: *This is Antonio's mother. Her name's Maria.*

Underline the possessive adjectives and remind students that they refer to the gender of the possessor not of the object or person possessed. Point out the use of the genitive apostrophe *'s* in *Antonio's.*

Ask students to copy the chart from their Students' Books into their notebooks. Copy a similar chart on the board leaving enough space to write in the names. Check that students know the names of the family members: *mother,*

father, brother and *sister,* used in the chart. Draw a simple family tree on the board if necessary. Practise the pronunciation of the words. Show how Exercise 3 works by asking a student the question:
T: What's your mother's/father's/brother's name?
S: Her/His name's Martha/George.

Write the student's own name under *Student 1* and fill in the name of the mother or father.

	Mother	Father	Brother	Sister
Student 1 *(Natalie)*	*Martha*			
Student 2				
Student 3				

Students question three different students and fill in their charts. For students who don't have the full quota of family members, you may like to teach: *I haven't got a brother/sister* or *My father's/mother's name was ...*

Exercise 4

Ask one or two students to tell the class about the names in their charts. Give an example using the chart on the board, e.g. *Student 1 is Natalie. Her mother's name is Martha.*

Check that students are producing the genitive *'s* and the short form *'s (is)*, e.g. *Her mother's name's Ann-Marie.* and **not** ~~Her mother name's Ann-Marie.~~ or ~~Her mother her name is ...~~

Exercise 5

Ask a student: *What's the name of your bank?* Elicit: *It's called (Credit Agricole).* Point out that you cannot say *What's your bank's name?* (because *bank* is an inanimate noun). Refer to the note and point out:
1 In reply to the question *What's the name of ...?* about places or objects, it is correct to say *It's called...* not *Its name is.*
2 *Its* in the phrase *Its name is* is the possessive adjective from *it*, and should not be confused with the verb *to be* in *It's called (Credit Agricole).*

Students now work in pairs using the questions in the book. At the end, check by asking about other local places, e.g.
T: What's the name of your favourite disco/your hairdresser?
S: My favourite disco's called.../It's called...

GRAMMAR FOCUS

Ask students to study the Focus box silently. Ask them to write the equivalents of the pronouns and possessive adjectives in their own language to make them aware of how the two systems relate. Then point out the rules for the possessive form of nouns. (The last rule need not be introduced until the example occurs in Unit 7.)

1 with singular nouns, add an apostrophe + *s*, e.g. *my father's name*
2 with plural nouns, add an apostrophe **after** the *s*, e.g. *my parents' house*
3 with proper names ending in *s* we put an apostrophe after the *s*, e.g. *Carlos' surname*
4 with irregular plural nouns which do not end in *s*, add an apostrophe + *s*, e.g. *my children's names are ...* (Unit 7)

Point out how contractions work (one or more letters are replaced by an apostrophe), e.g *He's = He is* and *You're = You are.* Explain when contractions are used. Try to explain in English, e.g. *When you speak and when you write notes and letters to friends, you say: 'I'm', 'You're', 'He's'. When you write compositions, you write: 'I am', 'You are', 'He is'.* Ask students: *Are there short forms in your language? When do you use them?*

Now ask students to complete the task at the bottom of the Focus box.

SUGGESTED LESSON BREAK

Exercise 6

Ask a student to look at the photographs of the famous people and ask who the first person is, e.g. *Who's that?* Elicit: *It's Mr Gorbachev.* Then point to Picture 7. Ask: *Who's that?* Elicit: *It's Mrs Thatcher.*

Practise *Who's that?* chorally and individually. Explain how *Mr* and *Mrs* are pronounced. You may like to add *Miss* and *Ms* to the list at this stage. Explain that *Ms* is a professional title used by women who do not wish to be identified as either married or single. Point out that we normally say: *Who's that? It's Mr ...* but *Who's he? He's Mr ...*

Ask students to work in pairs, matching the names to the photographs. Check the answers by asking students who the people are.

KEY
1 Mr Gorbachev /'gɔ:bətʃɒf/, the Soviet leader
2 Tom Cruise /kru:z/, an American film actor
3 Paul Hogan /'həʊgən/, an Australian film actor who played the character, 'Crocodile Dundee', in the films of the same name
4 Steffi Graf, a German tennis champion

5 Mother Theresa /təˈreɪzə/, a nun, world-famous for her work with the sick and the poor in India and for her campaign against world poverty and oppression

6 Mike Tyson /ˈtaɪsən/, an American heavyweight boxer

7 Mrs Thatcher /ˈθætʃə/, a British Prime Minister and leader of the Conservative Party

8 Mrs Cory Aquino /əˈkiːnəʊ/, President of the Philippines

Exercise 7 READING

Write the following sentences on the board:
1 What's your name in English? My name's (Anthony) in English.
2 What are you called for short? I'm called (Toni).

Ask the questions of one or two students. Elicit the English versions of their names or the answer *I don't know.* In answer to the second question you may like to teach: *I haven't got a short name.* The students then ask and answer both the questions in pairs. Refer to the photograph of Chris and ask students who she is. (She works in the travel agent's with Adam – see Preview Units 1–5). Students read the texts silently and answer the questions in Exercise 7.

Ask students if there are any names in their own language which are both boys' and girls' names.

Exercise 8 WRITING

Refer back to the Grammar Focus box and remind students about the rules for the use of the genitive apostrophe. Point out the examples of the *s* + apostrophe with plural nouns in *three boys' names* and *three girls' names* in the rubric. Ask them to look back at Exercise 7 and to note all the examples of the genitive apostrophe + *s* with singular nouns.

Read the example sentence aloud and ask students to work in pairs to complete the exercise. Summarise their answers on the board with an alphabetical list of names and their English versions. Finish the exercise by finding out what are some of the most popular names and short names at the moment in the students' own language.

EXTRA ACTIVITIES
1 First names
In advance, collect pictures of four leading world figures and/or their partners, four entertainers and four sports people, making sure you know their full names. Number and label them with their surnames only, e.g. *Mrs Bush* and display them prominently in the classroom. As an individual game, students compete to complete the list of first names, e.g.

s1: What's her first name?
s2: Her first name's Barbara.

2 Name game
Students sort out the jumbled letters below to make some popular names in English.

1 NAN	(Ann)
2 HNJO	(John)
3 ARBABRA	(Barbara)
4 LMIAWIL	(William)
5 TALIZEBEH	(Elizabeth)
6 HACILEM	(Michael)
7 DIRACRH	(Richard)
8 IADAN	(Diana)

UNIT 2 Greetings and goodbyes

Suggested lesson break: after Exercise 4

Exercise 1
Greet the class according to the time of day: *Good morning, everyone!* Elicit: *Good morning!* as the response. Write the exchange on the board, then introduce and practise chorally the other three greetings which begin with *Good ... .* Explain that *Good evening* is a greeting and is used after approximately 5 p.m. in the evening but that *Goodnight* is a form of farewell and is also often addressed to someone who is going to bed.

With a good class, play the tape and ask students to match each conversation with the correct picture. With complete beginners, read through the greetings and exchanges in the eight pictures before playing the tape. Point out that *sir* and its equivalent *madam* are normally used in service situations, e.g. in shops, restaurants and hotels.

TAPESCRIPT
Listen to the conversations and match them with the pictures.

1 MAN: Good evening, ladies and gentlemen! And welcome to tonight's fabulous show.

2 TEACHER: Good morning, everyone.
  CLASS: Good morning, Mrs Jackson.

3 MAN: Luisa let me introduce you, this is Clive Mortimer. Clive, this is Luisa Ferrero.
  LUISA: How do you do!
  CLIVE: How do you do!

4 MRS PORTER: We're leaving now.
  SALLY: O.K. Have a nice evening!
  MR PORTER: Thanks. And the same to you. See you tomorrow.

5 JAN: Roy! What a surprise!
  ROY: Oh, hello Jan. How are you?
  JAN: Fine, thanks. And you?
  ROY: Oh, not too bad.

6 MAN: Good afternoon, sir.
  ALAN: Good afternoon.
  MAN: Can I help you?
  ALAN: Er, well, I'm looking for a jacket.

7 MAN: And that is the end of the story. Off to
          sleep now.
  SAM: Yes.
  MAN: Goodnight, Sam.
  SAM: Night, Dad.
  MAN: Sleep well.

8 WOMAN: Have a nice time.
  MAN: Take care!
  ALL: Goodbye!
  GIRL: Bye! See you on Monday.

Exercise 2

Explain the words *formal* and *informal* with
reference to greetings. Say: *Listen. 'Hello, I'm
John.' This is informal. Now listen again. 'How
do you do? My name is Mr Richardson.' This is
formal.*

Now ask students to look at Picture 6. Ask: *Is it
formal or informal?* (It's formal.) Then ask them
to look at the exchange in Exercise 2. Ask again:
*Is it formal or informal? (*It's informal.*)* Practise
the informal introductions in Exercise 2 and then
ask students to choose a partner and walk around
the class taking it in turns to introduce their
partner informally. Finally, ask them to roleplay
formal introductions (see Picture 6).

Exercise 3

Do not attempt to teach the time or numbers here.
Write on the board (or explain) that:
Morning = 6.00 – 12.00
Afternoon = 12.00 – 17.00
Evening = 17.00 – 21.00

Ask if each time is *morning, afternoon* or
evening. Remind students that *Goodnight* is not
used as a greeting. Now ask students to work in
pairs and to greet each other according to the
times in Exercise 3.

Students can now practise acting out the other
greetings in the pictures in pairs.

COMMUNICATION FOCUS (1)

Refer to the Focus box and ask students to study
the columns of formal and informal greetings.
Practise the shortened informal greetings
Morning! Afternoon! and *Evening!* with a
cheerful manner and ask students to practise the
greetings in Exercise 3 again using the informal
forms this time.

In a multilingual class, ask students how they say
Hi! and *How do you do?* etc. in their own
languages.

Exercise 4

False beginners will probably already know the
days of the week, and will be able to do the
exercise quickly. When they have completed the
exercise, play the tape and practise the
pronunciation of the days of the week, especially
underlining the difference between Tuesday and
Thursday. With complete beginners, you may
wish to play the tape and practise the
pronunciation before students do the reordering
exercise. Point out the elision between the first
and second syllable in *Wednesday* /wenzdi/.
Write the abbreviated forms of the days of the
week on the board: *Mon, Tues, Wed, Thur, Fri,
Sat* and *Sun*. Point out the note on capital letters
with days of the week and ask if the same
punctuation rule applies in the students' own
language.

TAPESCRIPT
Listen and repeat the names of the days of the
week.

Monday Tuesday Wednesday Thursday
Friday Saturday Sunday

SUGGESTED LESSON BREAK

Exercise 5

Ask and answer the questions orally with the
whole class. Then ask different students to write
the answers on the board. Explain briefly that
was is the past form of *is*.

Exercise 6

Students practise saying goodbye using different
days of the week, first chorally and then in pairs.

Exercise 7 SPEECHWORK

To make sure that students understand the
convention of underlining the stressed syllable,
write the example on the board, saying it with an
emphasised stress and underlining the relevant
syllables. Ask students to copy all the phrases
into their notebooks before you play the tape.
Play the tape, then check students' answers,
practising each phrase chorally as you do so.

TAPESCRIPT AND KEY
Listen and underline the stressed syllables or
words.

<u>How</u> do you <u>do</u> He<u>llo</u> <u>How</u> are <u>you</u>
Good <u>morning</u> Good <u>afternoon</u>
<u>Morning</u> Good <u>evening</u> Good <u>night</u>
Good<u>bye</u> <u>See</u> you on <u>Mon</u>day

UNIT 2 / UNIT 3

COMMUNICATION FOCUS (2)

Students should now be able to use both formal and informal expressions with confidence. Ask individual students to 'greet' another student by name using one of the expressions in the box. The second student must respond with the same level of formality.

 Exercise 8 LISTENING

Ask students about the names of the people in the photograph. (Adam and Chris. They will not know Karen.) Then see if they can complete the dialogue in pairs. They can refer to the conversations on the left-hand page to help them. Play the tape for students to check if they are right. Finally, students can read the conversation in pairs and change parts.

TAPESCRIPT AND KEY

Listen and complete the conversation.

CHRIS: Hello, Adam. How are you?
ADAM: I'm fine, thanks. And you?
CHRIS: I'm O.K. Adam, this is Karen, a friend from Leeds.
ADAM: Hello, Karen.
KAREN: Hi!
ADAM: Sorry, Chris, but I must go.
CHRIS: That's O.K.
ADAM: See you on Monday.
CHRIS: O.K. Have a nice afternoon. Bye!
ADAM: Thanks. And the same to you. Bye.

Exercise 9

Arrange the students in groups of three to practise similar conversations.

Exercise 10

Practise the exchange and the variations chorally before the students walk around saying goodbye naturally to each other as they leave the room.

EXTRA ACTIVITIES

1 Days of the week

Ask students to write down the days of the week in the order in which they like them or in the order in which they dislike them. Students then compare their orders.

2 Greetings

In a monolingual class, ask students to say the greeting *Good morning* according to different moods. Give the mood word in the L1, e.g. *happy, sad, angry, excited, depressed, bored.* With a multilingual class, ask students to repeat the different variations on *Good morning* after you. Use mime to get the mood across.

UNIT 3 Nationalities

Suggested lesson break: after Exercise 7

PRESENTATION

Use a large map of the world for students to identify the names of their own country and other countries. Ask: *What country's this?* Elicit: *It's (England).* Ask: *And this?* Teach: *I don't know.*

Exercise 1

Ask students to find their own country on the map in their books. Then ask them to work in pairs to find all the countries listed in Exercise 1. Check the answers using the English alphabet. This initial introduction of some of the letters will help when the complete alphabet is introduced in Unit 4.

KEY

1 Italy = M 2 Argentina = C 3 France = K
4 Greece = N 5 Spain = J 6 Britain = H
7 The USA = A 8 Brazil = B 9 Turkey = D
10 China = F 11 Japan = G 12 The USSR = E
13 Portugal = I 14 West Germany = L

Practise the pronunciation of each country chorally and individually as you check the answers but do not be over-particular about the pronunciation of the countries at this stage. Point out the use of the article with *the USA* (the United States) and *the USSR* (the Soviet Union).

Ask students if they want to know the names of any other countries. Encourage them to ask questions like: *What's this country in English?*

Exercise 2

Ask individual students about each country. Say: *What's the capital of (Italy)?* and elicit the answer: *It's (Rome).* List the capital cities on the board as the students provide them.

KEY

1	Italy	Rome
2	Argentina	Buenos Aires
3	France	Paris
4	Greece	Athens
5	Spain	Madrid
6	Britain	London
7	The USA	Washington D.C.
8	Brazil	Brasilia
9	Turkey	Istanbul
10	China	Beijing/Peking
11	Japan	Tokyo
12	The USSR	Moscow
13	Portugal	Lisbon
14	West Germany	Bonn

Exercise 3

Present the example exchange in the Students' Book taking both sides of the conversation yourself, using your own country of origin. Write the exchange on the board. Point out:
– how to make questions with the verb *to be* using inversion of subject and verb
– that the personal pronoun *you* is the same for both singular and plural in both formal and informal use
– the short answers *Yes, I am* and *No, I'm not.*

Practise each line chorally and individually.

Students then ask and answer the question to each other around the class. If all your students come from the same place, some students may like to pretend that they come from different countries in order to provide variety in this exercise.

Exercise 4 SPEECHWORK

Practise the three patterns chorally, with extra emphasis on the stressed syllable, before playing the tape.

TAPESCRIPT
Which stress pattern can you hear? Listen to these examples.

1 Britain 2 Japan 3 Italy

Now say which pattern you hear. Is it 1, 2, or 3?

KEY
(The patterns are: 1 a two-syllable word with stress on the first syllable; 2 a two-syllable word with stress on the second syllable; 3 a three-syllable word with stress on the first syllable.)
China = 1   Portugal = 3   Turkey = 1
Brazil = 2   Germany = 3

Exercises 5 and 6

To introduce the new vocabulary, hold up the book and point to the photographs of the people. Say: *a girl, a boy, a man, a woman, some people, a couple (two people).*

Write the words in a list on the board. Show their relationship to the subject pronouns *she, he* and *they*. Ask students to copy the words into their notebooks. Practise the words chorally and individually. Now go through the list of nationality adjectives, asking students to say the country of origin, e.g. *Japanese, Japan.* Practise the pronunciation of the adjectives chorally.

Give an example of the exchange in Exercise 5 by taking the parts of A and B yourself. Then ask the students as a whole class to speculate about the nationalities of the people in the photographs.

Ask students to look at page 141 for the answers. While the students are checking the answers, write the following tables on the board:

Is	he / she	Italian?	Yes,	he / she	is.
No,	he / she	isn't.	He's / She's	Spanish	

| Are they Chinese? | Yes, | they | are. | |
| | No, | | aren't. | They're Japanese. |

Now point to the girl in Picture 1 and say: *Is she Japanese?* Elicit: *Yes, she is.* Practise this chorally and individually. Point to Picture 2 and ask: *Are they Italian?* Elicit: *No, they aren't. They're Spanish.*

Write the following questions on the board:

3 Is she Greek?
4 Is he French?
5 Are they American?
6 Is he Spanish?
7 Is she British?

Ask students to work in pairs using the key on page 141 for the correct answers. Go round and make sure that students are using short form answers.

Exercise 7

Ask students to write the sentence as well, and check spelling and use of capital letters for countries and nationalities.

SUGGESTED LESSON BREAK

Exercise 8 LISTENING

Point out the new nationalities: Thai, Dutch and Swedish. Ask students to look at the map in their Students' Book and identify the countries (Thailand, Holland and Sweden). Play the tape and ask students to note down which language they think the speaker is using each time. Play the tape twice if necessary. Discuss possible answers using the example exchange.

KEY
Speaker 1 = Spanish Speaker 2 = Thai
Speaker 3 = German

GRAMMAR FOCUS

Explain the three headings *positive, negative* and *question* using the examples given. Remind students, with arrows, how in questions with the verb *to be*, the subject and verb are inverted, i.e. they change place. Also remind them if necessary how questions are punctuated with a question mark.

Ask students to study the tables silently and to note the contractions. Students now complete the two tasks individually.

Exercise 9

For pictures of the Great Wall of China and the Taj Mahal see the Students' Book, Unit 33, pages 103 and 104. For a picture of the Kremlin, see Unit 23, page 72. The Prado Museum is an art gallery.

This exercise can either be done in pairs or as a whole class. If you wish, you can extend the list of buildings and places so that the students cannot prepare all the answers. Conduct the activity as a General Knowledge Quiz. Do not insist on an accurate British pronunciation of each place. Point out the use of the definite article *the* for specific places. The use of the definite article also has a special note in Unit 10, Places.

QUIZ ANSWERS
1 The Eiffel /'aɪfl/ Tower (Paris, France)
2 The Prado /'prɑːdəʊ/ Museum (Madrid, Spain)
3 The Great Wall (Peoples' Republic of China)
4 The Empire State Building (New York City, USA)
5 The Taj Mahal /ˌtɑːʒ məˈhɑːl/ (Agra, India)
6 The Kremlin (Moscow, Russia)

Exercise 10

If the class is monolingual and it is appropriate, this exercise can be used to start a brief discussion in the L1 on the role of English as an international language and the reasons why a knowledge of English may be important to the students' own lives.

SUGGESTED SENTENCES
People speak Spanish in Spain, Mexico and Argentina. (etc.) People speak English in Britain, the USA, Canada and Australia. (etc.) People speak French in France, Algeria and Senegal. (etc.)

Exercise 11 READING AND WRITING

In order to introduce the text about Youcef, ask students what they think the name Youcef is in other languages (Joseph in English). Ask students to find Algeria and Hungary on the map in their Students' Book. Ask them what languages they speak in Algeria (Arabic and French), and to name another country where Arabic is spoken. Students read the text about Youcef. Ask them to guess the meaning of *hobby*. Students write about themselves in class using the text as a model. In order to develop good study habits, tell students to read their paragraph twice through afterwards, once for spelling and capital letters, and again for correct use of apostrophes. With false beginners, ask the students to speculate about Youcef 's job, his career and his lifestyle, e.g. W*hy does he need to speak so many languages?*

EXTRA ACTIVITIES

1 Nationality quiz

Ask each student to prepare a list of five quiz questions about the nationality of an internationally famous person either alive or dead under the heading *What nationality is/was ...?* e.g.
What nationality is Boris Becker?
What nationality was Napoleon?
What nationality was Picasso?

Students can either ask each other the questions in pairs, or you can collect and collate the questions to create a quiz for the whole class.

2 Friends across the world

With a class of young adults, ask students who have a friend in another country to write about the friend and, if possible, include a photograph and a map of the person's country. The information could be written along these lines:

Friends across the world
My friend is called ... He/She is ... (nationality)
and he/she is from ... He/She speaks ...

UNIT 4 Objects

Suggested lesson break: after Exercise 4

PREPARATION

Bring to the class as many of the items in the photograph as possible, especially an apple and an orange. These will be useful at the presentation stage and for working with the Grammar Focus box.

PRESENTATION

Hold up a book and ask: *What's this?* Elicit: *It's a book.* Students repeat the answer chorally. Draw an apple on the board or produce one and ask the same question. Point out on the board the use of *an* before nouns beginning with a vowel. Now hold up some pens and ask: *What are these?* Elicit: *They're pens.* Students repeat the answer chorally.

Now point to a pencil at a distance on a student's desk and ask: *What's that?* Elicit: *It's a pencil.* Point to some books or magazines on a shelf and ask: *What are those?* Elicit: *They're magazines.* Repeat the four questions: *What's this?/What are these?* and *What's that?/What are those?* illustrating the difference by either holding things or pointing to things. Write the four questions on the board and ask students to repeat them chorally and individually. Draw attention to the /ð/ sound in *this, that,* etc. but don't worry if some students find this sound very hard. There will be plenty of practice of this sound in later lessons.

Exercises 1 and 2

Ask students to work in pairs. They should point to each item in the photograph and ask: *What's this?* and tick or write the items as they are identified. The items listed in Exercise 1 which are not in the photograph are *an umbrella* and *a key.*

Give extra choral practice of any difficult words, e.g. *drawer* /drɔː/, *chair* /tʃeə/, *envelope* /'envələʊp/

Exercise 3 SPEECHWORK

First ask students to write the words in their notebooks, then play the tape for them to mark the stress patterns. Check the stress patterns, then play the tape a second time for students to repeat each word.

TAPESCRIPT AND KEY

Listen and underline the stressed syllables.

<u>pen</u>cil <u>en</u>velope <u>wa</u>llet <u>ap</u>ple <u>di</u>ary <u>or</u>ange <u>te</u>lephone <u>add</u>ress

GRAMMAR FOCUS

Draw three columns on the board and head them as follows:

a	*an*	*plurals*
book	apple	pens

Collect the objects you have brought to class and hold up each in turn. Get students to say what they are, e.g. *a pen, an orange, pencils.* As students say the words, write them in the appropriate column on the board. In a monolingual class, ask students in the L1 to explain the rule for the use of *a* or *an* and how to make singular words plural.

Now put some of the items **on** something, e.g. on a notepad or a book, and some of them **in** something, e.g. in an opened bag or drawer.

Ask where the items are:
T: Where's the apple/pen/orange?
S: It's on the table/book/desk. *or*
   It's in the bag/drawer.
T: Where are the pens/pencils/apples? etc.
S: They're on the table. *or*
   They're in the bag.

Write some of the questions and answers on the board.

| *Where's the apple?* | *It's on the desk.* |
| *Where are the apples?* | *They're in the drawer.* |

Exercise 4

Go through the exchange orally and remind students that the final syllable of *drawer* is not pronounced /drɔː/. Students work in pairs. One student uses the book to ask the questions, and the other student covers the photograph or closes the book and answers from memory.

SUGGESTED LESSON BREAK

Exercises 5 and 6

Students who are not familiar with the Roman alphabet will need extra time and practice to learn how to write the letters in both upper and lower case forms. Ask students to copy each letter into their notebooks in both small and capital letters. Many students will already know most of the English alphabet but they may still make mistakes with the vowels and some of the consonants, e.g. G, J, H, R. Spend time particularly on practising these letters. Play the tape for students to repeat.

Exercise 7

Practise the example exchange by asking about the spelling of other words used in the lesson, e.g. *How do you spell 'envelope'? How do you spell 'drawer'?*

Ask students to close their books and then choose individual students to spell different words. As they give you the letters, complete the words in a list on the board. As a final spelling check, dictate the spelling of ten words which you have chosen from the list in Exercise 1.

Exercise 8

Read each example exchange aloud choosing a different student each time to take the part of B. Now practise the conversation with other students, using items from your collection. Ask students to repeat the two questions chorally and individually. Then ask individual students to produce similar personal items for the other students to name and spell, e.g. *a mirror, some credit cards, some sweets, a ticket, a travel card, a foreign stamp, an identity card.* Write these words on the board.

Exercise 9 LISTENING

Read the rubric aloud, checking the understanding of the words *birthday* and *present* and the three items listed. Play the tape for the students to listen and a second time for them to note down what the present is.

TAPESCRIPT

Listen and say what present Adam got for his birthday from his mother and father. Choose from the following: a cassette recorder, a CD (compact disc) player, a radio.

MOTHER: Happy birthday, Adam. Here you are.
ADAM: Oh, thanks! What is it?
FATHER: Aha.
ADAM: Is it a cassette recorder?
MOTHER: No, it isn't.
ADAM: It's a radio, isn't it?
MOTHER: Open it!

ADAM: Oh no! A CD player! That's really great! Thanks, Mum. Thanks, Dad. Thanks a lot!

FATHER: Glad you like it.

Exercise 10

Some students may already know the names of the primary colours. Find out which of the colour words are unfamiliar to them by asking about objects in the photograph, e.g.

T: What colour is the address book?
S: It's red.
T: What colour is the apple?
S: It's green.

Practise the example exchange in the book, then students ask each other about the colours of things.

Exercise 11

This is a version of Kim's Game. Instead of using the picture, you may like to prepare your own tray of items for the students to remember. It can also be made more difficult by asking the students to remember the colours of objects as well.

EXTRA ACTIVITIES

1 Picture dictation

Ask students to draw a number of objects in different places, e.g.

Draw:
a stamp on an envelope
a pen in a mug
an umbrella on a chair
an apple on a table
some keys in a hand
a pencil on a diary

Students compare their drawings. Check their work to make sure that the items are correctly positioned.

2 Goal! A spelling game

Think of any English word already presented in the book, the longer the better, e.g. *birthday* and write a line of dashes (– – – – – – – –) on the board with a dash instead of each letter. Ask the students to try to guess the word by taking it in turns to say a letter they think is in the word. If they guess a letter correctly, write it above the appropriate dash where it occurs. If they guess a wrong letter, draw in turn part of a goalpost , a stick-figure goalkeeper and a ball as in the diagram.

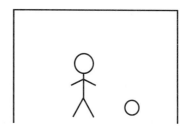

Ten 'no's' will mean that the 'goal' is complete and that the person who has chosen the word is the winner. The students can take turns to 'play in goal', choosing a different word each time.

UNIT 5 Personal information

 ## Exercise 1

If you think the numbers *one to a hundred* are already familiar to the students, check their knowledge by writing random numbers on the board and asking students what they are. Ensure that students can distinguish between and reproduce the pronunciation difference between numbers like *13* (*thirteen*) and *30* (*thirty*). With absolute beginners ask students to look at the numbers in their Students' Book and repeat them after the voice on the tape. Check afterwards with random numbers on the board. (You may also wish to use the tape with false beginners who need pronunciation practice.)

Exercise 2

Give some more practice in the difference between numbers such as *sixteen* and *sixty*. Then play the tape, pausing for the students to write down each number as they hear it.

TAPESCRIPT AND KEY
Listen and write the numbers you hear.

3 13 11 30 14 15 23 40 60 59 18 90 100

Exercises 3, 4 and 5

BACKGROUND NOTE
Health Club: A health club offers a variety of facilities for its members. Among other things, you can usually go to exercise classes, work on special exercise machines in a gym, swim, play tennis or squash, have a sauna, etc. These clubs have become quite popular in Britain during the last five years and membership of a health club is similar to membership of a social club.

To check that students understand the concept of *surname* and *first names*, ask for names round the class. Point to one student and ask:

T: What's your first name?
S: (It's) Daniel.
T: What's your surname?
S: (It's) Delano.

or elicit from different students the sentence:
My first name is Daniel and my surname is Delano.

Ask students to look at Adam's membership card for The Palms Health Club and to copy the headings into their notebooks. These will be used for interviewing their partner during the following three exercises.

Ask one student to take the part of Adam and practise the example exchange in Exercise 3 with you taking the part of A. Students now work in pairs asking their partner the questions in Exercises 3 and 4 and completing the relevant part of the card.

Practise the question for Exercise 5 chorally. Illustrate the point about the pronunciation of O /əʊ/ and double figure numbers. Check by asking different students their telephone numbers until examples of both points have occurred a few times. Ask students to continue the 'interview' with their partners, completing the card as they go along.

Exercise 6
Give students roles A or B. Ask them to cover their partner's information so that it becomes a genuine information gap task. Practise the two questions chorally first, using back-chaining techniques to practise the longer question, e.g *Blake's restaurant...the telephone number of Blake's restaurant...What's the telephone number of Blake's restaurant?*

Exercise 7
Illustrate the question and answer by asking a student in the class: *How old are you?* (Choose a student whom you know will not object or be embarrassed about revealing his/her age.) Point out that it is incorrect to say: ~~What age are you?~~ or ~~What age have you?~~. Avoid pair work in classes where you think students might be sensitive about their ages and move on instead to the next exercise.

Exercise 8
Use the photograph to revise: *people, man, woman, child, boy, girl* and to introduce the adjectives: *young, old* and *middle-aged*. Hold up the book and say:
T: Look at these people. Is this a boy or a man?
S: It's a man/boy.

T: Is he young or old?
S: He's old/middle-aged/young.
T: How old do you think he is?
S: I think he's about ...

Students then look at the example exchange and do the exercise in pairs. There is no key. You may like to extend the exercise to speculating about the ages of popular personalities of the moment.

Exercise 9
Ask students to take their notebooks, leave their places and walk round the classroom, collecting the information. If this is not possible, ask the students to interview the person sitting in front, behind and to one side of them, e.g.
S1: What's your full name?
S2: It's ...
S1: What's your address?
S2: It's ..., etc.

Ask students to keep this information to use later in Exercise 11 and Extra activity 3.

Exercise 10 LISTENING
First ask students to copy the application form into their notebooks. Remind them that Chris is Adam's friend and works in the same travel agency. Students can look back at Preview Units 1-5 and Unit 1 to see photographs of Chris. Play the tape for students to note the information. Play it several times if necessary. Check the students' answers by writing them on the board.

TAPESCRIPT
Listen and complete the form for Adam's friend Chris.

MAN: O.K. First I need some personal information. Your name please.
CHRIS: Furness.
MAN: Can you spell that please?
CHRIS: Yes, it's F.U.R.N.E.S.S.
MAN: Thank you. And your first name?
CHRIS: Christine.
MAN: Christine. That's C.H.R?
CHRIS: Yes.
MAN: And is it Miss or Mrs?
CHRIS: Miss.
MAN: And your address?
CHRIS: 15, Clifton Street, York.
MAN: Clifton Street. Is that double F?
CHRIS: No, one F. C.L.I.F.T.O.N, Clifton Street.
MAN: Do you know the postcode?
CHRIS: Yes, it's YO3 4RD
MAN: 4RD. Telephone number?
CHRIS: 0904 642091
MAN: And how old are you Miss Furness?
CHRIS: I'm nineteen.
MAN: Fine. Now can you just sign your name here please? Good. Right, well let's see ...

Exercise 11 READING AND WRITING

Ask students to read the paragraph about Adam silently. Explain *full name = all my names*. Check that students understand *grandfather*. Students write about themselves in the same way. Answer any queries which may arise. Afterwards, ask students to check their work once for capital letters and commas, and again for the use of apostrophes.

Now ask students to use the information they collected in Exercise 9 to write about another student in the class. With complete beginners, build up an example passage on the board with their help. Alternatively, students can write about a friend or someone in their family. This part can be done as homework.

ABOUT NAMES AND ADDRESSES

Ask students to look at the Title section on the application form in Exercise 10 and ask them what the parallel titles are in their own language. Students repeat the English titles after you. Write on the board:

Miss
Mrs (**not** ~~Missis~~)
Mr (**not** ~~Mister~~)
Ms = Mrs or Miss
(See note in Unit 1 on *Ms*)

Ask students to read the note about how to talk about people by name. Check by asking students:
T: What's my name?
S1: Angela.
T: What else can you call me? (prompting) Miss...?
S1: Miss Angela?
T: No.
S2: Miss Robinson?
T: Yes, that's right.

Ask students to look at the address on Adam's envelope on page 11. They then read the note on how to write addresses on envelopes, and also read the two notes under the box. To check the points, ask: *What is Laura's address? What's her postcode?* Find out if the students have similar postcodes in their country. Complete the two tasks with the whole class.

Now ask students to draw an envelope in their notebooks and address it to Chris. They should use the address given in the listening activity in Exercise 10.

EXTRA ACTIVITIES
1 Find the mistakes
Write this form on the board for students to copy.

> *Surname:*
> *First Names:*
> *Address:*
> *Telephone number:*
> *Status: single* ☐ *married* ☐ *divorced* ☐
> *Nationality:*
> *Age:*

Ask students to complete it for themselves but to include four mistakes in the information. For example, they can write the wrong house number or postcode, or give the wrong age, or spell their surname incorrectly. Ask them to pair up and exchange forms with someone in the class they do not know very well. They must then ask questions to find the mistakes on each other's forms like this:
A: What's your surname?
B: Marrone.
A: How do you spell it?
B: M.A.R.R.O.N.E.
A: O.K. That's one mistake. And what are your first names? (etc.)

2 Bingo
This game is best limited to a range of twenty-five numbers, e.g. 1 to 25 or 25 to 50. Ask each student to draw 4 x 4 squares and put a different number between 1 and 25 (or between 25 and 50) in each box in any order. For example:

6	8	13	11
23	19	1	5
17	9	21	15
12	3	10	2

When everyone has prepared their squares, the teacher calls out the numbers one to twenty-five in any order. Each student puts a cross through the number as it is called out. The winner is the first person to get a line of crosses vertically, horizontally or diagonally.

FLUENCY Units 1–5

With monolingual classes, explain to the students in the L1 that in this lesson they have a chance to try to use all the language they have learnt so far.

Exercise 1
Ask students to look at the title of the competition on page 13. Explain *surprise* and *prize*. Ask students to read the advertisement for the competition and to answer the questions in Exercise 1. Check the answers. Do not draw attention to the use of the present simple in the unit. (At this stage students do not need to

read the competition form in the bottom right-hand corner of the advertisement.)

📻 Exercise 2 LISTENING

Ask students to read the questions first. Explain *caller* and, if necessary, *boy/girlfriend*. Notice that the word *present* refers to the *prize*. Play the tape at least twice for students to answer the questions. Check the answers.

Explain to the students that the taped conversation is a model and that they should try to memorise the DJ's questions for their roleplay in Exercise 4. Play the tape again once or twice. Some students may find it helpful to write the DJ's questions down.

TAPESCRIPT

Listen to a telephone call to 'What a Surprise!' and answer the questions.

NARRATOR: Radio York has a new radio phone-in programme. It's called 'What a Surprise!' It's very simple. Think of a friend and give them a surprise! All you do is phone us!

DJ: Hello there! I'm Jeff Andrews, from Radio York. Let's listen to another call on 'What a surprise!'

Hello! What's your name and where are you from?

GIRL: Hello, my name's Maggie and I'm from Leeds.

DJ: Hello, Maggie. And what's your friend's name?

GIRL: He's called Jonathan. He's my boyfriend actually.

DJ: I see. And where's Jonathan from?

GIRL: He's from York.

DJ: And how old is Jonathan?

GIRL: He's twenty-one.

DJ: And what present do you want for your boyfriend?

GIRL: A T-shirt please.

DJ: Great. O.K. Now Maggie, here's your quiz question. 'What nationality is Steffi Graf?'

GIRL: She's German.

DJ: Yes, you're right. She's German. And your friend Jonathan wins a Radio York T-shirt! Congratulations and thanks for calling.

GIRL: Thank you! Bye!

Exercise 3

Ask students to read the competition form in the advertisement and to copy and complete it in their notebooks. This is to be used in the roleplay in Exercise 4 when the student is the caller. Now ask students to prepare one or two nationality questions, as in the example. These should not be shown to anyone else. One of the questions will be used in the roleplay when the student is the disc jockey.

Exercise 4 ROLEPLAY

Both students need the competition form and the 'disc jockey' also needs the nationality questions which he/she prepared in Exercise 3. Demonstrate how the roleplay works, and how to interpret the cues. (For a suggested conversation please see the tapescript.) Students then work in pairs and change parts afterwards. Select a pair of students to perform for the class. Tell the 'disc jockey' to ask a different nationality question this time.

Exercise 5 WRITING

Students use the text as a model to write about one of their friends who has 'won' the competition.

CHECK Units 1–5

If you wish, before the lesson, photocopy the key or copy it onto an OHT or stencil. Then, when students have completed all the check exercises, they can exchange them and correct each other's answers. Alternatively, they can correct their own. Students should complete the whole test in one lesson.

KEY

Ex. 1 1a 2b 3c 4a 5b 6c 7b 8c 9a 10c (10 marks)

Ex. 2 1 What's your name?
2 What's her name?
3 What's his name?
4 What's her name?
5 What's the name of the college?
(5 marks)

Ex. 3 1 chair 2 umbrella 3 mug 4 hello 5 Greek (5 marks)

Ex. 4 1 She's from the USA.
2 He's from Britain.
3 They're from Italy.
4 We're from Brazil.
5 She's from France.
6 They're from Germany.
7 He's from Spain.
8 We're from Switzerland.
9 She's from Portugal.
10 He's from Japan.
(10 marks)

Ex. 5 1 American 2 Brazilian 3 Japanese 4 Spanish 5 Portuguese 6 Chinese 7 Argentinian 8 Mexican 9 Italian 10 French
(10 marks. Deduct 3 marks if no capital letters.)

Ex. 6 1c 2d 3e 4b 5a (5 marks)

Ex. 7 1 I'm Karen.
       2 She's a friend from work.
       3 They're from Brazil.
       4 What's your mother's name?
       5 He's Adam's friend.
       (7 marks)

Ex. 8 b a a a b (5 marks)

Ex. 9 1 My name's Adam.
       2 I'm from Paris.
       3 He's Italian.
       4 Good morning, Mrs Gibson.
       5 My name's John. What's your name?
       (12 marks)

Ex. 10 1 Monday 2 Tuesday 3 Saturday
4 Thursday 5 Wednesday (5 marks)

CHECK YOUR PROGRESS

Give students time to look through their test results and to assess their difficulties. Ask individual students which exercises they found easy and which difficult. Encourage them to label their problems, e.g. capital letters, nationality adjectives. This will help them to be more aware in later lessons of what they need to concentrate on.

Ask students to correct all their mistakes, including their spelling mistakes. They should study any grammar focus points again if necessary. It might be a good time for students to look at some of the relevant grammar points in the Language review (page 135 onwards).

LEARNING TO LEARN 1

Go through each of the questions, giving further examples of each. Students practise the questions chorally and individually until they are confident of using them. Do not go into the 'grammar' of the present simple question forms with *do* or *does* yet. Treat them as set phrases to learn. Set students the tasks 1-3 and try to hear as many students as possible. As you continue with the course, try to encourage the use of these questions whenever the students want to ask for your help. Do **not** accept questions beginning with ~~Please, what means ..?~~

PREVIEW Units 6 –10

> BACKGROUND NOTES
> Use maps to show the position of York and San Diego.
> *York*: An old city in north-east England, famous for its history.
> *San Diego*: A modern city in Southern California just south of Los Angeles. (For further information on York and San Diego see Unit 10.)
> *The photographs*: These show the medieval architecture typical of many parts of York. This particular street , College Street, is very close to the Cathedral (York Minster).

The photographs and the dialogue

Ask students to look at the main photograph and to answer the following questions: *Who are the people? What nationality are they? Where are they? What day of the week do you think it is?*

The tape

Play the tape and ask students to follow the conversation in their Students' Books. Explain that the conversation on the tape is slightly longer but that the information is the same. After playing the tape, check or gloss the meaning of *remember, work* (v), *lovely, live* (v), *coast, cousin, surf* (v) and the expression *Give me a ring*, i.e. telephone me.

TAPESCRIPT
Listen and follow the conversation in your Students' Book.

ADAM: Hello! Remember me? I'm Adam – from the travel agent's.
LAURA: Oh, yes. I remember.
ADAM: Have you got time for a coffee?
LAURA: Yes, lovely.
ADAM: Do you work near here?
LAURA: No, I'm a student at the university.
ADAM: Oh, are you? What are you studying?
LAURA: English literature.
ADAM: Do you like York?
LAURA: Yes, very much. It's a lovely city.
ADAM: Yes, I like it a lot, too. Where do you live in the States?
LAURA: I come from the west coast, from San Diego in California.
ADAM: Really? I've got a cousin in California. He's a surfer. Can you surf?
LAURA: Yes, but not very well. Can you?
ADAM: No, no I can't.
LAURA: Look, I must go. Give me a ring some time.
ADAM: O.K. Bye!
LAURA: Bye!

The exercise

Read aloud each sentence in the comprehension exercise and ask the students to say *Yes, No* or *Don't know* after each sentence.

Play the tape again and ask students to try to 'shadow' the printed conversation (i.e. speak at the same time as the voice on the tape). Then ask them to read the dialogue in pairs.
Revise the vocabulary in the pictures, e.g. *table, chair, man, woman, bag, street*. With false beginners, build up more vocabulary items, e.g. *watch, cup, saucer, camera, house*, etc. With very good false beginners, you may also like to use the present continuous (which is taught in detail in Unit 15) to ask what is happening in each of the pictures.

The learning objectives box

Ask students to read the list of objectives in the box, and then see if they can find examples of each one in the printed dialogue.

Skills and abilities: *Can you surf? Yes, but not very well.*
The family: *I've got a cousin in California.*
Jobs and lifestyles: *I'm a student at the university.*
Likes and dislikes: *Do you like York? Yes, very much.*
Geographical location: *I come from the west coast.*
Cities of the world: *York, San Diego*

UNIT 6 Skills and abilities

Suggested lesson break: after Exercise 3

PRESENTATION

To present *can* (ability), ask a student:
T: Can you speak (L1)?
S: Yes.
T: Say 'Yes, I can'.
S1: Yes, I can.

Now ask another student:
T: Can Gisela speak (Ll)?
S2: Yes, she can.

Turn back to the first student and ask:
T: Can you speak Chinese?
S1: No, I can't.
T: Can she speak Chinese?
S2: No, she can't.
T: What about English? Can you speak English?
S1: Yes, a little.
T: Yes, you can speak English a little. In fact, you can speak English quite well. What about me?
S1: You can speak English very well.
T: Thank you. But I can't speak Chinese at all.

Write on the board the following tables:

Can	you he she	speak	English? Chinese?

Yes,	I he she	can.	No,	I he she,	can't.

I can speak English	a little. quite well. very well.

I can't speak Chinese	very well. at all.

Students practise the questions, answers and statements chorally and individually. Some students may ask if they can say: *I can speak a little English*. Explain that this is also possible. In fact it is more common than *I can speak English a little* but point out that they cannot use the other adverbs in the same way, i.e. you **cannot** say ~~I can speak very well English.~~ Leave the charts on the board to refer to later.

Now ask a quietly-spoken student: *Can you speak Russian?* When the student answers, put your hand behind your ear (or use a similar appropriate gesture) and say: *I can't hear you.* Ask students to repeat this after you. Then write something illegible on the board, and ask: *What's that word?* Elicit: *I can't read it.* Ask: *Can't you read my writing?* Student responds: *No.*

Then point at something out of the window and ask someone on the opposite side of the classroom: *What's that over there?* Elicit: *I can't see (it).*

Write on the board:

I can't	see read hear	it/you. it. it/you.

Exercise 1

Ask students to look at the pictures. Then ask the following questions to establish the situation for each one, e.g.
1 *What is this?* (pointing to the letter)
2 *Where are the man and the boy?* (In a cinema) *What's the boy's name?* (Robert)
3 *Where are the two men?* (In a restaurant) *What nationality is this man?* (pointing to the man on the left)

Now refer to the sentences in Exercise 1 and ask students to match a sentence with each picture. Ask students to read the completed exchanges and to change parts.

22

GRAMMAR FOCUS

To show that *can* never changes from its base form, ask students to make similar sentences to those in the Focus box, using the other personal pronouns: *he, she, you, they,* etc. Point out that the full form of *can't* is *cannot.*

Move on to the diagram showing the levels of ability. These adverb phrases should now be familiar from the presentation. Refer back to the charts on the board and point out the position of the adverbs after, not in between, the verb and object. Ask students to copy the charts on the board into their notebooks.

Exercise 2

Ask a student to ask you if you can speak French.
s: Can you speak French?
T: No, not very well. Now ask me about Spanish.
s: Can you speak Spanish?
T: No, not at all. Ask me about English.
s: Can you speak English?
T: Yes, very well.

This will give students an example of how to respond without needing to give full sentences. Now ask students in pairs to work through all the languages listed. Go round and monitor, correcting where necessary.

Exercise 3 SPEECHWORK

Say sentences with *can*, the first with weak stress and the next with strong stress, e.g.
I can speak English. (weak) *Can you speak English?* (weak) *Yes, I can.* (strong) Write the two phonetic symbols on the board: /kən/ (weak) and /kæn/ (strong). Play the tape and ask the students to say if they hear /kən/ or /kæn/

TAPESCRIPT AND KEY
Yes, she can. /kæn/ strong
I can speak English. /kən/ weak
He can speak French. /kən/ weak
Yes, I can. /kæn/ strong
Can you speak Italian? /kən/ weak
What can you do? /kən/ weak

SUGGESTED LESSON BREAK

Exercise 4

Refer students to the questionnaire chart and use mime or pictures to demonstrate and explain what each of the words mean. A set of flash cards showing each activity would be particularly useful here. Add other sports and games if they are topical. As you explain the words, the meaning of the three categories: *sports, practical* and *artistic* will emerge. Practise the pronunciation of each new word chorally. Point out the use of the definite article with musical instruments in *play the piano/guitar* but not in *play tennis/football.*

Ask students to look at the example exchange and select a student to take the part of B. Encourage B to ask *What about you?* at the end so that you can show how the conversation can continue to cover the different activities.

Students then ask the questions in pairs or groups. Tell them to ask the questions out of sequence, e.g. *Can you swim? Can you change a wheel? Can you draw?* This will encourage them to use the full question form each time rather than a shortened version like *Can you swim? ski? windsurf?* etc. Students make a note of each other's answers for use in Exercises 5 and 6. Monitor as students work. As you do so, you may like to make a note of any special talents revealed in your class so that these can be used in a later social event you may wish to organise.

Exercise 5

Students should select from their notes two things their partner can do and two things he/she can't do, to give practice in both positive and negative forms of the verb. Point out the use of *or* when two negative items are linked, e.g. *She can't swim or ski.*

Exercise 6 WRITING

To show the use of conjunctions *and, or* and *but* orally, give true examples of your own skills, following the order of the headings in Exercise 6. Then refer to the examples in the Students' Book showing how the conjunctions are used to link and to contrast statements. Students can start the exercise in class so that you can check the use of conjunctions and the position of adverbs. They can finish the work at home.

Exercise 7 READING AND LISTENING

BACKGROUND NOTE
The survey comes from a MORI Poll in the Sunday Times Magazine published in October 1988. Explain that *the Brits* is short for *the British* and is a form of slang used more often in spoken English than in written English.

Go through the survey explaining or translating any categories which students don't understand. Ask them to look at the figures. Then ask the following comprehension questions. Accept one-word answers.
1 How many British people between fifteen and thirty-four can speak French fluently? (3%)
2 How many British people of your age can speak French fluently?
3 How many British people of your age can have a simple conversation in French?
4 How many British people over fifty-five can read a menu in French? (22%)
5 How many British people between thirty-five and fifty-four can't speak French at all? (63%)

Ask students to listen to a British man talking about what he can do in French. Students note what he can and can't do. As this is an authentic recording of a native English speaker, explain to the students that they should not worry if they do not understand every word. Play the tape twice.

TAPESCRIPT

Listen to a British person living in Paris. Look at the survey and note down what the speaker can and can't do.

PETER:

Read a menu…Yes, I can do that. Um, ask directions… Um no, I'm not so good at that. I don't really think I can do that.. Um, no I can't ask directions. Read a French newspaper… Er, no I can't do that at all, er, my level of French isn't up to that at all… Um, have a simple conversation… I think I can do that. It has to be a very simple conversation otherwise I can't understand it but, er, I can do that, yes. Understand a TV and radio programme… Er, no I can't do that. That's much too difficult for me. Speaking French fluently… No I can't do that at all.

Students now work in pairs to find out what they can do in English and/or another language. Tell them to use the questions listed in the book. Check with a few students afterwards. Ask: *What can you do, (Julio)?* Elicit: *I can …, and I can … but I can't …*

Make sure students use the weak form of *can*. With false beginners, discuss which of the skills listed they think are the most important to acquire first. Ask: *Is reading a menu important? What about asking directions?* etc. To make it more challenging, they could rate each on a scale of one to five.

EXTRA ACTIVITIES
1 Foreign language survey
In a multilingual class, collect information about the number of foreign languages which people in the class can speak. Collate the numbers and prepare a chart on the board, e.g.

	a little	quite well	fluently
English	25		
French	5	6	
Japanese	1		

2 Foreign words
In groups, students think of between five and ten 'loan' words in their own language which have been 'borrowed' from other languages. They say which country the words originate from.

Examples in English might be:
tango = Argentina, *ski* = Norway, *samovar* = Russia, *sari* = India, *geisha* = Japan, *opera* = Italy, *chic* = France, *rock 'n roll* = USA. These words can be used for a quiz between the groups.

TEAM 1
A: (Calls out a word) Sari

TEAM 2
B: It's an Indian word.
TEAM 1
A: Yes, that's right./No, it isn't. It's a … word.

UNIT 7 Family
Suggested lesson break: after Exercise 6

PRESENTATION
Start by drawing your own or an invented family tree on the board. As you draw the different parts of the tree, identify the words for the family members listed in Exercise 1, e.g. *John is my father and Ann is my mother*. Leave this diagram on the board for later use in Exercise 5. Point out the irregular plural forms: *wife – wives, child – children*.

Exercise 1
Ask students to look at both the photographs and Laura's family tree in their Students' Book and to discuss and identify all the people in the family tree, following the example exchange in Exercise 1. When they have finished, ask students to draw their own family tree, starting from their parents.

GRAMMAR FOCUS (1)
Point to your family tree and say: *I've got (two sisters and one brother)*. Now ask a student the first question in the Focus box: *Paolo, have you got any brothers or sisters?* Elicit: *Yes, I have. I've got (two brothers)*. Practise the question and answer chorally and individually.

Now ask a different student: *Carmen, has Paolo got any brothers or sisters?* Elicit: *Yes, he has. He's got (two brothers)*. Practise chorally and individually. Then ask: *What about you, Carmen?* Elicit: *I've got (a sister and a brother)*. Practise chorally and individually. Continue round the class until most students have spoken. Introduce the phrase *I'm an only child*.

Ask students to look at the box silently for about half a minute. Write the contracted forms from the task on the board and ask individual students to come up and write the full forms next to them.

Exercise 2

Ask students to prepare at least ten questions to ask about Laura's family. Some of these should contain *have/has got* but other possible questions are:

What's her sister's name? (Silvia)
What are her brothers' names? (Danny and Steve)
What's her mother's name? (Barbara)
What are her parents' names? (Barbara and Tony)
Is Steve married? (Yes, he is.)
What's his wife's name? (Debbie)
Have they got any children? (Yes, they have./ Yes, they've got two.)
What are their names? (Robert and Lisa)

Give some examples orally first of some possible questions and answers. Students then ask their prepared questions in pairs.

Remind students to use contracted forms where possible, e.g. *What's* rather than *What is* and *She's got* rather than *She has got.*

Exercise 3

This can be done orally with the whole class or students can complete the sentences individually.

Exercise 4 SPEECHWORK

Practise the words chorally before or after playing the tape. Many students will find this sound difficult and will substitute /z/ or /d/. Show them that the tongue must come between the front teeth to make the /ð/ sound.

Exercise 5

Refer back to your own family tree on the board and increase it to show the additional family members: *grandmother/grandfather, aunt/uncle, niece/nephew, cousin.* Show how the exercise works by writing the first completed sentence *Laura is Lisa's aunt,* on the board next to the prompt. Ask students to work individually to complete the remaining sentences.

Exercise 6

Ask one student to think of the name of someone in their family and to tell you their name, e.g. *Antonio.* Ask: *Who's Antonio?* and elicit the answer: *He's my (brother/cousin),* etc.
Now tell all students to write down five names of family members (not just brothers and sisters, as this information will be familiar from the work in the Grammar Focus box) and exchange lists with their partner. They then ask and answer who the people are, according to the example.

SUGGESTED LESSON BREAK

Exercise 7 LISTENING

Draw a skeleton family tree for Adam on the board and ask students to copy it into their notebooks. Choose a skeleton of **one** of the two possibilities below. Refer students to the names in the Students' Book and ask them to listen and complete Adam's family tree. Play the tape twice and then check by asking a student to come to the board and complete Adam's family tree. With a good class, see if they can deduce the second possible tree (see key A or B). (The tape does not say if Mary and Jim are William's parents or Dorothy's parents.)

TAPESCRIPT
Listen to Adam talking to Laura about his family. Use these names to draw his family tree: William, Michael, Dorothy, Mary, Jim.

LAURA: Tell me about your family, Adam.
ADAM: Well, there's my mother - she's called Dorothy, and my father. His name's William.
LAURA: And are your grandparents alive?
ADAM: Yes, they are. They're called Jim and Mary. They're quite old now, over eighty.
LAURA: Mm. My grandparents are both dead. Have you got any brothers ... or sisters?
ADAM: Just one brother, Michael.
LAURA: How old is he?
ADAM: Twenty-four. He's my 'big brother'. I share a flat with him.
LAURA: Oh, that sounds fun!
ADAM: Mmm. Sometimes!

KEY

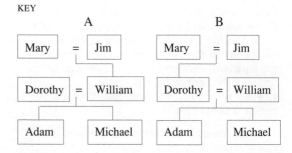

Then ask: *How old are Adam's grandparents? Is Adam an only child? Has he got any sisters? How old is his brother, Michael? Who does Adam share a flat with?* Explain *share a flat* as you ask the question. Play the tape again if necessary if students find the first and last questions difficult.

Exercise 8

Work through the conversation, with a student taking the part of A and you taking the part of B. Make your answers sound as natural as possible. Introduce the words *alive* and *dead.* Students then work in pairs.

Now ask students to try to draw a family tree for their partner. Some of this they can now do from memory but they will need to ask further questions to complete an extended tree, e.g. *Has your father got any brothers?* Give an example first by working Teacher–Student, drawing the student's family tree on the board as you go along. At this stage, you may want to introduce *the youngest/eldest* and even *older/younger.* Comparative adjectives are not introduced formally until Unit 28 and teachers must use their own judgement as to whether this would overload the lesson structurally or not.

Exercise 9 READING

Ask students to look at the picture of Cher. Ask: *Do you know Cher? What nationality is she?* (American) *Do you know the names of any of her films or songs?*

Ask students to cover the text. Read the questions in the Students' Book aloud and see if students can answer them before they read the text. Gloss *ancestors,* e.g. *great-grandparents,* etc. Now ask students to read the text and find the answers to the questions. Check the answers.

Check that students understand the meaning of: *real, together, won, actress.* Ask further questions on the text, e.g. *What is her real name? What's the name of her son/daughter? How old is she now? What was the name of her Oscar-winning film?*

GRAMMAR FOCUS (2)

Refer back to the use of the past tense *was* and *were* in the text about Cher, e.g. *Her ancestors were French. Her first husband was called Sonny Bono.* Read aloud the sentences in the box and work Teacher–Student asking about the nationality of people's grandparents or great-grandparents/ ancestors using the present and past forms of the verb *to be,* e.g.

T: What nationality was your grandmother?
S: She was Spanish.

The past tense of the verb *to be* is introduced again in Unit 19.

Exercise 10 WRITING

Ask students to look back at their own family trees from Exercise 1. Introduce the expression *I come from a large family.* Ask students to start the exercise in class and help them with any extra vocabulary, e.g. *great-grandparents.*

EXTRA ACTIVITIES
1 Family trees

Students elaborate on their family trees by introducing other branches of the family and adding photographs and ages.

2 Star!

Students who are interested in music and film personalities may like to write a paragraph about a personality of their choice. Ask them to collect the information and to use the text about Cher as a model. When these are completed, ask students to bring them to class and choose some students to read their work aloud for the class. Ask them to omit the name of the personality so that the other students guess who the person is.

UNIT 8 Jobs and lifestyles

Suggested lesson break: after Exercise 3

BACKGROUND NOTES
Houston: The largest city in Texas, USA, famous for its oil refineries and chemical industries. It is also a major port.
Leeds: An industrial city in Yorkshire, in Britain. Its main industries are engineering and textiles. It also has a famous cathedral, university and football team.
Madrid: The capital and commercial centre of Spain. Its industries are engineering and light manufacturing. The Prado, the national museum, contains one of the greatest painting collections in Europe.
Perpignan: The chief town of Pyrenees-Orientales, France, and the historic capital of Rousillon. It is fifteen miles from Spain. It has a famous cathedral, fortress and market.
Recife: A port in Brazil and the commercial centre of the north-east of the country.
Belfast: The capital of Northern Ireland and a seaport. Its main industries are shipbuilding and linen.
Lisbon: The capital of Portugal and a large port. Its main industries are food processing, textiles and shipbuilding. It was rebuilt after an earthquake in 1755.

PRESENTATION

Select a good student and ask: *What do you do?* Elicit*: I'm a student/factory worker.* Then ask: *Where do you study/work?* Elicit: *I study/work at ... School/the ... factory.* Ask: *Where do you live?* etc.

Write the three questions on the board and practise them chorally and individually. Write the answers next to them on the right-hand side. Practise these also. Now ask different students the same questions. (Students with jobs can look up the English equivalent in a bilingual dictionary.) You may wish to do Exercise 2 now, but please read the note on Exercise 1 below first.

Exercise 1 READING

If the students are false beginners, they can now read the texts silently and find the answers to the questions. With complete beginners, however, it is best to leave the reading comprehension questions until later in the class (after Exercise 4). The reading texts themselves can be introduced gradually throughout the lesson and exploited for different purposes (see below).

Exercise 2 SPEECHWORK

Practise the question forms chorally before playing the tape.

TAPESCRIPT AND KEY

Listen and underline the stressed syllable or word.

Where do you work?   Where do you live?
What do you do?   Where do you come from?

Reading texts (1)

Play the tape of the first three people. Students follow the texts as they listen. After each character has finished, show the class a world map and ask where each person lives. Give or elicit any information which you think appropriate from the background notes. Check the comprehension and pronunciation of the following words and phrases.

Shirley: *telephone operator, look after herself, grown-up*
Brenda: *bus driver, housewife, teenage, factory*
Carlos and Helen: *flat, journalist, musician, violin*

Now ask one student to be Shirley and ask: *What do you do, Shirley?* Elicit: *I'm a telephone operator.* (Give some choral practice of the pronunciation of this job.) Then ask: *Where do you live?* etc. Work Teacher–Student with other students taking the part of Brenda and Carlos.

GRAMMAR FOCUS (1)

Ask students to look at the first Focus box. Read the questions and answers aloud including the Yes/No questions. Give students some practice of short answers by asking: *Do you live in Milan/ London? Do you live in a flat/house? Do you work (have a job)?*
Ask the task question in the Focus box to the whole class.
Point out the use of *do* to form the question and *don't* to form the negative.

Exercise 3 ROLEPLAY

Choose a good student and act out a conversation based on the suggested conversation below. Prompt the student to keep the conversation going by saying *What about you?* Make the *Oh, really?* and *That's interesting* responses yourself.

Ask students to work in pairs roleplaying two of the characters they have read about so far. They should try to memorise the information about their character before they start. Then ask them to shut their books and start their conversations.

SUGGESTED CONVERSATION

A: What's your name?
B: Brenda.
A: Where do you come from?
B: I come from Leeds in England. What about you? What's your name?
A: My name's Carlos and I'm from Spain.
B: Oh, really? What do you do?
A: I'm a journalist. What about you?
B: I'm a bus driver .
A: That's interesting. Do you live with your family?
B: Yes, I do. I live with my husband and children. I'm also a housewife.
A: How many children have you got?
B: I've got two teenage children. What about you?
A: I live with my wife in a flat in Lisbon.
B: Have you got any children?
A: No, we haven't.

SUGGESTED LESSON BREAK

Reading texts (2)

Play the tape of the next two characters and get students to follow the texts. Check that students understand the following words and phrases:

Michel: *at home, the country* (opposite: *the town*), *farm*
Selma: *airline, airport, check-in desk*

Now recycle the information about these characters orally using the 3rd person singular. Students can repeat some of the sentences after you. Ask questions about the characters and give the answers yourself, e.g. *Where does Michel come from? He comes from France.* The students then ask and answer questions about Selma.

GRAMMAR FOCUS (2)

Read the questions and answers aloud or ask students to study the box silently. Ask the task question to the whole class. Point out the spelling of *Does*. Ask some questions about people in the class, e.g. *What does Angela do? Where does she live? Does she live with her parents?* Remind students about the 3rd person singular *s* each time they answer.
Ask them to tell you something about their partner, e.g. *She lives at home* or *He works in Madrid* or *She's a housewife.* They can now ask and answer questions across the class about Shirley, Brenda and Carlos/Helen.

Do not expect complete accuracy at this stage. Even advanced level students make mistakes with this tense. From now on the present tense occurs regularly and consistently in texts and activities throughout the book, so students will have thorough practice of this tense as the course progresses.

Reading texts (3)

Play the tape of the remaining two characters: Kevin and Vera. Check the meaning of: *hostel, suburb, alone, the government*. Practise Yes/No answers with *does/doesn't*.

Exercise 4

This exercise gives special practice of short form answers. Do it as a class game. If students guess the person after one question, move rapidly on to another student/character.

Now turn back to the reading comprehension questions from Exercise 1.

Exercise 1 READING (continued)

Ask a few general questions so that students scan all the texts again briefly. *What nationality are the couple? What are their names? Who comes from the USA? Which two people come from Britain? What nationality is Vera Laucas? What nationality is Michel Moulin?*

Use the questions at the top of the page to check detailed comprehension of all the texts with the whole class. After the first few questions, students can work in pairs asking and answering about the people. Students need only give a name for each answer. Draw special attention to the use of prepositions with *live* and *work*.

Exercise 5 LISTENING

The students will probably recognise the voice immediately as Carlos. As they listen ask them to note other 'clues', e.g. *It's a man speaking and there are only three men. He's not English. He lives in a flat in the centre of the city. He's married so he's not Michel. He works for a newspaper.* Ask them to tell you what else they learn about him, e.g. *the flat is small, he speaks English in his job,* etc. Explain the following words: *cosmopolitan, travel, correspondent*.

TAPESCRIPT

Listen and say which of the people in the photographs is talking. How do you know?

CARLOS:

It's a nice city. I like it very much. It's big and cosmopolitan. We live in the centre near my work. We've only got a small flat but that's fine at the moment because we haven't got any children. I have to speak English very well for my job and I often travel to Britain and the USA. My wife travels a lot in her job too. Next year

I'm going to work in London as the British correspondent for my newspaper.

Exercise 6

Students work in pairs. They should try to choose someone who lives in a different country. Give some examples of questions to ask, e.g. *Where does she come from?* or *Where does she live? Does she live with her parents? Is she married? Does she work?* etc.

Ask students to make a few notes about their partner's friend as they listen. These can be used for the next writing exercise.

Exercise 7 WRITING

Allow time for students to plan what they are going to write and to ask about any new vocabulary items they may need. After they have written the paragraph, ask them to check carefully the use of the 3rd person singular and the prepositions *in, on, at* and *for*.

Refer students to the Language review on page 139 which summarises the present simple tense in tabular form.

EXTRA ACTIVITIES
1 Use your imagination

Collect a set of magazine photos and stick them up on the board. Students talk or write about each person from their imagination and compare with each other.

2 Who am I?

Students pretend they are a famous person. Other students ask Yes/No questions to guess the person, e.g. *Are you Italian? Do you live in Rome?*

UNIT 9 Likes and dislikes

Suggested lesson break: after Exercise 3

PREPARATION

To save valuable class time, copy the chart in Exercise 1 on to a sheet of paper and make a photocopy or stencil for each member of the class. Make sure that you leave plenty of space for students to write in their answers. Alternatively, ask students to prepare in advance by copying the chart into their notebooks at home before the lesson.

The photograph

Ask students what they can see in the photograph and if they know where it is. Ask a few students: *Do you like it?* Elicit: *Yes, I do./No, I don't.* Point to each of the 'reply bubbles' in the picture and ask: *Does he like it?* Elicit: *Yes, he does.* Ask: *Does she like it?* Elicit: *No, she doesn't.*

COMMUNICATION FOCUS

Prompt students to ask you certain questions. You reply to the questions using the range of responses in the box. At the same time use an appropriate facial expression, e.g.
T: Ask me: 'Do you like tea?'
S: Do you like tea?
T: Yes, I do. I love it. Now ask me: 'Do you like coffee?'
S: Do you like coffee?
T: Yes, I like it very much. (etc.)
Practise the responses in the box chorally and individually.

Now ask students a range of simple questions (but avoiding questions about people at this stage), e.g. *Do you like tea/coffee/swimming/beer?* etc. Elicit some different responses.

Exercise 1

Write the first section of the chart on the board and complete the *I like...* column for yourself. Don't forget to include the name of a band so that you can illustrate clearly the object pronouns *him, her* and *them* listed in the Grammar Focus box. Now go through the four names with parallel sentences using the object pronouns, e.g. *I like Prince. I like him very much I like Cher. I like her very much. I like Police. I like them very much.* etc.

GRAMMAR FOCUS

Refer students to the Grammar Focus box and ask them to study the lists of pronouns, including *me, you,* and *us.* Read aloud the sentence *I like cooking* and illustrate other verbs like *boxing, jogging* and *reading.* Show on the board the relationship between the base form of the verb and the *ing* form, e.g *jog/jogging, box/boxing, run/running, read/reading, write/writing.* Point out the spelling changes in passing. These will be taken up in Unit 15 when dealing with the present continuous. Give a few more examples of how the *ing* form is used with other verbs which express likes or dislikes, e.g. *I like swimming. I hate cooking/cleaning. I love walking in the country. I enjoy watching television/keeping fit/ playing cards.*

Exercise 1 (continued)

Refer students to the pre-prepared chart or allow students time to copy it into their notebooks, leaving plenty of space to write in their responses to the questions. Explain *politician, horror, war.* Tell students to add to the categories if they wish, e.g. *opera singer, comedian, newspaper* or *magazine.* Students now individually complete the left-hand column with their likes. When they come to the list of leisure interests, tell them to use their dictionaries to translate the words for any other special interests they have. When students have written their likes, ask individual students to tell the class about some of them, e.g. *I like romantic films, I like watching TV.*

Exercise 2

To demonstrate how the exercise works, choose a student to work Teacher–Student. Ask the student his/her opinion of the people you have included in the first category, e.g.
T: Do you like Prince?
S: Yes, I do./Yes, I like him very much.

Encourage the use of the object pronouns where appropriate. Work across the class and ask a few students to ask others in the class about the people on their lists. Students then work in pairs to ask about their partners and to complete the right-hand column of their charts. As they work, monitor their accuracy and check that they are following the instruction about the answers, *Yes, No, O.K.* If any pair is spending too much time on one category, move them on to the next.

Exercise 3

Draw the class together. Give students time to look at the information on their lists and find the most interesting points of disagreement between themselves and their partners - no more than three or four. Ask them to write the sentences first and then check by selecting a few students to read their sentences aloud.

SUGGESTED LESSON BREAK

 Exercise 4 READING AND LISTENING
Explain the words *advertisement* and *interview.* Read the small advertisement (a *small ad*) aloud with the whole group, glossing the vocabulary and expressions, e.g. *20ish,* as you read.

Ask students to make a chart with headings in their notebooks like this:

	Man 1	Man 2	Man 3
Name			
Age			
Job			
Interests			

Play the tape, stopping after each interview for students to complete the information in their chart. Check if there were any special difficulties before continuing. Play the tape a second time without stopping and then ask students to say which they think is the best partner for the woman. Encourage them to try to explain why. There is no correct answer.

TAPESCRIPT

Read the dateline advertisement, then listen to three interviews. Note each man's name, age, job and interests. Say which you think is the best partner for the woman, and why.

1

INTERVIEWER: Now, your name's Tony, isn't it?
TONY: That's right.
INTERVIEWER: And you're...?
TONY: I'm a teacher.
INTERVIEWER: How old are you?
TONY: Twenty-five.
INTERVIEWER: Right. And what sort of things are you interested in?
TONY: Well, I like reading, and gardening. I'm a stay-at-home person, I suppose.
INTERVIEWER: Do you enjoy travelling?
TONY: No, not much. I like staying at home.

2

INTERVIEWER: What's your name?
DAVID: David.
INTERVIEWER: And how old are you, David?
DAVID: I'm thirty-one.
INTERVIEWER: What do you do?
DAVID: I'm a doctor. I work at St Thomas's Hospital.
INTERVIEWER: What are your interests?
DAVID: Well, I like classical music, going to the theatre, going to restaurants...
INTERVIEWER: What about sports?
DAVID: No, I don't really like sports at all.
INTERVIEWER: And what sort of person would you like to meet?
DAVID: Um, someone not too old, not too young, someone who likes the same things as me.

3

INTERVIEWER: And your name is...?
SIMON: Simon.
INTERVIEWER: And what do you like doing in your spare time?
SIMON: I like keeping fit, playing tennis, walking and so on.
INTERVIEWER: Anything else?
SIMON: I like going to the cinema and going to discos.
INTERVIEWER: What about music?
SIMON: I don't like classical music very much. I like rock music.
INTERVIEWER: And how old are you, Simon?
SIMON: I'm nineteen.
INTERVIEWER: What do you do?
SIMON: I'm a student.

Exercise 5 READING AND WRITING

BACKGROUND NOTE
Whitney Houston: A popular black American female singer (see picture in Unit 24).

Divide the class into three groups. Allot one advertisement for each group to read. They should use a dictionary to look up the meaning of any new words. One person from each group must then elect to 'report' the main points about their person to the other two groups, e.g. *This is from a woman called Cezary. She is twenty-three. She is a student. She likes photography,* etc. On the basis of this, students can select which person they would most like to write to.

Ask students to look at the letter. Ask: *Who is it to? Who is it from? What nationality is she? What is her address in England?* Then ask students to read the letter and find the answers to the following questions which you can write on the board:

How old is she? What does she do? What does she like doing in her spare time? Which singer does she like? What else is she interested in? Does she like studying English?

After students have read the letter and answered the questions, prepare them for the letter-writing activity. Point out the layout of the letter, with the address at the top right-hand corner and the date underneath. Read the letter aloud. Point out that *Dear* is the way to start all letters, but draw attention to the ending: *Yours sincerely.* This is used when writing to someone you do not know but is not as formal as *Yours faithfully*. A letter to a friend would end with *Best wishes.* Students can write to either Cezary or Christine or to one of the pupils in Maria's class in Portugal.

EXTRA ACTIVITIES
1 Penfriend corner
Everybody writes an advertisement (real or imaginary) for a penfriend as in Exercise 5, folds it over and puts it in a box. As in a raffle, each student chooses one of the advertisements and answers it. If they choose their own, they have to put it back and choose again.

2 Likes and dislikes consequences
This is a version of the 'Consequences' game. Write a set of headings (see below) on the board and ask students to copy them onto a piece of paper. Students fill in information next to one heading, fold the paper over and pass it on to the next student, who completes the next category and so on, until all four categories are completed, e.g.

Name:	Margaret Thatcher
Nationality:	Russian
Age:	93
Likes:	disco dancing and aerobics
Hates:	speaking English

The student who unfolds the completed paper must read it out in proper sentences, e.g. *My name is Margaret Thatcher. I'm Russian. I'm ninety-three. I like disco dancing and aerobics but I don't like speaking English.*

UNIT 10 Places

Suggested lesson break: after Exercise 4

First photograph and map
Ask students to find London and York on the maps in their Students' Books. Ask: *What city is near York?* (Leeds) *What river is York on?* (The Ouse)

Draw a simple compass on the board and do choral practice of the four points: *north, south, east* and *west*, and the intermediate points: *north-east, north-west, south-east* and *south-west*.

Refer students back to the map. Ask: *Is London in the north or the south of England?* (In the south) *Is it in the south-east or south-west?* (In the south-east) *What about York?* (It's in the north-east.)

Ask students to look at the photograph of York. Ask: *What can you see?* (A church/cathedral) *Is York an old or a modern city?* (It's old.) *What other buildings do tourists visit?* Elicit: *historical buildings/museums*. Write the new words on the board and practise their pronunciation.

Exercise 1 READING (York)
Ask students to read the text about York. While they read, draw the chart from Exercise 1 on the board, leaving space to write notes next to each heading. Ask students to suggest what to write in each category.

Second photograph and map
Students look at the map of the USA in their Students' Books. Ask: *What part of the USA can you see?* (California) *Is it on the east or the west coast of the USA?* (On the west coast) *What city is San Diego near?* (Los Angeles) *What other famous cities do you know in California?* (San Francisco) *What is the name of the ocean near San Diego?* (The Pacific Ocean) *Do you think California has good beaches?* (Yes)

Ask students to look at the photograph of San Diego. Ask: Is S*an Diego an old or a modern city?* (It's modern.) *What can you see in the picture?* (The sea, buildings, a harbour, palm trees, a road) Write the new words on the board and practise their pronunciation.

Exercise 1 READING (San Diego)
Students copy the chart with the heading *San Diego*. They read the text on San Diego and complete the information. Check the answers afterwards.

Use one text for choral reading practice, making breaks according to sense-units, e.g. *York is a beautiful old city/in the north-east of England/on the River Ouse.*

The note
To revise the use of the articles, write these sentences on the board and ask students to complete them.

Leeds is ... English city.
San Diego is ... city in California.
Canberra is ... capital of Australia.

Point out the use of the definite article *the* in the reading texts with oceans, seas and rivers. Check the rule by writing these names on the board: *Atlantic, Indian, Mediterranean, Baltic, North, Thames, Rhone, Seine.*

Ask students to complete the names, using the words *ocean, sea* or *river*, e.g. *the Atlantic Ocean, the Indian Ocean, the Mediterranean Sea, the Baltic Sea, the North Sea, the River Thames, the River Rhone, the River Seine.* Explain that sometimes you do not need to use the words *river, ocean, sea*, e.g. *the Atlantic, the Pacific, the Mediterranean, the Baltic, the Thames, the Rhone, the Seine.* (Note that you **cannot** say: ~~The Indian~~ or ~~The North.~~

Exercise 2
Use pictures, mime or examples to illustrate the meaning of the following words: *university, industrial, ugly, interesting, boring.* Practise their pronunciation chorally and individually. Explain

that a city usually has a cathedral and is bigger than a town. Students work in pairs to think of examples from their country of each item in the list. They then join another pair to compare their lists. Encourage differences of opinion like: *But ... isn't a beautiful building. It's ugly.*

GRAMMAR FOCUS
Ask students to look at the information in the Focus box as a reminder. Then check by asking questions about the position of a few towns and cities in their own country, e.g.
T: Where's Milan?
s: It's in the north of Italy.

Exercise 3
Students can use atlases for this exercise, or the exercise can be made into a competition with teams answering the questions. Students can make up additional questions. (See Extra activity 2.)

KEY
1 Bilbao is in the north of Spain.
2 Naples is in the south of Italy.
3 Paris is in the north of France.
4 Madrid is in the centre of Spain.
5 New York is on the east coast of the USA.
6 Malaga is on the south coast of Spain.
7 Izmir is on the west coast of Turkey.
8 Acapulco is on the west coast of Mexico.
9 Thessaloniki is in the north-east of Greece.

Exercise 4
Explain any new words in the box. Students write about the cities in pairs or groups. When checking, elicit full sentences as in the example.

KEY
Florence is famous for its museums and art galleries.
Sydney is famous for its harbour.
Paris is famous for its shops and nightlife, museums and art galleries.
Madrid is famous for its football team, museums and art galleries.
Rio de Janeiro is famous for its beaches.
Chartres is famous for its cathedral.

Remind students that *its* is not *it is* but the possessive adjective from *it* (c.f. *his/her*).

Exercise 5 LISTENING
Before playing the tape, ask: *What do you think the person is going to talk about?* Elicit: *art galleries, cafés, bars, shops.* Play the tape, stopping at intervals to check comprehension and elicit guesses. Before playing the final sentence, ask the students if they know what the city is. (The answer is Paris.) Play the recording again for students to appreciate the description.

TAPESCRIPT
Listen to someone describing a city in Exercise 3. Which city is the speaker describing?

DAVID:
I think it's my favourite city in the world. It's very big but it has the feeling sometimes of being really very small because there, there are certain parts of the city which have very small streets and very small shops and, and bars. There are millions and millions of things to do there, there are museums, discos – the nightlife is terrific. It's a city that is never boring. It's full of historical buildings and also there are a lot of modern buildings there as well. So there's a, a, an extraordinary mixture. There are many many different ways of seeing the city, apart from the Metro. A ride in a cab in this city is quite an event! Another way of seeing it is to take a trip down the river on a *bateau mouche*. From the boat you can see pretty well everything – everything from the Eiffel Tower to Notre Dame.

Exercise 6
Ask students to list the adjectives in a separate vocabulary book. (See Learning to learn 3: Recording vocabulary on page 48.) Explain that *large* and *big* mean the same but *large* is often used when describing cities.

KEY
large – small	historical
big – small	famous
beautiful – ugly	best
old – modern	industrial
old – new	
interesting – boring	

Exercise 7 SPEECHWORK
Ask students to copy the words into their notebooks. Play the tape while students listen and underline the stressed syllable. Practise the words afterwards chorally.

KEY
beautiful   interesting   industrial   gallery
historical   restaurant   cathedral   university

Exercise 8 ROLEPLAY
Before starting, refer to the note below the roleplay and explain the meaning of *What's it like?* Build up a series of replies that students can use about their own city, e.g. *What's Rome/ Istanbul/Athens like? It's very nice. It's a very beautiful city. It's a very interesting place to live. It has a very big harbour. It's the best place to live in Italy/Turkey/Greece.*

Ask all students to prepare answers to A's questions. Then divide students into pairs to act out the roleplay. Write a simple framework on the board.

A: *Excuse me, is this seat free?*
B: *Yes, it is.*
A: *Nice day.*
B: *Yes, very nice.*
A: *Excuse my asking but where do you come from?*
B: *I come from York.*
A: *Where's that exactly?*
B: *It's in the north-east of England.*
A: *What's it like?*
B: *It's an interesting old city with a beautiful cathedral.*
A: *Do you like living there?*
B: *Yes, very much. And you? Where do you come from?*
A: *I come from ... (etc.)*

Exercise 9
Students use the texts about York and San Diego as a model for their writing.

Exercise 10
Ask students to look at the three lists. Ask:
Which is the best place in Britain for a weekend break? (York) *Where does London come on the list?* (Number 3) Ask similar questions for the other two lists.
(You may like to introduce the ordinal numbers: *first, second, third, fourth* and *fifth* at this point.)

Ask students to make their own list of three places for each category, substituting their own country for Britain in the first list. Involve the whole class in deciding on the five top places in each category.

EXTRA ACTIVITIES
1 Famous places
Write these headings and list on the board:

PLACE	CITY OR COUNTRY
The ... Gallery	...
The ... Museum	...
... Cathedral	...
... Beach	...
... Mountain	...
The River ...	...
... Airport	...

Ask students to add specific names to make real places and to say where they are, e.g. *The Tate Gallery - London*. The first person to complete his/her list correctly wins.

2 Goal!
One student thinks of a word from Unit 10 and other students must try to guess the word. See Unit 4, Extra activity 2 for detailed instructions.

FLUENCY Units 6–10

> BACKGROUND NOTE
> *A shanty town*: A town made up of wooden or metal huts where poor people live. These are sometimes found on the outskirts of large cities.

PREPARATION
If possible, copy each text, A and B, onto separate sheets of paper and photocopy or stencil equal numbers of A and B texts so that each student has a copy of one text only.

Exercise 1 READING
Ask students to cover the right-hand page of their Students' Book and to look at the map. Ask:
What part of the world does this show? (Latin/South America) *What is the capital of Peru?* (Lima) *What is the capital of Ecuador?* (Quito).
Now ask students to look at the photograph of the boy. Ask: *What has he got?/What is he holding?* (A hat) *Why?* (He's selling hats.)

Give a copy of one of the texts, A or B, to each student. If you have not got copies, ask A students to cover B's text and vice versa. Students read their appropriate text twice; once for general meaning and a second time to answer the questions in Exercise 1. They should use dictionaries or ask you the meaning of any unfamiliar words.

Exercise 2
Take the part of A yourself and choose a student to take the part of B. Give an example of how the exercise works, e.g.
T: His full name is Victor Raul Manani.
S: No, it isn't. His full name is Victor *Jorge* Manani.
T: He's ten years old.
S: No, he isn't. He's *twelve* years old.

Encourage Student B to stress the corrected word each time, i.e. *Jorge, twelve*.
Students work with their partner. Student A starts as shown in the example and Student B interrupts at each point of difference.

Exercise 3 LISTENING
Ask: *What can you see in the photograph? Is it an old or a modern part of Lima? Are there any buildings like these in your town/city?* Find out what the students know about Lima under the headings in the listening exercise. Remind students of the features of cities in Exercise 1 of Unit 10. Play the tape once through without stopping, then again, pausing for students to take notes. When they have finished, check their answers. It is important that students note the correct answers in order to do the writing in Exercise 4.

TAPESCRIPT
Listen to two people talking about the city of Lima and make notes under the headings in your Students' Book.

A: You've been to Lima, haven't you Simon?
B: Yes, I have.
A: Tell me about it. What's it like as a city?
B: Ah... Well ... as you know Lima is the capital of Peru.
A: Is it mainly a tourist city?
B: Well, yes, it is a tourist city but it's also an industrial city.
A: Where exactly is it situated? On the coast?
B: Yes, it's on the coast.
A: Is it a large city?
B: Yes, it is. About five million people live in Lima.
A: Five million. That is quite large. And is it a beautiful city, do you think?
B: Yes and no. Some parts are very beautiful. It has a very old university, a beautiful cathedral, a palace and many old Spanish buildings but there are a lot of modern buildings and industries now in Lima and they aren't exactly beautiful.
A: But that's true of any big city.
B: I agree. Yes.

Exercise 4 WRITING
Students complete the paragraph using their notes from Exercise 3. Students can refer back to the texts on York and San Diego in Unit 10 for a model.

EXTRA ACTIVITY
Roleplay
Write the following notes on the board. Ask students to copy them and to prepare questions to use in a roleplay with a street-seller in New York.

Name:	Bernie Miguel Sanchez
Home town:	Brooklyn, New York
Age:	36
Family:	one brother, two sisters, parents both dead
Job:	sells hamburgers
Likes:	watching football on TV, fishing, making money
Doesn't like:	New York policemen
Languages:	Spanish and English

Help students with some of the questions, e.g.
What's your name?
Where are you from?
How old are you?
Have you got any brothers or sisters?
Are your parents alive?
What do you do?
What do you like doing in your spare time?
What don't you like?
What languages do you speak?

CHECK Units 6 –10
(For advice on handling this section, see the notes for Check Units 1–5.)

KEY
Ex. 1 1a 2c 3b 4a 5b 6b 7a
8b (a = American English) 9a 10c
(10 marks)

Ex. 2 1 Do you like cycling?
2 She doesn't like him very much.
3 Where do they live?
4 Does he live with his parents?
5 I don't like this music.
(5 marks)

Ex. 3 1 an 2 the 3 a 4 The 5 the (5 marks)

Ex. 4 1 from 2 on 3 of 4 in 5 for (in) 6 of
7 in 8 with 9 at 10 from (10 marks)

Ex. 5

mother	father
morning	evening
love	hate
near	far
interesting	boring
big	small
brother	sister
old	modern
aunt	uncle
north	south

(10 marks)

Ex. 6 1g 2c 3e 4b 5a 6h 7j 8d 9f 10i
(10 marks)

Ex. 7 1 it 2 them 3 her 4 him 5 them 6 it
7 him 8 her 9 it 10 you (10 marks)

Ex. 8 'My name's Laura and I'm twenty-two years old. I come from California in America but I'm in York at the moment. I'm a student at the university. York is a very beautiful old city and I like living here very much.' (15 marks)

CHECK YOUR PROGRESS
(See notes for Check Units 1–5.)

LEARNING TO LEARN 2
As the course progresses, the students should be getting used to the teacher referring to points of grammar in English. Learning to learn 2 is designed to help students to become familiar with the main grammar words so that they can benefit fully from the Grammar Focus notes and from the Language review section. Teachers can gradually introduce other words like *pronoun, possessive, conjunction* as the need arises. The list of verb tenses allows students a quick overview of the

main tenses of English. This should not be seen as an occasion for presenting these tenses for active use. The idea is that students should simply become aware of the shape and form of these tenses. False beginners may find this early introduction useful for experimenting with the language in roleplays or writing tasks.

Go through the lists and ask students to give other English examples of each word class. Do the tasks with the class as a whole. Do not insist on everyone remembering all the names of the tenses at this stage. There will be plenty of opportunity in the future to become more acquainted with the terms.

KEY
What are these words?
1 noun   2 verb   3 adjective   4 article
5 adverb   6 verb/adjective   7 adjective
8 preposition   9 verb

What are these tenses?
1 present continuous   2 present simple
3 present perfect   4 past simple   5 *going to* future

PREVIEW Units 11–15

BACKGROUND NOTES
The background map: This shows the campus of the University of York, the university where Laura is studying.
J. B. Morrell: The library at the University of York is named after one of the founders of the university.
In San Diego they're just going to bed: The time difference between the west coast of the USA and the UK is eleven hours later than GMT (Greenwich Mean Time).
Zambia: A country in East Africa, bordering on to Zimbabwe, Mozambique, Tanzania, Zaire and Angola. The capital city is Lusaka.

The photographs and the captions
If you have a class of false beginners, use the photographs to find out how much students know about the grammar and vocabulary presented in the next five units. For example ask questions to find out if students can:
– tell the time: *What's the time in Picture 1?*
– use the present continuous: *What's Laura doing in Picture 2?*
– talk about journeys: *How does Laura go to college?*
– use the present simple: *What time does the library open?*
– talk about routines : *What does Laura usually do in the morning?*
– name the rooms of the house: *What room are the people in? Where's Laura studying?*

Let students experiment with the language and try to express what they want to say even if it is incorrect.

If you have a class of complete beginners, ask simple questions about the pictures, e.g.
Picture 1
Where is Laura? (In bed)
What's that near the bed? (An alarm clock)
What time is it? (Half past seven/7.30)
Picture 2
Is Laura in a car? (No, she isn't. She's on a bike.)
What's that building? (The university)
Picture 3
What's the library called? (The J.B. Morrell Library)
Picture 4
Who are the people? (Laura and Mr and Mrs Gibson)
Picture 5
Is Laura in bed? (No, she isn't.)
What's that on the table? (It's a radio cassette recorder.)
Where are the pens? (In a mug)

The tape and the exercise
Play the tape and ask students to follow the captions. Explain any difficult words or expressions, e.g. *It only takes me ten minutes.* Ask different students each to read a sentence of the True/False exercise and to select another student to answer it. Ask students to try to correct the sentences which are false.

TAPESCRIPT
Listen and read the captions in your Students' Book.

MRS GIBSON: Laura, time to get up! It's half past seven!
LAURA: I get up at 7.30 on weekdays. Back home in San Diego they're just going to bed.
I cycle to college. It only takes me ten minutes.
MAN: Morning, Laura.
LAURA: Morning!
I usually go to the library in the morning. It opens at 9. I'm staying with a couple called Mr and Mrs Gibson. Their daughter's working in Zambia. I've got her room. It's a nice room. There's a bed, a wardrobe, and a big table near the window. I like working there.
MRS GIBSON: Laura! Cup of tea?
LAURA: Thanks. I'm coming.
I like Mrs Gibson. She's really friendly.

The learning objectives box
Ask students to read the objectives in the box and then find examples of the language in the captions under the pictures.

Tell the time: *I get up at 7.30.*
Say what time things happen: *It opens at nine.*
Describe your daily routine: *I usually go to the library in the morning.*
Talk about journeys: *I cycle to college.*
Describe your home: *It's a nice room. There's a big table near the window.*
Talk about present activities: *In San Diego they're just going to bed.*

UNIT 11 Times

Suggested lesson break: after the Grammar Focus

PRESENTATION
With books closed, use a model clock or draw a clock on the board to show how to ask and tell the time Ask: What time is it?/What's the time? Demonstrate or elicit: *It's one o'clock.* Ask: *What time is it now?/What's the time now?* Elicit: *It's ten past one.* etc.

Practise the stress patterns of different time phrases chorally and individually, e.g.

one o'clock   two o'clock   three o'clock
half past two   half past three   half past four
five to two   ten to two   quarter to two, etc.

Exercise 1
Play the tape, asking students to repeat the times. Finish by asking what the time is on the large clock above the title.

Exercise 2
Ask students to open their books and look at the clock faces in Exercise 2. Students work in pairs and change parts to ask about each different clock. Check by asking individual students what the times are.

KEY
1 It's seven o'clock.   4 It's quarter past nine.
2 It's twenty past three. 5 It's half past eleven.
3 It's ten to six.   6 It's quarter to three.

Note
Go through the note with the students. Give some practice of the main points. Write some times on the board like *9.30, 10.45.* Ask: *What time is it?* Elicit: *It's nine thirty* (or *It's half past nine*), etc. Then write some a.m .and p.m. times on the board, e.g. *6 p.m., 3 a.m.* Ask students: *What time is it?* Elicit: *It's six o'clock in the evening. It's three o'clock in the morning.* etc.

With false beginners, point out that you can say *It's ten to six.* or *It's ten minutes to six.* but the first is more common. However, explain that when talking about one, two, three or four minute intervals, the word *minutes* **must** be added, e.g. *Three minutes to six* **not** ~~three to six.~~ Demonstrate with a clock, e.g. *It's eleven minutes to nine. It's two minutes to six. What's the exact time now?* Elicit: *It's three minutes to eleven.*

Exercise 3 VOCABULARY
Allow students time to see if they can do the exercise on their own with a dictionary.

KEY
1 second 2 minute 3 hour 4 day 5 week
6 fortnight 7 month 8 year 9 century

Ask students to work in pairs with the exercise. You may want to introduce the structure *are there* at this stage. If so, expand the question, e.g. *How many seconds are there in a minute? How many minutes are there in an hour?* etc.

KEY
60 seconds in a minute   (2 fortnights in a month)
60 minutes in an hour   4 weeks in a month
24 hours in a day   12 months in a year
7 days in a week   100 years in a century
2 weeks in a fortnight

Exercise 4 READING

> BACKGROUND NOTES
> The extracts show:
> *A poster for the ballet, 'Coppelia'*: a classical ballet with music by Tchaikovsky.
> *A cinema advertisement in a newspaper*: for the film 'Gorillas in the Mist', an American film set in Africa and starring Sigourney Weaver.
> *A train timetable*: for journeys from Scarborough and York to London. Scarborough is a holiday resort on the north-east coast of England, in Yorkshire.
> *A invitation to a birthday party.*
> *Television programme times in a newspaper*: for ITV (Independent Television), one of the commercial television channels on the British television network.

Ask students to look at the advertisements, etc:
What's the ballet called? ('Coppelia /kə'peɪlɪə/)
Where is the performance? (At the York Theatre Royal - See Preview Units 26–30)
What's the name of the cinema? (The Odeon)
What's the timetable for? (Trains to London)
Whose birthday is it? (Sue's)
What's the name of the programme at five past eight? ('Murder She Wrote')
Which times are circled in the cinema advertisement and the rail timetable? (Eight oh five/five past eight and six fifty/ten to seven)

Ask the questions about the different times to the whole class. Encourage students to express the times in alternative ways, e.g. *It's half past seven./It's seven thirty.* Point out that we say *eight oh five* not ~~eight zero five~~ or ~~eight five~~ and get the students to practise several times which are a few minutes past the 'o'clock', e.g. *8.05 = eight oh five; 10.03 = ten oh three; 6.05 = six oh five.* Explain that the word *o'clock* is often omitted, e.g. *The party starts at nine (o'clock).*

If you wish, students can then do the exercise in pairs.

GRAMMAR FOCUS

Draw the students' attention to the examples in the Focus box. Do the exercise with the whole class. Give further practice by calling out words and phrases and getting the students to supply the preposition, e.g.

T: Wednesday   S: On Wednesday
T: The evening   S: In the evening
T: Midnight   S: At midnight
T: Eight o'clock   S: At eight o'clock

If you have a class of false beginners, add phrases such as: *on Monday morning, on Tuesday afternoon, tomorrow morning*, etc.

KEY
Which preposition?
1 at noon   2 in the afternoon   3 from 10 a.m. to 5 p.m.   4 at 1.30 p.m.   5 on Tuesday

SUGGESTED LESSON BREAK

 Exercise 5 LISTENING

> BACKGROUND NOTE
> *King's Cross*: A mainline London station serving the north and north-east regions of Britain. It is also an important London underground station.

Read aloud the situation. Explain where King's Cross is and that York is about two hours from London. On the board write the two questions:

What time does your train leave London?
What time does your train arrive in York?

Point out that you *arrive in* or *arrive at* a place not ~~arrive to.~~

Play the tape once or twice for the students to write down the times. Students then ask each other the two questions on the board.

TAPESCRIPT
You're going to York tomorrow. You want to be there by ten o'clock. You phone King's Cross Station to find out the train times. Listen to the recorded information and choose a suitable train.

This is British Rail's talking timetable giving details of British Rail services from London

King's Cross to York, on weekdays. Departures are at 6 o'clock arriving at 8.32, 7.30 arriving at 9.39, 8 o'clock arriving at 10.10, 9 o'clock arriving at 11.01, 9.30 arriving at 11.45, 10 o'clock arriving at 12.01, 10.30 arriving at 12.25, 11 o'clock arriving at 13.01...

Exercise 6

> BACKGROUND NOTES
> *Derwent College:* One of the colleges which together comprise York University.
> *Halifax:* A large town in Yorkshire, not far from York.
> *Approx:* Approximately (about)
> *Entrance:* The price of the ticket to see the film.

To show the meaning of the words *open, close, start, finish, leave, arrive,* etc. write the following information on the board:

Bank: 9.30-15.30
Film: 20.15 - 22.30
Train: dep. 6.20 arr. 7.15

Ask: *What time does the bank open?* (It opens at half past nine.)
What time does it close? (It closes at half past three.)
What time does the film start? (It starts at eight fifteen.)
What time does it finish? (It finishes at half past ten.)
What time does the train leave? (It leaves at six twenty.)
What time does the train arrive? (It arrives back at quarter past seven.)
Explain that the word *depart* is used for travel timetables but that *leave* is used in conversation.

Practise chorally the pronunciation of third person singular form of the present simple with the verbs e.g.

closes /kləʊzɪz/:   *It closes ... It closes at half past three.*
finishes /fɪnɪʃɪz/:   *It finishes ... It finishes at half past ten.*
starts /stɑːts/:   *It starts ... It starts at eight fifteen.*
leaves /liːvz/:   *It leaves ... It leaves at six twenty.*

Go through the example exchange in Exercise 6 and practise the question chorally with the students. Make sure that *does* is pronounced as a weak form /dəz/, and that the 3rd person singular *s* is not forgotten in the answers. Different students around the class ask other students about the times on the notices in the Students' Book.
S1: What time does the library open?
S2: It opens at nine.
S3: What time does the library close on Tuesday?
S4: It closes at ten. (etc.)

Extend this practice to local places and events.

Exercise 7

Go through the questions, asking individual students to reply. Do not necessarily expect full sentence answers, e.g.

T: What time does this school open in the morning?
S: (I think it opens) at seven thirty.

Students can write out full sentence answers for homework. If students ask if they can use *when* instead of *what time*, explain that this is also possible and vary your questions with *when* and *what time* so that they get used to hearing both expressions. Note that *when* is presented later in Unit 19 with months and seasons.

Exercise 8 READING

> BACKGROUND NOTES
> *Bureau de change* /ˌbjʊərəʊ də ˈʃɑːdnʒ/: A French expression meaning a place where you can change money from one currency to another. There is no English expression for this.
> *Until quite late*: Means up to 9 p.m. or 10 p.m., in some big cities, i.e. well after the normal bank working hours.
> *National holiday*: Official holiday when banks and other businesses are closed.

Ask students to read the information silently and report back the answers to the questions. Explain *except* and give some more example sentences, e.g. *The museum is open every day except Monday*.

Ask students to give similar information for their own country. Elicit full sentences by saying: *Tell me about the opening times of ... (banks, post offices, cinemas, etc.)*. Elicit: *Banks open at ...*

Exercise 9 WRITING

On the board, write headings similar to those in the box in the Students' Book and ask the students to present their information in the same way. Ask them to include any other information about opening times in other places which they think is useful, e.g. museums, libraries, swimming pools, etc. The students can start the work in class and continue it for homework.

EXTRA ACTIVITIES

1 Information gap

Write the following timetable on a piece of paper and copy it so that you have enough copies for half the class. Give it to half of the class.

Edinburgh	*11.15*
Newcastle	*13.23*
Darlington	*13.55*
York	*14.51*
Doncaster	*15.21*
Peterborough	*16.20*
King's Cross	*17.30*

Give each student in the other half of the class a slip of paper with some travel plans, e.g. *York to King's Cross, Doncaster to Peterborough*.

Explain that these students must find out from someone with the complete timetable what time the train leaves and arrives in the places on their pieces of paper, e.g. *What time does the train leave Doncaster? What time does it arrive in Peterborough?*

2 Fast and slow

The class must understand the meaning of *fast* and *slow* in expressions like *My watch is fast/slow*. Divide the class into two teams: a Fast Team and a Slow Team. The teacher is the 'game leader' and calls out a time, e.g. *ten past eight*. If the teacher points to someone in the Fast Team, that person must add five minutes and say: *quarter past eight*. If the teacher points to someone in the Slow Team, that person must subtract five minutes and say *five past eight*. (Explain that you will work in five minute differences.) A point is awarded for each correct answer. Continue until everyone has given a time.

UNIT 12 Routines

Suggested lesson break: after Exercise 4

PREPARATION

Write the routine below on the board.

My daily routine
6.30	*get up and make coffee*
	have a shower
	get dressed
7.30	*have breakfast*
7.45	*go to work*
12.00	*have lunch*
5.30	*go home*
6.30	*have supper*
9.30	*go out dancing*
11.30	*go to bed*

Presentation

Present each stage of your daily routine in a complete sentence, illustrating it using mime, drawings of stick figures or a set of magazine pictures, e.g. (miming) *I get up at seven o'clock. Then I have a shower and get dressed*. etc.

Then ask and answer about your routine: *What do you do at six thirty? I get up and make coffee.* Ask one or two students: *What time do you get up/have breakfast/go to school/college/work?*

To illustrate the first two adverbs of frequency: *always* and *usually* (the others occur later in Grammar Focus 2) write the following table on the board:

	get up	go to bed
Mon	*6.30*	*11.00*
Tues	*6.30*	*11.00*
Wed	*6.30*	*11.30*
Thurs	*6.30*	*11.30*
Fri	*6.30*	*11.30*
Sat	*6.30*	*11.30*
Sun	*6.30*	*11.00*

Then say: *I always get up at 6.30. I usually go to bed at eleven thirty.* Then ask one or two students: *What time do you usually go to bed?*

Now ask students to open their books and look at the pictures at the top of the page.

Exercise 1
Ask students what they can see in the pictures, e.g. (Picture A) *What's that?* Elicit: *It's an alarm clock.* Supply any necessary vocabulary, e.g. *a shower, a plate of cornflakes/a plate of breakfast cereal (and a spoon), a plate of food (and a knife and fork), a key, a disco notice, a house, a light in the bedroom window, the sky at night, the moon and stars.*

Read out each sentence in turn. Students either call out or write down the letter of the picture which matches the sentence.

KEY
1 B 2 D 3 E 4 F 5 A 6 H 7 G 8 C

Now ask students to read out the sentences in the correct order round the class and then write them in their notebooks in the correct sequence.

GRAMMAR FOCUS (1)
Practise the use of the article as explained in the Focus box. Get students to give you full sentences in answer, e.g. *I have breakfast at seven./I have lunch at one. What time do you have breakfast?* etc. Elicit: *I have breakfast at seven too. I go to work/get home in the evening at ...*

Exercise 2
Ask students to look at the pictures again and say:
T: Picture A. Laura always gets up at seven thirty. What time does Laura get up?

s: She gets up at seven thirty.
T: Picture B. What does she do after that?
s: She has a shower and gets dressed.

Go through the question cues making sure all the students know how to expand them correctly. Practise the stress and rhythm of the questions chorally with the whole class. Weaker students may need to write the full version of the questions in their notebooks. Do not insist on full answers to all the questions but insist on any relevant preposition, e.g. *at seven thirty.* Students do the exercise in pairs.

Exercise 3
Work Teacher–Student with a couple of questions to give students an example:
T: What time do you get up?
s: I get up at six.
T: What time do you have breakfast?
s: I have breakfast at six thirty.

Tell students to use the question cues in Exercise 2 to help them in their interviews.

Exercise 4
Draw out the information like this: *Tell me about the time you get up.* Elicit: *Well, (Anna) gets up at (seven thirty) but I get up at (seven fifteen).* or *We both get up at ...*
Point out the position of *both* in this type of sentence: before the principal/main verb but after the verb *to be.* Try to hear as many pairs as possible.

SUGGESTED LESSON BREAK

GRAMMAR FOCUS (2)
Refer back to the chart about your own routine on the board and revise and expand the adverbs of frequency. Introduce *never* and *sometimes* by saying: *I never go to bed at 11.15. I usually go to bed at 11.30 and I sometimes go at 11.00.* Introduce *often* by saying: *I go to the cinema every Monday night. I often go to the cinema. What about you?* Elicit: *Yes, I often go to the cinema, too.*

Ask students to rearrange the jumbled adverbs: *always, usually, sometimes,* etc. in order of frequency starting with *never.*

KEY
never sometimes often usually always

Ask students to look at the three sentences in the second part of the Focus box and say them aloud. Say: *Which is the adverb in each sentence?* (always, usually, never) *What do you notice about the position of the adverbs in the sentences? Can you make a rule about the position of adverbs?* Then read the question in the Focus box for the students to answer.

KEY
Adverbs of frequency normally come **before** the main verb. They come **after** the verb *to be*.

Ask students to give you more sentences using adverbs of frequency with different verbs, including the verb *to be*. Write some prompts on the board, e.g.

HABITS
Newspapers: *I ... read ...*
TV: *I ... watch ...*
Breakfast: *I ... have ...*
Time: *I'm ... late for work/school.*

After students have done this, ask one or two to tell the class about their habits and routines.

As a final check, call out some sentences for the students to say if they are right or wrong and to correct them if necessary, e.g.
T: I go always home at two thirty.
s: Wrong! I always go home ...
T: I am asleep by midnight always.
s: Wrong. I am always asleep by midnight.
T: I always have breakfast at eight.
s: Right!
T: I never am late for school.
s: Wrong! I'm never late ...

Exercise 5 LISTENING
Note that in the listening passage *when* and *what time* are both used. If you have not already done so, point out that these mean the same in this case. Now ask students to copy the chart into their notebooks. Play the tape, pausing where appropriate for students to tick the right columns. Play the tape once more without stopping, for students to listen and check their ticks. Check the answers with the class.

TAPESCRIPT
Listen to Adam talking about his daily routine. How often does he do things?

INTERVIEWER: Adam, you say you get up at seven thirty.
ADAM: On Monday to Friday I usually get up at seven thirty. But not at the weekend.
INTERVIEWER: What about breakfast?
ADAM: Oh, yes. I always have a big breakfast. Cornflakes, toast, fruit, tea, you know ...
INTERVIEWER: And when do you leave home?
ADAM: I usually leave home at 8.15.
INTERVIEWER: What about the evening? When do you get home?
ADAM: Well, I never get home before seven in the evening.
INTERVIEWER: I see. That's quite late. Then do you go out in the evenings?
ADAM: Yes, sometimes. Maybe to a pub with friends or to the cinema.

INTERVIEWER: And what time do you go to bed?
ADAM: It depends. But I never go to bed before midnight.

Exercise 6
Ask students to look at their completed charts in Exercise 5. Give an example of the first sentence. Either ask individual students to say the sentences, or ask them to write the sentences for homework.

Exercise 7 READING

BACKGROUND NOTE
In the photograph, both the man in white uniform and the woman are nurses. Male nurses are quite common in Britain.

Ask students to look at the picture. Ask questions about the man in the white uniform. Ask:
What's his job? (He's a nurse.)
Where does he work? (In a hospital)
What time does he start work if he's on night duty, do you think? (Perhaps/I think he starts work at 10 p.m.)
How many hours a day does he work? (I think he works 8 hours a day.)
What time do nurses usually finish work after night duty? (Perhaps at 9 o'clock)
What do you think they do during the day? (I think they sleep, go shopping and watch TV.)

Now ask students to study the text in pairs and to fill in the words (or note down the missing words in their notebooks). Check by asking individual students to read a sentence each of the completed text round the class.

Ask: *Which verb is used most frequently?* (go)
Write on the board a list of useful verbal expressions with *go* for students to copy into their notebooks, e.g.

WITH 'TO' AND THE ARTICLE	*WITH 'TO' AND NO ARTICLE*
go to the cinema	*go to work*
go to the theatre	*go to school*
	go to college
	go to university
	go to church
	go to bed
WITHOUY 'TO' AND NO ARTICLE	*WITH 'ING'*
go home	*go shopping*
	go swimming
	go skiing

Exercise 8 WRITING
Ask students to look at the example paragraph and to read the sentences aloud. Refer back to your routine. Show how to connect the stages of your routine by saying: *I always get up at six thirty and have a shower.* **After that** *I get dressed*

and have breakfast. **Then** I go to work. **After lunch**, I sometimes go shopping.

Write these sentences on the board, underlining the linking words *After that* and *Then*. Point out the following:

It is wrong to write: *I work in the morning. ~~After, I have lunch.~~* You must write instead: *I work in the morning. After that I have lunch. After lunch I ...* or: *I work in the morning. Afterwards, I have lunch. After lunch...* There is no article in the phrases: *After lunch/breakfast/work.*

Ask students first to write simple sentences in a list about their routine and then to combine them with *Then I ..., After that I ..., After (lunch) I ... .* Students then start writing their paragraphs while you go round and monitor. Ask one or two students to read out their finished paragraphs.

EXTRA ACTIVITIES
1 Shift work
Ask students to work in groups and make a list of jobs which involve shift work, or jobs with unusual hours, e.g. *nurse, doctor, waiter, night porter, ambulance driver, police officer, fire fighter, actor, night club disc jockey.* Ask them to see how quickly they can make a list of ten jobs. The jobs must be expressed in English so each group must have a good dictionary.

2 Information gap
In advance, make copies of the two texts A and B below. Divide students into pairs and give Text A to one student in each pair and Text B to the other student. Tell students that they must not look at each other's texts or read out any part of their text to each other. They have to ask questions to obtain the missing information in their texts.

TEXT A Bob and Carol Brown
Bob's a [1].... He plays the violin but he hasn't got a job at the moment. [2]..., his wife, is a student. They have a baby daughter called Jenny. She is [3]... old.

They get up at [4]... and have breakfast. After breakfast, Carol [5]... . At 10 o'clock, Bob goes shopping with the baby.

In the afternoon, Bob [6]... and the baby sleeps. Then he makes supper. Carol gets home at about [7]... .

In the evening, Carol usually studies and Bob often goes out with friends or watches TV. They usually go to bed at [8]... .

TEXT B Bob and Carol Brown
Bob is a musician. He plays the [1] ... but he hasn't got a job at the moment. Carol, his wife, is a [2]... . They have a baby daughter called [3]... . She is eighteen months old.

They get up at 7.00 and have breakfast. After breakfast, [4].... cycles to college. At [5]... o'clock, Bob goes shopping with the baby.

In the afternoon, Bob usually plays the violin and the baby [6]... . Then he makes supper. Carol gets home at about 6.30.

In the evening, Carol usually [7]... and Bob [8]... . They usually go to bed at 11.30.

Students should first write down the questions they need to ask to get the information. Give some examples on the board, e.g:

STUDENT A QUESTIONS
1 What does Bob do? (He's a musician.)
2 What's his wife's name? (Carol.)

STUDENT B QUESTIONS
1 What (instrument) does Bob play? (He plays the violin.)
2 What does Carol/his wife do? (She's a student.)

Students now work in pairs and take turns to ask questions on each paragraph, e.g. Student A starts by asking the questions relating to paragraph 1 of Text A, then B asks his/her questions on paragraph 1 of Text B, and so on until both texts are complete.

UNIT 13 Journeys

Suggested lesson break: after Exercise 2

PRESENTATION
With books closed, draw on the board or use magazine pictures to show the following: a car, a bus, a train, an underground train, a plane (an aeroplane), a boat, a bicycle, a person walking. The students probably know a proportion of these items in English already. Elicit the words for each type of transport, write them on the board in a list and practise them chorally and individually. Then say: *How do you get to work?* Point to each method in turn and say: *I go by car/I go by bus,* etc. (Do not introduce the verbs *I drive* or *I cycle* yet.) Write *I go by* in front of the transport words on the board (with the exception of *walk*). If you wish, teach the expression *on foot* but point out that it isn't used very often. Now ask a few individual students the same question and elicit different answers. Then ask:

T: How does Anna get to work?
S: She goes by train. (etc.)

Explain that *get to*, when used about journeys, means *arrive at* or *travel to*.

Now write on the board:

home → work/school = 3 kilometres

Ask: *How far is it from your home to work/school?* Elicit: *It's 3 kilometres.* Then ask: *Is that near or a long way away?* Elicit: *It's quite near.* Ask one or two students the same question.

Now write on the board:

Leave home: 7.30
Arrive at work: 7.45

Ask: *How long does it take you to get to work/school?* Elicit: *It takes me fifteen minutes/a quarter of an hour.*

Write the following table on the board:

15 minutes – quarter of an hour
30 minutes – half an hour
45 minutes – ?
60 minutes – ?

Ask if students can complete the table. Write in: *three quarters of an hour* and *an hour*. Practise the periods of time chorally and individually. Now ask a few students: *How long does it take you to get to school?* Elicit: *It takes me about half an hour/twenty minutes.*

The photograph
Now ask students to open their books and look at the photograph. Ask: *What does the picture show?* (A station) *Is it a station in a big city?* (No, it isn't.) *How many people can you see?* (Two) *What are the numbers of the two platforms?* (Two and three)

Before you read
Now ask the two questions at the top of the page. Elicit: *early in the morning.*

The text

> BACKGROUND NOTES
> *The title*: A pun on the title of a 20th century play by the American playwright Eugene O'Neill: *A Long Day's Journey into Night*.
> *Liverpool Street Station*: A mainline station as well as an underground station in central London. It is situated near the business and financial centre of London.
> *King's Cross Station*: (See note in Unit 11.)

Translate *accountant* or ask students to look it up in their dictionaries. Write the following words on the board and ask students to guess their meaning as they read: *village, local, smile.*

Write the following questions on the board:

Where does David live?
How far is it from London?
How long does it take him to get to work every day?
Does he like his job?

Ask students to read the text and find the answers to these questions.

Exercise 1 READING
Ask students to copy the chart into their notebooks and to read the text a second time to complete the information. Explain that *bus* and *car*, etc. are *methods of transport*. After completing the charts, students ask each other questions to check if their information is correct, e.g.
S1: What's his name?
S2: David Ross

GRAMMAR FOCUS
Refer back to the list of different methods of transport which you wrote on the board at the beginning of the lesson. Point out that you can also say: *I drive/cycle/fly/walk* and *I catch/take the train/bus/underground*. Ask a few more students how they get to school or college and get them to use one of these verbs above.

Exercise 2
Present the example exchange and if necessary practise it chorally. Then ask different students to make and ask the rest of the questions and other students to answer them.

SUGGESTED LESSON BREAK

 Exercise 3 LISTENING

> BACKGROUND NOTES
> *Leeds*: A large industrial city in Yorkshire.
> *Newbury*: A large market town in Berkshire.
> *Charing Cross*: A mainline railway station in London, serving the south-east of England. It is also an underground station.

Say: *You are going to hear three people talking about their journeys to work. Look at your books. One is John Gardener. What does he do?* and so on for the other two people.

Translate the job words or ask students to look them up in a dictionary. Now write on the board:

How long does John/Sara/Joan take to get to work? How does he/she travel?

Students listen to the tape at least twice, and then check their answers by working in pairs.

TAPESCRIPT
Listen and note how long the people take to travel to work.

1

JOHN: I usually leave home at eight fifteen and I get to work at about eight forty-five. It depends on the traffic.

2

SARA: I'm a solicitor. I work in the centre of London near Charing Cross. I always travel by underground. My journey to work isn't too bad. It takes me forty minutes approximately from door to door.

3

JOAN: I cycle to work. It's about a fifteen minute journey from my house to the surgery. I leave at half past seven and I'm at the surgery at quarter to eight.

Exercise 4 ROLEPLAY

Prepare Student B's questions with the whole class. Ask different students to make a complete question from each prompt. Give an example of one or two of Mrs Ross's answers. Give an example of a suitable time (e.g. 4.15) in answer to the first question. (The answer is not in the text.) Now divide the students into As and Bs and ask them to ask and answer the questions working from the text and then to change parts. Finally, ask them to close their books and to conduct the roleplay from memory.

SUGGESTED CONVERSATION

B: What time does your husband get up?

A: He gets up at (4.15) in the morning.

B How does he travel to London?

A: By train.

B: How long does the journey take?

A: It takes about an hour to get to York and then it takes two hours from York to London, and about fifty minutes from King's Cross to his office.

or It takes three hours and fifty minutes.

A: What time does he get home in the evening?

B: At about nine o'clock.

A: Why don't you move to London?

B: Because he likes living in the north - and he likes travelling by train!

Exercise 5

Work Teacher–Student with one student, e.g.

T: Anna, how do you usually get to school/college/work?

S: I walk.

T: How far is it?

S: It's about four hundred metres.

T: How long does it take (you)?

S: It takes (me) about ten minutes but if I go by bus it takes two minutes.

Students now copy the chart into their notebooks and ask questions to complete it for different students. The results of the survey can be shown in a bar chart.

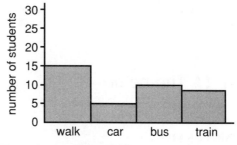

Exercise 6 WRITING

Ask students to read the rubric, then ask them questions about the man on the bicycle: *What's his name?* (John Ellis) *What does he do?* (He's a cycle messenger.) *What does a cycle messenger do?* (He collects and delivers letters and packets.) *Where does he live?* (In North London) *Where does he work?* (In the centre, near Liverpool Street Station) *How do you think he gets to work?*

Ask students to use their imagination and to think what John's day is like, starting from the time he gets up. Write the following prompts on the board:

Get up?   Go to work?
When/Where have lunch?   Get home?
Likes job?   After work?

Students should make notes and write them in connected sentences in a paragraph. Ask one or two students to read their paragraphs aloud to the class. Make a note of any errors to correct with the whole class later.

EXTRA ACTIVITIES

1 Miming game: methods of transport

Students form groups and choose one method of transport to act out in front of the class. They should all involve more than one person, e.g. travelling on an underground train, driving to work with two children in the back seat, travelling by boat. The other students must guess by saying *You're on a boat/train/bus/bicycle/in a car,* etc.

2 Draw it!

Divide the class into two teams. They must sit as far away as possible from each other. Make a list of words on a separate card for students to draw. One person from each team comes up to you and you show them a card with a word written on it, e.g. *train.* That person now goes back to the team and draws it, without saying anything or writing words to help the team. As soon as one person in the team guesses the word, that person goes up to get the next word. It is best if you give the same words to each team but in a different order so that they are not trying to overhear the other team guessing the same word. Suggested words to draw: *underground train, cycle messenger, aeroplane, accountant, doctor, railway station.* Try not to make the words too easy. The team which guesses all the words first is the winner.

UNIT 14 The home

Suggested lesson break: after Exercise 5

PRESENTATION

Ask students to look at the first photograph. Ask: *Is this an American house, do you think?* Elicit: *No, it isn't. It's English.*

Exercise 1

Ask students to look at the other photographs and the list of rooms. Hold up the book and ask questions about each room: *What room is this? Can you see a dining room? Can you see a hall?* Practise the pronunciation of the rooms chorally. Ask them which rooms aren't shown in the photographs (the hall and the dining room).

Exercise 2

Use the classroom and its surrounding buildings to illustrate all the words listed by saying: *Please point to a door/window,* etc.
Practise the pronunciation of the words chorally. Then ask students in pairs to find these parts of the house in the photographs.

Exercise 3

Build up a simple plan on the board of an imaginary sitting room. Say: *This is my sitting room. In my sitting room, there's a sofa, there's a table, there are two armchairs, there are two lamps,* etc. As you talk, draw each piece of furniture and write the words on the board in a list, e.g.

SITTING ROOM
a sofa
a table
a bookcase
a mirror
a carpet
two armchairs
two lamps

Now point to the list again and say: *There's a sofa and there's a table. There are two armchairs and there are two lamps.* Practise the sentences chorally. Then ask: *How many armchairs are there?* Elicit: *There are two.* Ask: *How many lamps are there?* etc.

Divide the class into pairs or groups and ask them to list the main *furniture words* in each

room in the photographs. To give an example, start with the kitchen and ask a student: *What is there in the kitchen?* Elicit: *There's a table ...* Ask: *What else?* Elicit: *There are three chairs.*

Students now work in pairs or groups with the list of words in Exercise 3. They can use a dictionary if necessary. Correct any pronunciation errors while they are working. Bring the class together to check the vocabulary. Say: *Anna, tell me about the furniture in the kitchen. How many chairs are there?* Anna replies: *There are three.*

Practise the pronunciation of all the words chorally, paying special attention to the difficult words, e.g. *wardrobe* /ˈwɔːdrəub/ *mirror* /ˈmɪrəʳ/ *cupboard* /ˈkʌbəd/ *curtains* /ˈkɜːtnz/

Now ask students to list the words in their notebooks. Students who are already familiar with most of the words in the list can help to build up further vocabulary items, e.g. *radiator, plant, tap,* etc. Remind students how to ask about the meaning of new words, e.g. *How do you say ... in English? What's that in English?*

📼 Exercise 4 SPEECHWORK

Ask individual students to say the words aloud. Point out the silent *r* in *carpet.* Play the tape for confirmation.

TAPESCRIPT AND KEY
/læmp/ /hɔːl/ /bɑːθ/ /wɔːl/ /ˈteɪbəl/ /ˈkɑːpɪt/

GRAMMAR FOCUS

Ask students to look at the tables in the Focus box silently. Ask the question about *any.* (It is used with plural nouns in negative sentences and in questions.) Ask students to look at the photographs again. Ask questions to produce short answer forms, and to practise *any.*
T: Is there a television in the sitting room?
S: Yes, there is.
T: Is there a television in the bedroom?
S: No, there isn't.
T: Are there any chairs in the kitchen?
S: Yes, there are.
T: Are there any chairs in the bedroom?
S: No, there aren't.

Now students ask each other similar questions about the pictures.

Exercise 5

To revise *how many,* ask: *How many lamps are there in the sitting room?* Elicit: *There are three.* Explain that tables and chairs are *furniture* (a collective noun which is always singular).
Now select a student to ask you the questions in the book. Then students work in pairs, taking notes. They can then report back, e.g. *There are three rooms in Anna's flat.* Some students may like to talk about another house they know well, or invent their ideal house.

SUGGESTED LESSON BREAK

Exercise 6 WRITING

Read aloud the letter about the Gibson's house. Use the first photograph, or another picture, to illustrate the meaning of *upstairs* and *downstairs, garden at the front, garage,* etc. Ask students if they live in a flat or a house. Students who live in flats may want to know how to say *I live on the ground/first floor.* If so, present the necessary ordinal numbers, e.g. up to *tenth.* Ask any students who live in a house if they have a garden or garage, and what rooms are upstairs or downstairs. Now draw a ground plan of your own home on the board and describe your home as if you were writing a similar paragraph about it.

Students now write a paragraph describing their own home. Help them with any other words they might want, e.g. *balcony, basement.* Students may like to know a few more prepositions, e.g. *next to, in front of,* so that they can describe their bedrooms in more detail. A ground plan of their house or flat could accompany the paragraph.

Exercise 7 LISTENING

Before you listen, use the questions in the rubric to talk about the house in the picture.

Play the tape through once for general understanding. Then write the following questions on the board before playing the tape a second time. Students answer the questions orally and you write the answers on the board.

Who owns the house?
Where is it?
How many rooms has it got?
What else is there?
What car has John got?
Why is the house unusual?
Where is John's office?

TAPESCRIPT
Listen to someone describing the house in the photograph. What is unusual about it?

And now 'House and Gardens' has this interesting report from our American reporter, Dee Crandall.

Multi-millionaire John Amos and his wife Elena have certainly got the house of their dreams in Columbus, Georgia. It's a big, white mansion with a red roof. There are fifteen rooms, a gymnasium, a swimming pool, a summer house and a large patio garden. But what about a garage for the Cadillac? Well, there's no problem. The mansion is on top of a car park! And when I say 'on top of' I mean 'on top of'! The car park, for 750 cars, is seven floors high and the house is right on the very top of the building! John likes his house because it's next door to his office, and, he says, 'Because I'm closer to heaven!'

This is Dee Crandall, for 'House and Gardens', Columbus, Georgia, USA.

Thank you, Dee. And now let's have a look at what's new in bathrooms ...

KEY
The house is on top of a seven-storey car park.

ABOUT LIVING STANDARDS IN BRITAIN

Present and teach, by drawing or showing pictures, the new words, e.g. *washing machine, freezer, central heating.* Then ask students: *Have you got a television?* etc. Elicit: *Yes, we have./No, we haven't.* Remind students of the meaning of *to own.* Say: *This is my car. I own it. I don't rent it.*

Ask students to read the paragraph and look at the graph. Ask: *How many people in Britain own their homes? Do most people live in flats or houses?* Explain: *They live in houses **rather than** flats.*
Ask students: *Is it the same in your country?*

Introduce the following phrases so that the students can make generalisations:
Most people have got ...
Many people (or a lot of people) have got ...
Not many people have got ...

EXTRA ACTIVITIES

1 Blob! A vocabulary game

A student thinks of an object in one of the photographs on the page, e.g. a roof or a curtain and calls it *blob.* Others have to guess what the *blob* is by asking Yes/No questions:

s1: Is the blob in the house?
s2: Is there a blob in the bathroom?
s3: Is the blob big?
s4: Can you sit on a blob?
s5: Have you got a blob? etc.

2 Vowels only

This game helps spelling awareness. Write a selection of the words from the lesson on the board leaving out the consonants. Students work in pairs to see who can complete the list first, e.g.

— — A I — (chair)
— O I — E — (toilet)
— U — — O A — — (cupboard)
— O O — — A — E (bookcase), etc.

UNIT 15 Present activities

Suggested lesson break: after Exercise 6

Note

The present continuous tense may already be familiar to the students if you have used it in classroom instructions and in discussing the Previews. Common mistakes are: omitting the verb *to be*, e.g. ~~He having a shower~~ and misspelling the main verb.

PRESENTATION

Pretend to start writing a letter on the board and ask students: *What am I doing?* Elicit: *You're writing a letter.*

Draw a stick figure of someone watching TV and ask: *What's he/she doing?* Elicit: *He's/She's watching TV.*

Now draw two people having a meal. Ask: *What are they doing?* Elicit: *They're having (lunch).*

Exercise 1

Now ask students to look at the pictures on the left-hand page and get different students to ask and answer the questions. Students can look at the table in the Focus box as they do so.

GRAMMAR FOCUS

When they have completed Exercise 1, ask a student how to spell having and making, in order to draw attention to the spelling rules in the Focus box. Get students to study the rules in the box and then ask the 'grammatical questions'. Illustrate the questions as you ask them, e.g. write on the board:

1 make – making 2 lie – lying 3 run – running

KEY

The *e* disappears./There is no *e* in *making*.
The *ie* becomes *y*./The *ie* is *y*.
The consonant doubles./There are two *n*s.

In the last rule, give the students the exception to the rule: that if the single consonant is *k* it doesn't double, e.g. *cooking, looking.*

Check that students have grasped the rule by writing other verbs on the board. Ask individual students to come up to the board and write the continuous form next to the base form, e.g.
*swim (swimming) hope (hoping) send (sending)
 sit (sitting) look (looking) do (doing) tie (tying)*

 Exercise 2 LISTENING

Play the tape and ask different students to guess the answers.

TAPESCRIPT
Listen and say what the people are doing.

1 Susan (piano playing)
2 Robert (rock music on Walkman)
3 The Gibsons (TV news)
4 Laura (coffee-making noises)
5 Adam (shower running)

Exercise 3

Ask students to see how many different combinations they can make. Get individual students to tell you their answers. Collect their answers and write them on the board.

 Exercise 4 SPEECHWORK

Explain the rubric and give an example of the weak form *to* in *going to work*. Ask students to think of how they are going to say each phrase first. Then play the tape for students to repeat.

Exercise 5

Mime an activity as an example and elicit questions from the students as you do so, e.g. Mime watching TV. Say:
T: What am I doing?
S: You're looking at the wall!
T: No, I'm not. Find out where I am.
S: Are you in the cinema?
T: No, I'm not.
S: Are you watching TV?
T: Yes, I am.

Make sure you answer the students' questions with short form answers. Now ask students to form groups to play the game. Have a list of activities ready. Each student comes to you for their activity and then goes back and mimes it for the rest of the students in the group. Continue the game until everyone has had a chance to mime.

LIST OF ACTIVITIES

reading a paper	writing a postcard
travelling on the	listening to music
underground	repairing a puncture
driving a car	changing a plug
playing cards	skiing
cooking	having breakfast
watching TV	making coffee/tea

Exercise 6

Students may include cousins and grandparents or wives, husbands and children if they like. Explain *probably* by saying: *I think my mother is shopping. She usually goes shopping in the afternoon so she's probably shopping now.* Help students with extra vocabulary and point out that it is more common to say *He's asleep* than *He's sleeping.*

Exercise 7

BACKGROUND NOTES
The picture: By William Strang, a British painter (1859-1921), it is in the Tate Gallery in London.
Bank Holiday: This is a national holiday on a weekday when all banks, work places and schools are closed.

Let students work on their own with a dictionary. They can also make sentences with *there is/are*. Give some examples on the board.

POSSIBLE SENTENCES
The couple are sitting at a table.
They are having a meal.
There's a dog on the chair near/next to the woman.
There are some flowers on the chair near/next to the man.
The man is wearing a hat.
He is looking at the menu.
The waiter is standing next to the table.

🎧 Exercise 8 READING AND LISTENING

BACKGROUND NOTES
Barbados: An island in the Caribbean and a popular holiday destination.
Rum punch: A drink of rum and tropical fruit juices.

Ask students who Chris is and, if necessary, remind them that she works with Adam in the travel agent's. Read the postcard aloud. Ask students to guess the meaning of any new words and expressions, e.g. *great, having a wonderful time, to get fit, beach, next week, maybe, all (= everyone)* and *This is the life!* Ask questions about the postcard, e.g. *Where is Chris having a holiday? Are they having a good time? What's Chris doing at the moment? What's she drinking? What's Keith doing?*

Play the tape once and ask students to listen and silently prepare what they want to say. Play the tape a second time and select one or two students to talk to Adam. All students can write the dialogue for homework.

TAPESCRIPT
You work with Chris and Adam at the travel agent's. Chris is on holiday at the moment and sends you a postcard. Read it and then answer Adam's questions about it.

ADAM: What are you reading?
YOU: (bleep)
ADAM: Oh? Who's it from?
YOU: (bleep)
ADAM: Where is she?
YOU: (bleep)

ADAM: Is she having a good time?
YOU: (bleep)
ADAM: What's she doing?
YOU: (bleep)
ADAM: What about Keith?
YOU: (bleep)
ADAM: Well, it's all right for some people. Come on, let's get back to work.

SUGGESTED CONVERSATION
ADAM: What are you reading?
YOU: A postcard.
ADAM: Oh? Who's it from?
YOU: It's from Chris.
ADAM: Where is she?
YOU: She's in Barbados.
ADAM: Is she having a good time?
YOU: Yes, she is. She's having a wonderful time.
ADAM: What's she doing?
YOU: She's swimming and getting fit.
ADAM: What about Keith?
YOU: He's learning to windsurf.
ADAM: Well it's all right for some people. Come on, let's get back to work.

Exercise 9 WRITING

Give an example on the board, eliciting sentences from the students. List some suggestions for some of the gaps, e.g.

– *a wonderful/great/lovely time*
– *visiting museums/doing a lot of sightseeing*
– *walking/sailing/climbing/camping/fishing/swimming/sunbathing*
– *relaxing/reading/sleeping*
– *in a café/on the beach/in bed/in my hotel room*

SUGGESTED POSTCARD
Hi Helen!
Here I am in Budapest. I'm having a wonderful time. I'm visiting museums and art galleries and doing a lot of sightseeing. I'm writing this in a beautiful café in the old part of the city. See you on Monday.
Love,
Nico

EXTRA ACTIVITIES
1 Coffee-potting

One student thinks of an activity. The others must try to guess what the activity is by substituting the word *coffee-pot* and asking Yes/No questions, e.g.
s1: Do you coffee-pot every day?
s2: Are you coffee-potting now?
s3: Can you coffee-pot in water?
s4: Are Chris and Keith coffee-potting?

Ask students to give short form answers to each 'coffee-pot' question.

2 Spot the mistake!

Use a picture which shows a number of different activities. Ask students to look at the picture and, in turn, say a sentence which describes something or somebody in the picture either correctly or incorrectly. Other students look at the picture and say: *Yes, that's right.* or: *No, that's wrong.* and give the correct information, e.g.

s1: The car is black.
s2: Yes, that's right.
s3: A man's driving the car.
s2: No, that's wrong. A woman's driving.

FLUENCY Units 11–15

BACKGROUND NOTE
The Bolshoi Ballet: The leading Soviet ballet company based at the Bolshoi Theatre in Moscow.

Exercise 1 Before you read

Collect a selection of the students' questions and write them on the board. Tell students that they will probably find answers to some but not all these questions in the text. Write the following words on the board and ask students to look them up in a dictionary if they cannot guess their meaning from the text: *diplomat, performance, energy, earn, queue, laugh.*

Exercise 2 READING

Students read silently. Check with them afterwards which of their questions were answered. Check the meaning of the words on the board. Ask students to count how many paragraphs there are in the text (five). Ask them to tell you the number of the paragraph which corresponds to each topic listed in Exercise 2. Ask one student finally to read out the list of topics in the order in which the article is written. By doing this, students will be able to see the logical sequence of topics contained in the article. Help students with any other queries they may have about the text.

Exercise 3 ROLEPLAY

Ask students to look at the question cues and elicit examples of the full questions and answers from them. Students then work in pairs, preferably with their books shut.

Exercise 4

Allow a few minutes for discussion to let students tell you what they found interesting about the text, e.g. that Nina and her husband live in such a small flat, that she uses three pairs of shoes for every performance, etc. Students who have done some ballet dancing in the past will be able to explain what sort of 'preparation' needs to be done on the ballet shoes, e.g. sewing on the ribbons. Make sure that male students are included in the discussion.

Exercise 5 LISTENING

Ask students to look at the photograph of Nina and Guya's flat and see if they can describe what is in it before listening to the tape. Play the tape twice if necessary and ask students to complete the list of items in their notebooks. Ask if any details of the flat were surprising.

TAPESCRIPT
Listen to the description of Nina and Guya's Moscow flat and follow the instructions in your Students' Book.

It really is surprising how small the flat is. When you go into their flat you go straight into the sitting room. It isn't very large and there isn't a lot of furniture. There's a sofa, a table, an armchair, a very big television and a video recorder. Nina's husband, Guya, has every performance of Nina dancing on video, and watches them all the time. Um, there's a cupboard for all the video tapes, and there's also a bookcase with lots of books in it. There isn't a bedroom. They sleep on the sofa in the sitting room. The kitchen is very small. There's just enough space for a small table and two chairs, a cooker and a cupboard. That's all. There's no fridge.

EXTRA ACTIVITY

Parts of the text can be copied on to an OHT in a later lesson and be used for a gap-filling exercise.

CHECK Units 11–15

(For advice on handling this section, see the notes for Check Units 1–5.)

KEY
Ex. 1 1 lives 2 gets up 3 makes 4 prepares
5 milks 6 works 7 has 8 watch 9 go
10 listens to (10 marks)

Ex. 2 1 she is having 2 I like 3 are you doing
4 Do you listen 5 Are you listening (5 marks)

Ex. 3 1 Eight o'clock in the morning.
2 Two o'clock in the afternoon.
3 Eleven o'clock at night.
4 Seven o'clock in the evening.
5 Six o'clock in the morning.
(5 marks)

Ex. 4 1 What time/When do you start work?
2 How do you get to work?
3 How long does your journey take?
4 How far is it?
5 Where do you park your car?
6 What time/When do you finish work?
7 What time/When do you get home?
8 Does your wife work?
9 What do you do after supper?
10 What time/When do you go to bed?
(10 marks)

Ex. 5 1 from 2 for 3 from 4 in 5 to (until) 6 in
7 at 8 by 9 to 10 on 11 to 12 at (12 marks)

Ex. 6 1 He always has breakfast in bed.
2 She is never late for work.
3 We sometimes play cards all night.
4 I often eat my lunch in the park.
5 They are usually at home on Saturday morning.
(5 marks)

Ex. 7 1 There's a 2 There are 3 Are there
4 Is there; there isn't 5 There are
6 Is there; there is 7 Is there 8 Are there
(10 marks)

Ex. 8 1 a 2 – 3 the 4 a 5 – 6 – the 7 –
8 an the (10 marks)

Ex. 9.

KITCHEN	BATHROOM	BEDROOM	SITTING ROOM
sink	bath	bed	sofa
cooker	washbasin	dressing table	television
fridge	shower	wardrobe	armchair
freezer	toilet		table
(15 marks)			

CHECK YOUR PROGRESS
(See notes for Check Units 1–5.)

LEARNING TO LEARN 3
If you have not already done so, ask students to create a separate vocabulary book (i.e. a slim exercise book in which they can write new vocabulary).

Ask a student to show you his/her ordinary notebook. Look through it and find some examples of words which the student has copied down during a lesson. Show on the board your suggestions on how to record these in the vocabulary book (see examples under point 3). Obviously not all new vocabulary will need an example sentence but it is a good habit to get into.

Suggest that students reserve the front of the vocabulary book for general words and leave the back for word fields. To consolidate what you have said, the students can now read through the *Learning to learn* notes silently.

For homework, students can look through their notebooks and select all the major word fields they have had so far, e.g. days of the week, colours, family members, rooms of the house, furniture, etc. and group them in the back of their vocabulary books. The next homework could be to transfer all the general words to the front of the vocabulary books, with translations (or synonyms) and example sentences where useful. If students complain that this is a waste of time, explain that copying out new words helps to fix them in the memory.

As the course progresses, if it is appropriate to the class, it may be a good idea to keep a check on the students' vocabulary books. Warn them a week in advance that you would like to collect them in and check them.

PREVIEW Units 16–20

BACKGROUND NOTES
Caravan Park: A caravan (also called a 'mobile home') is a popular type of holiday accommodation. In this case a caravan park consists of caravans in a park-like setting with facilities and services. (See the advertisement on page 49 of the Students' Book.) People can rent the caravans for a short time for a holiday.
Yorkshire Moors: The county of Yorkshire has two areas of great natural beauty: the Yorkshire Moors and the Yorkshire Dales. These are favourite holiday spots for walking, climbing and touring.
Helmsley: One of the many picturesque villages in North Yorkshire. The main photograph shows the ruins of Helmsley Castle, just outside the village.
Rievaulx Abbey /'ri:vəʊ/: A medieval abbey just outside Helmsley. It is now in ruins.

The photographs and the dialogue
Ask students to look at the main photograph. Then ask: *Who can you see in the photograph?* (Adam, his brother Michael, who has blond hair and glasses, and his friends) *Where are they?* (In the country/near a castle/near some ruins) *What are they doing?* (They're walking/sightseeing/talking/smiling) Use the photograph to illustrate the meaning of the words: *wall, tower, church, trees, grass, path, rucksack.*

Students read the poster for the caravan park. Teach or elicit new vocabulary. Refer to the small inset map to show Helmsley in relation to York and, if possible, show its location on a larger map.

Ask students the following questions:
Where are Adam and his friends? (In the North Yorkshire Moors. Near/in Helmsley)

How long does it take to get from the caravan park to Rievaulx Abbey? (Five minutes)
Is there a shop in the caravan park? (Yes, there is.)
Are there showers? (Yes, there are.)
Is there a swimming pool? (No, there isn't.)
Is there a laundry (a place where you can wash your clothes)? (Yes, there is.)
Can you fish there? (Yes, you can.)
How far is the caravan park from Helmsley? (Three minutes)
What is the telephone number of the caravan park? (0439 8871)

Now ask students to look at the photographs on the right-hand page. Ask where they think Adam and his friends are and what they are doing there.

▣ The tape and the exercise

Play the tape and ask students to listen and follow the conversations. Explain *carton* and *corner*. Ask the comprehension questions of the whole class.

TAPESCRIPT
Listen and follow the conversation in your Students' Book. Adam is on a weekend break in the Yorkshire Moors

ADAM:	Come on. Let's go into Helmsley now and get some postcards.
MICHAEL:	And some orange juice. I'm thirsty.
ADAM:	How much are these postcards of Helmsley?
WOMAN:	They're 25p each.
ADAM:	Can I have two, please.
WOMAN:	That's 50p.
ADAM:	Oh, and I'd like some orange juice. Have you got any small cartons?
WOMAN:	Yes, they're over there.
ADAM:	Thanks.
ADAM:	Excuse me, is there a post office near here?
MAN:	Yes, there's one on the corner.
CHRIS:	Hi. Did you have a good weekend?
ADAM:	Yes, it was great. We went walking on the moors and went to see Helmsley Castle.
CHRIS:	What was the weather like?
ADAM:	It was O.K. Well, it didn't rain!

The learning objectives box
Go through the list of objectives in the box and ask students to find examples of each objective in the dialogues.

Ask and say how much things cost : *How much are these postcards? They're 25p.*
Ask for things in shops: *I'd like some orange juice. Have you got any small cartons?*

Talk about food and drink: *orange juice* (drink)
Ask and say where places are: *Is there a post office near here? Yes, there's one on the corner.*
Talk about the weather: *What was the weather like? It didn't rain.*
Talk about the recent past: *Did you have a good weekend? Yes, it was great. We went walking on the moors.*

UNIT 16 Prices

Suggested lesson break: after Exercise 3

> BACKGROUND NOTE
> *The photograph*: This shows the interior of a newsagent's selling newspapers, sweets, chocolates, cigarettes and other small items. Many newsagent's now sell food and drink.

PRESENTATION
If possible, bring some English money into the classroom, i.e. coins and notes in the following amounts. Coins: £1, 50p, 20p, 10p, 5p, 2p, 1p. Notes: £5, £10, £20. Hold up each coin/note and say: *This is a penny or one p. Say after me. A penny... One p...*, *This is two pence or two p.* etc. Point out here that the plural of *penny* is *pence* but that the plural of *p* is *p*. Then give different combinations of the coins and notes to different students, e.g. £5.50 and ask: *How much is that? It's five pounds and fifty pence.* Say: *Yes, or five pounds fifty. Say after me. Five pounds fifty.*

Note that, when giving prices which have both pounds and pence, people do not usually say *pence*. They often do not say *pounds* either. The numbers alone are usually sufficient, e.g. (£8.99) *eight ninety-nine*. However, it is probably clearer for students to say *pounds*: *eight pounds ninety-nine*.

The photograph and the dialogue
Ask students to look at the photograph and say what items they can see. Elicit: *boxes of chocolates, cigarettes, sweets, newspapers.* Read the dialogue. Explain the word *expensive* and its opposite *cheap*. Now practise the lines of the dialogue chorally and then ask students to read the dialogue in pairs.

Provide extra practice of the indefinite pronoun *one/ones* by holding up or pointing to pairs of coloured pens and pencils and different sizes of books. Ask: *Which one/ones do you want?* Elicit: *The red one/The big ones, please.* This can be extended to practise prices by giving prices to objects in the classroom or drawn on the board.

s: How much is the pen?
t: Which one?
s: The red one.
t: It's 25p.

Exercise 1 LISTENING

> BACKGROUND NOTES
> *Black Magic*: The name of a well-known brand of chocolates sold in boxes. (They are made in York by the firm of Rowntrees.)
> *Small, medium, and large*: Clothes sizes.
> *Minolta*: The name of a Japanese camera company.
> *Zoom lens*: When attached to a camera, this makes objects in a photograph larger.

Ask students to copy the chart into their notebooks. Before they listen, give the explanations in the background notes.

Play the tape once, pausing after each sequence to give time for the students to fill in the information on their charts. Play the tape a second time for the students to check their notes. Check by asking which items they think are expensive and how much they are in their own countries.

TAPESCRIPT
Listen to some people shopping. Write the price of each article and tick the items which the customer thinks are expensive.

1
a: Excuse me, how much is that box of chocolates up there?
b: What, the Black Magic?
a: No, the big one with the flowers on it.
b: It's eight pounds fifty.
a: Eight pounds fifty! That's expensive! I think I'll leave it.

2
a: T-shirts! Postcards! T-shirt?
b: No, thanks.
a: Come on, buy a T-shirt for your girlfriend!
b: How much is that one?
a: They're all one price. Seven ninety-nine. Do you want small, medium or large?
b: Oh, O.K. A large one, please. Here's the money. Seven fifty ... seventy ... ninety ... there ... seven ninety-nine exactly.

3
a: Can I help you?
b: Yes, please. I'd like a camera ... an automatic camera.
a: We have several automatics. The Minolta is probably the best of the range. It's fully automatic and it has a zoom lens.
b: How much is it?
a: It's a hundred and nineteen pounds ninety-nine.

b: A hundred and nineteen pounds ninety-nine! It's too expensive, I'm afraid.

COMMUNICATION FOCUS

Ask students to study the tables in the Focus box silently. Explain that *can/could* are nearly the same in this case, but that *could* is slightly more formal and polite. Remind students of the demonstrative pronouns (*this, that, these, those*) which were introduced in Unit 4. Ask them to make different questions from the table, e.g. *Could I have that pen, please? How much are the large ones?*

Exercise 2

Collect some containers similar to those in the pictures, e.g. a bottle, a packet, a can, a tube, a box, a carton, a loaf and a bar. Introduce and practise these items chorally and individually. Students now write in their notebooks the completed list of items in Exercise 2. With false beginners you may prefer to do the exercise orally first, without presenting the objects, to see if students can provide the vocabulary items themselves.

Exercise 3

Practise the exchange Teacher–Student, with one student taking the part of B. Then ask students to work in pairs and to change parts so that they each ask as well as answer.

SUGGESTED LESSON BREAK

The photographs

> BACKGROUND NOTES
> *Picture 1*: This shows a busy fast-food restaurant selling mainly hamburgers, e.g. Wimpy or MacDonald's.
> *Picture 2*: This shows a counter in a bakery (baker's shop). In Britain a bakery sells cakes and pastries as well as bread.
> *Picture 3*: This shows the counter of a chemist's shop, where you can buy toiletries (e.g. shampoo, make-up, combs, etc.) as well as medicines. It is also possible to buy films and get them processed at a chemist's.

Ask students to look at the photographs and the price lists and say what you can buy in each shop, e.g. *What can you buy in a ...?* Elicit: *You can buy ....* Explain *King-size* (big) and *portion* in the restaurant price list. Ask students to find some rolls and sandwiches in Picture 2 (they're on the right of the counter) and some films in Picture 3. Write on the board:

How much is (a King-size hamburger)?
It's (£2.75)

Students then work in pairs asking and answering about the prices of at least three items on each price list.

Exercise 4 ROLEPLAY

Ask one student to be the assistant and work through the roleplay with you as the customer. Point out that the cues which are in brackets only apply when choosing between large or small items, e.g. portions of chips, packets of aspirin, etc. Also point out that the response to *How much is that?* may be *That's ...,* or *It's ... .* Students then work in pairs to complete a roleplay for each picture. Ask them to make new pairs for each situation. Monitor their work and ask one or two pairs to act their conversation for the whole class. Complete beginners can write out one or two of the conversations for homework.

SUGGESTED CONVERSATION

A: Can I help you?
B: Yes, could I have a packet of aspirin, please?
A: A small one or a large one?
B: A large one, please.
A: Yes, anything else?
B: Yes, I'd like a film, please.
A: Anything else?
B: No, thank you. How much is that?
A: That's four pounds, please.

Exercise 5

Students look at the items in Exercise 2. Ask:
T: How much does a box of tissues cost?
S: 80p.
T: How much does it cost in this/your country?
S: About ... /I don't know.

Write on the board the question and answer form and practise chorally and individually. Explain that if you are discussing prices in the abstract, you can say *How much is (a box of tissues)?* or *How much does (a box of tissues) cost?* Students ask and answer about other prices in Exercise 2 across the class, using *How much does ... cost?*

Now ask students to look at the list of items and prices in Exercise 5. (Note that the prices given are approximate at the time of writing.) Teach any vocabulary which students do not know, e.g. *three-star hotel* = a medium-priced hotel. Practise the example exchange chorally and explain *leaded/unleaded petrol* and *It depends.* The discussion is best handled as a whole class, but with large classes, divide the students into groups.

Exercise 6

Refer to a list of current exchange rates printed in a daily newspaper and ask students to work out the value of the items in Exercise 5 in their own currency and to compare them with prices in their own country. They should comment on which they consider to be expensive and which are cheap items. Introduce *cheaper* and *more expensive* if students need to use them. (Comparatives are introduced in Units 28 and 29.)

EXTRA ACTIVITIES
1 Shopping cards

Collect pictures from magazines of as many items as you can from this unit, e.g. a tube of toothpaste, a cheese roll, a litre of milk. Attach each of them to thin card about 16cm x 12cm. These are the 'item' cards. On an equal number of small cards about 16cm x 3cm print the name of the item with its price, e.g. *A tube of toothpaste = £1.20.* These are the 'price' cards. Shuffle both sets of cards and hand them out to the students so that they have either an item card or a price card. Ask a student with an item card to look at the card and say *Could I have ... , please?* The student with the equivalent price card replies: *Certainly,* and then the first student goes on to ask: *How much is it?/are they?* The second student replies: *It's/They're ... .* Another student then reads out an item card and so on around the class.

2 Memory game

This is another version of Kim's Game presented in Unit 4, Exercise 11. Collect magazine pictures of vocabulary items from this unit. Mount the pictures on a large piece of card about 50cm x 30cm, in the form of a collage, with the pictures overlapping. Give students one minute to look at the collage. They then write down as many items as they can remember.

UNIT 17 Food and drink

Suggested lesson break: after Grammar Focus (2)

PRESENTATION

Prepare a set of pictures taken from magazine advertisements which show some of the food items listed in Exercise 1, e.g. *apples, oranges, coffee, milk, yoghurt, eggs, bananas, biscuits.* (Some teachers may want to introduce all the words in this way.)

Hold up each card and point to the item(s) and say: *An apple, some apples. An orange, some oranges. A banana, some bananas. Some coffee, Some milk, Some yoghurt,* etc. Get students to repeat the words chorally and individually. Make sure students produce the unstressed form of *some* /səm/.

The picture and Exercise 1

BACKGROUND NOTES
Bread: The picture shows two slices of brown bread. This is bread made from brown wholemeal flour. Both brown and white bread are sold in loaves or in packets of sliced bread.
Sugar: The sugar in the picture is a type of brown sugar (called 'Demerara') it is usually used for coffee. White sugar is used for tea. Either may be used on cereals or for cooking.
Salt and pepper: The salt container has one hole and the pepper container has several.

Ask students to look at the picture and, in pairs, to find the items on the list, noting those which are not in the picture (*tea, yoghurt, chicken, oil, vinegar*). Practise the pronunciation of all the words on the list. Draw attention to the spelling, with *es*, of the plural forms of *potato* and *tomato*. (For a general overview of plurals, refer students to the relevant section in the Students' Book Language review on page 135.)
Teach the words *bowl, jug, plate, knife, fork, spoon*. Revise the prepositions *in* and *on*. Ask and answer:
Where's the milk?   *It's in a/the jug.*
Where are the tomatoes?   *They're on a/the plate.*
Where's the sugar?   *It's in a/the bowl.*

Exercise 2 SPEECHWORK

These phrases are important for students to practise not only for the elision of *and* but also because they represent common collocations with food and drink. Many students will be familiar with the spoken elision of *and* to *n* in phrases such as *rock 'n' roll* and *rhythm 'n' blues*.

GRAMMAR FOCUS (1)

Explain the concept of 'countable' and 'uncountable' nouns. Say: *One egg. Two apples. Three oranges. You can count eggs, apples and oranges. They are called 'countable' nouns. Can you give me some other examples of countable nouns?* Elicit: *banana(s), biscuit(s)*. Now say: *Coffee, tea, milk. You can't count coffee, tea or milk. They are called 'uncountable' nouns. Can you give me some other examples of uncountable nouns?* Elicit: *butter, oil, bread*.

Now ask students to work in pairs and to write the items in Exercise 1 in two groups in their notebooks.

KEY

Countable nouns		Uncountable nouns	
eggs	oranges	bread	tea
biscuits	bananas	milk	yoghurt
(chicken)	potatoes	butter	cheese
apples	tomatoes	salt	(chicken)
		pepper	oil
		sugar	vinegar
		coffee	

Point out that some nouns refer to different things in their countable and uncountable form, e.g. a chicken (animal)/some chicken (meat), a fish (animal)/some fish (food) (countable = the animal, uncountable = food). Also point out that *some* is used with both plural countable nouns and uncountable nouns, but that you will deal with the uses of *some* later in the lesson.

Exercise 3 DIALOGUE

BACKGROUND NOTES
TV Times: A magazine listing ITV (Independent Television) programmes for the coming week.
Share a flat: In Britain it is quite common for young people to move away from home and share houses and flats.

Read the rubric aloud, explaining that *to share a flat* means *to live with somebody in a flat*. (See the background note above.) Remind students of Adam's brother Michael (Unit 7 Listening and Preview Units 16–20 – main photo). Ask students to write the heading *Shopping list* in their notebooks and to read the dialogue silently noting down what Adam has to buy. Ask students what they think *lazy* means from the context.

Exercise 4 LISTENING

Play the tape and ask students to look at the lines from the printed dialogue as they listen. Tell them to say *Stop, please!* when there is a difference, e.g.
s: Stop, please!
t: Yes, what is it?
s: It's not bread, it's milk.

TAPESCRIPT
Look at the dialogue in Exercise 3. Listen to a similar conversation and note four differences.

MICHAEL: Are you going to the shops?
ADAM: Yes, I need some new batteries for my radio.
MICHAEL: Well, we haven't got any eggs or bread. Can you get some?
ADAM: O.K.
MICHAEL: And we need some tea too.
ADAM: All right. Have you got any money?
MICHAEL: Here's a five pound note. Oh, and can you get me a magazine too – *Motorsport*.
ADAM: Why can't you go to the shops yourself?
MICHAEL: Because I'm lazy!

KEY
bread not milk, tea not coffee, £5 not £10, *Motorsport* magazine, not *TV Times*

Students can now practise reading the dialogue in pairs.

GRAMMAR FOCUS (2)

Refer back to the use of *some* and *any* in the dialogue. Say:

T: Look at the dialogue again. Adam says: 'I need some new batteries.' What does Michael say then?
S: He says: 'We haven't got any eggs or milk.'
T: What question does Adam ask about money?
S: 'Have you got any money?'

Write the three sentences with *some* and *any* on the board. Now ask students to look at the grammar box. Ask:

T: In what sort of sentences is *some* used?
S: In positive sentences.
T: What about *any*?
S: In questions and negatives.

(Teachers should note that there are exceptions to the rule, but that these are best handled later when the examples occur, e.g. with *Would you like ...* , *some* not *any* is used: *Would you like some milk?* (Unit 31). It is possible to use *some* in questions where you are fairly sure the answer will be *yes*: *Is there some/any milk left?*

With false beginners, point out that *some* is also used as an indefinite pronoun in the dialogue, e.g. *We haven't got any eggs. Can you get me some?* In this case, the word *some* is given its full value and pronounced /sʌm/.

SUGGESTED LESSON BREAK

Exercise 5 ROLEPLAY

To help students to make their lists, ask them to think of their own needs at home or give them a specific situation, e.g. they are on a camping holiday.

SUGGESTED CONVERSATION
A: Are you going to the shops?
B: Yes, I am.
A: We haven't got any sugar or milk. Can you get some?
B: O.K. Anything else?
A: Yes, we need some coffee and biscuits.
B: O.K. Have you got any money?
A: Yes, here's £10.
B: Thanks. Bye.
A: See you soon.

Exercise 6

BACKGROUND NOTES
curry /'kʌri/: Highly-spiced food associated with India
sweet and sour: A combination of sharp and sweet flavours found particularly in some Chinese dishes.
hamburgers: Associated with fast food from the USA. These are flat portions of minced beef, grilled and served in a bread roll.

bolognese /bolə'neɪz/: A meat sauce originating from Bologna in Italy.
sachertorte /sæʃə'tɔ:t/: A rich chocolate cake. Its name derives from the Hotel Sacher in Vienna in Austria.
fish and chips /ˌfɪʃən'tʃɪps/: A British take-away food of fish fried in batter, and chips.
sauerkraut /'sauəkraut/: A German dish made from sliced cabbage and salt.
gazpacho /gæz'pætʃəʊ/: A soup from Spain always served cold, and made from raw peppers, onions, tomatoes, cucumber, vinegar and water.
bouillabaisse /ˌbu:jə'bes /: A strong-tasting fish soup or stew from the south of France.
kebabs /kə'bæbz/: Cubes of meat or fish served on a skewer and grilled over charcoal, typical of Turkey, Greece and the Middle East.
chilli con carne /ˌtʃɪlikən 'kɑ:ni/: A dish of meat and beans cooked with red chilli powder, originating from Mexico.
borscht /bɔ:ʃt/ (also *borsch*): A beetroot soup often served with sour cream, associated with Russian cuisine.
port: A strong, sweet, dark Portuguese wine usually drunk after a meal. It originates from Oporto in Portugal.

Students can either work as a whole class, in groups or in pairs. Give an example of what you would like the students to say. Ask: *What about chicken curry?* or *Where's chicken curry from originally?* Elicit: *It's from India.* (The key to the nationality of the dishes is on page 141 of the Students' Book.)

Write the names of the categories on the board and elicit an example for each category, e.g.
T: What sort of dish is gazpacho?
S: It's a soup. It's a cold soup.

Students then work in pairs to sort the food and drink. Check students' answers. With a class of false beginners, encourage them to try to explain to each other what the dishes are and what they consist of (see the background notes above), e.g.
S1: What is sachertorte?
S2: It's a chocolate cake.

Write on the board the expressions: *It's made from .... It's hot. It's spicy.* Introduce the following food vocabulary if necessary: *cucumber, cabbage, onion, beetroot.*

KEY

Soups	**Fish dishes**
gazpacho	fish and chips
bouillabaisse	bouillabaisse
borscht	

Meat dishes   **Vegetable dishes**
chicken curry   sauerkraut
sweet and sour pork
hamburgers   **Drinks**
spaghetti bolognese   coffee
kebabs   port
chilli con carne

Desserts
sachertorte

Exercise 7 READING

The diagram is from the *Sunday Times* newspaper and is based on an opinion poll. Ask students to look at the diagram. Ask: *How many people think the evening meal is the main meal of the day?* (79%) Ask about breakfast and lunch in the same way. Then ask the two *Before you read* questions. Do not give the full answer to the second question yet.

ABOUT MEALS IN BRITAIN

> BACKGROUND NOTES
> *Muesli*: A Swiss breakfast cereal made from dried fruits, nuts and cereals.
> *Fried bread*: Thin slices of bread fried in butter, oil, or animal fat until it is crisp.

Write the following questions on the board and ask students to read the text and find the answers.

Where do most people think that the British eat their evening meal? (In front of the television)
Is this true? (No, they sit down at a table)
What is a typical English breakfast? (Sausage, bacon, eggs and fried bread)
What sort of breakfast do people now prefer? (Cereal or muesli, toast and marmalade and a cup of tea or coffee)

Exercise 8 About you

Ask the first two questions to different students around the class. Students then work in pairs and make a note of their partner's answers. Draw the class together and ask them to report back about their partner's eating habits. Try to hear as many students' answers as possible.

For homework, students can write a paragraph about meals and mealtimes in their own country. You may like to write a skeleton paragraph on the board, e.g.

The main meal of the day for most people in ... is lunch. People have a big lunch every day at about one o'clock. A typical lunch is ... .
Breakfast is not a big meal. People usually have ... for breakfast. They usually have ... for dinner.

EXTRA ACTIVITIES
1 In my fridge: a chain game
One student begins by saying a sentence and the next student in turn adds to the sentence, repeating what has gone before in the same order, e.g.
S1: In my fridge I've got some cheese.
S2: In my fridge I've got some cheese and some butter and so on.

2 What's my dish?
Ask students to think of a simple food dish for five or six people. They write down a complete list of the ingredients they need to make the dish (but not the method) and then dictate it to the class. The class must write down the ingredients and guess what the dish is.

UNIT 18 Location

Suggested lesson break: after Exercise 5

PRESENTATION
Draw on the board a sketch of two roads crossing each other. On one of the corners draw a building and mark it *bank*. Now ask and answer the following question yourself. *Excuse me, is there a bank near here? Yes, there's one on the corner of the street.* Write the two sentences on the board.

Extend your sketch map so that it looks similar to the one in Exercise 3, but you do not need to write street names. To illustrate the meaning of each of the prepositional phrases listed in the Grammar Focus box, draw in a building and then say, e.g. *The post office is next to the bank. The supermarket is opposite the post office. The car park is behind the supermarket,* etc. You may need to use a different perspective of drawing to illustrate *over, under, outside* and *inside.* Ask students to repeat each sentence chorally as you say it and write all the prepositions and prepositional phrases on the board.

GRAMMAR FOCUS
Ask students to open their books and look at the list in the Focus box.

The picture
> BACKGROUND NOTES
> *Black taxis*: Black taxis (or *cabs*) are a feature of London and other British cities. (In New York cabs are yellow.) Some taxi drivers are now breaking with tradition and have different coloured taxis with advertisements on them.
> *Red post boxes*: These red post boxes (or *pillar boxes*) are part of the British street scene.

Exercise 1

Ask students to look at the picture and to find the following: *a woman, a bus stop, someone on a bicycle, a man and a dog, a post box, a hairdresser's, a bank, a restaurant, a post office, a taxi,* etc. Practise the pronunciation of the words *supermarket, restaurant* and *hairdresser's*. Then ask students to work in pairs, making as many sentences as they can to describe where people and places are in the picture. To check, draw an outline sketch of the street illustrated in the picture and, as students give you sentences, mark the buildings and people on your sketch map. Ask complete beginners to write their sentences in full in their notebooks.

SOME POSSIBLE SENTENCES
There's a taxi/car outside the supermarket.
The bank is on the corner of the street, opposite the post office.
There are some people inside the restaurant.
There's a restaurant between the supermarket and the baker's.
There's a man with a dog in front of the bank.
There's a bank opposite the post office.
There's a man on a bicycle. He's behind the taxi.
There's a hairdresser's over the newsagent's.
There's a newsagent's under the hairdresser's.

Now on the board, make a list of five or six real places and buildings in your locality and ask students to say where they are, e.g.
T: Where's the post office?
S: It's in the main square next to the supermarket.
T: Where's the Miramar Cinema? etc.

Exercise 2 SPEECHWORK

Check that students understand the meaning of *taxi rank*. Find out where the nearest taxi rank is.

TAPESCRIPT AND KEY
Listen and underline the main stressed syllable.

<u>su</u>permarket   <u>post</u> office   <u>ci</u>nema   <u>res</u>taurant
<u>bus</u> stop   <u>taxi</u> rank

Exercise 3 ACTIVITY

Ask all students, both A and B groups, to copy a larger version of the map into their notebooks. Then ask A students to put the other places listed below the diagram, i.e. *bank, post office,* etc. anywhere they like on their street maps. (So that they can't see, B students should go to other parts of the classroom while A students are marking their maps. While they wait, they can start to write out some of their questions.) B students then have to ask questions to find out where the listed places are, and place them on their maps.

Practise the example exchange chorally and individually first, e.g.
B: Where's the bank?
A: It's in King Street opposite the railway station.

Students then do the activity in pairs. When they have finished, B students can check their maps by comparing them with those of the A students.

Exercise 4 ROLEPLAY

Ask students to work individually first, making notes about the places to go to for each enquiry, e.g. *guide book – book shop, parcel – post office*. Go through the example exchange in the Students' Book, working Teacher–Student. Then ask students to do the roleplays working across the class, rather than in pairs.

Exercise 5 WRITING

BACKGROUND NOTES
Launderette: A place where you can take your washing, and wash and dry it yourself. It has coin-operated, automatic washing machines. Launderettes are used a lot by students and other young people.
Lloyds: the name of a bank, c.f. *Barclays, The Midland,* and *The National Westminster,* the 'big four' banks in Britain.

Ask students to look at the rubric above the note. Ask: *Who is Mrs Gibson?* and elicit the fact that Laura is staying in her house. (See Preview Units 11–15 in the Students' Book.) Refer to the note and point out that in notes it is common to omit *Dear* before the name of the person to whom the note is addressed.

Read the note aloud, sentence by sentence, asking the following questions as you read:
What's Mrs Gibson's friend called? (Vicky)
What is the note about? (The local shops)
Where's the newsagent's? (On the corner of Heath Road)
Where's the launderette? (Opposite the newsagent's)
Where's the chemist's? (Next to the launderette)
Why does Mrs Gibson use the supermarket next to Lloyds Bank? (Because the one in her street isn't very good)
What's Mrs Gibson's first name? (Sheila)

Point out the use of apostrophes with shops, e.g. *newsagent's/chemist's/baker's/hairdresser's*. (Students resident in Britain will notice that this usage is becoming less common.)

Now ask students to write a similar informal note to a friend about the shops, services and facilities in their local area. Ask them to start and end their note in the same way, e.g. *Just a short note ... / Enjoy your stay*.

To check, ask one student to read his/her note aloud and write it on the board. As you do so, the other students can comment on the accuracy of the grammar and information.

SUGGESTED LESSON BREAK

▣ Exercise 6 LISTENING

> BACKGROUND NOTES
> *The Brontë* /'Brɒnti/ *family*:
> Charlotte Brontë (1816-1855)
> Patrick Branwell Brontë (1817-1848)
> Emily Brontë (1818-1848)
> Anne Brontë (1820-1849)
> *Haworth* /'haʊəθ/: The village in West York-
> shire in which the Brontë family lived. In fact,
> Haworth is two villages. The old village, with
> its church and parsonage, is on the top of a hill
> and the new village is in the valley below. The
> two villages are linked by a steep, cobbled
> street with old houses and shops on either side.
> *The Black Bull Pub*: Pub is short for *public
> house*. This is a place typical to Britain, which
> sells alcoholic and soft drinks. All pubs have
> names similar to *The Black Bull*. Names of
> animals and birds, kings and queens and
> famous people are popular. Nowadays most
> pubs sell food and coffee as well as the more
> traditional drinks, and sometimes provide
> accommodation.
> *The portrait:* The Brontë sisters' brother,
> Patrick Branwell, painted this famous portrait
> of himself and his sisters, but he later erased
> himself from the portrait. The sisters are, from
> left to right: Anne, the youngest, Emily and
> Charlotte, the eldest.

You may prefer to do the reading text first in
order to provide a richer context for the listening.
If not, use the background notes to explain briefly
why Haworth is famous, and explain that the
reading text which follows is about the Brontë
family.

Make sure students are familiar with the streets
and places on the map by asking simple
questions, e.g. *Where's the Tourist Information
Office/the community centre/the post office?*

Play the tape for the first time and ask students to
point to the locations on their maps as they listen.
Play the tape a second time for students to note
the information. Check by asking certain students
to tell you or show you on their map.

TAPESCRIPT
Laura is in Haworth. Listen and mark on your
map where the following are: a) Laura b) The
Brontë museum c) the pub called 'The Black
Bull'.

SARA: I wonder where the Brontë Museum is.
LAURA: Oh look, here's the Tourist Information
Centre. Let's ask in there.
Excuse me. Can you tell me where the
Brontë Museum is?
MAN: Yes, of course. Right. Well, we're here on
the corner of Changegate and West Lane.
LAURA: Yes, O.K.

MAN: Now, can you see immediately opposite
there's a small street called Church Street?
LAURA: Where? Oh, yes, I see it. Church Street.
MAN: You go down that street, there's a church
on your left, and then you go up the hill.
LAURA: Up the hill.
MAN: You'll see a school on your right.
LAURA: A church and then a school. Yes.
MAN: O.K. Well, just after the school there's the
Brontë Museum.
LAURA: On the same side as the school?
MAN: No, on the opposite side. Almost opposite
the school. You can't miss it.
LAURA: O.K.
MAN: Look, you take this map. See, here's the
Museum.
LAURA: Oh yes. And where's the Black Bull pub?
MAN: It's here on Main Street next to the
church. See?
LAURA: Oh yes, great. We can have lunch there
afterwards. Thanks very much.
MAN: You're welcome.

KEY

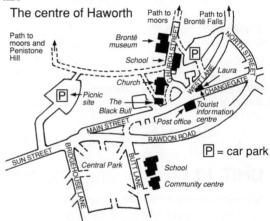

The centre of Haworth

P = car park

Exercise 7 READING

In a monolingual class use the L1 to find out
what the students know about the Brontë sisters
and if they have read any of their novels or seen
any TV or film versions of them.

In a multilingual class, read through the
questions. Explain *novel* (a long written story),
e.g. *War and Peace* is a novel by Tolstoy. Also
explain *setting* (where the novel takes place), e.g.
the Yorkshire moors is the setting for *Wuthering
Heights*.

Ask students to read through the text silently and
to answer the comprehension questions. Check by
asking these questions of the whole class. Finally
ask: *What happened to Patrick Branwell Brontë?*
(He drank himself to death.) Point out that *drank*
is the past tense of *drink*.

Find out if students know of any other places in
their own country, or in others, which are famous

because of a literary figure. Say: *Stratford-upon-Avon is famous because Shakespeare lived there. Do you know any other places which are famous because a writer lived there?*

EXTRA ACTIVITIES
1 Picture dictation
Ask students to take a large sheet of clean paper. Say: *As I tell you about the picture, can you draw it.* Dictate the following slowly for the students to draw:

'In the middle of the picture there's a house with an upstairs, a downstairs and a door in the middle. On each side of the door there are two windows upstairs and two windows downstairs. In front of the door there's a dog. Next to the dog there's a cat. On the right of the house there's a very big tree. Between the tree and the house there's a woman with an umbrella. On the left of the house there's a church. Behind the church you can see the sea.'

Students then compare their drawings in pairs and check if they have drawn all the details.

2 Video
If you have access to a video, arrange a showing of the section of the Longman video *Introducing Great Britain* which shows York, Haworth and other parts of Yorkshire. This will give the students an idea of the setting of the Brontë novels.

UNIT 19 Weather and seasons

Suggested lesson break: after Exercise 4

PRESENTATION
Ask and answer a question about the weather yourself: *What's the weather like today? It's warm and sunny.* Write the question and answer on the board and practise it chorally and individually.

Draw on the board a sun, a cloud, some rain, some snow (snowflakes). Ask: *What's this?* Elicit: *It's the sun/a cloud/rain/snow.* Write the noun under each picture. Then introduce the following weather words and expressions and write them beside each noun on the board, e.g.

sun   *It's sunny.*
cloud   *It's cloudy.*
rain   *It's raining.*
snow   *It's snowing .*

Ask students to repeat the sentences chorally. Now introduce and add to the list: *fog, foggy, wind, windy.* Say:
(foggy) *In San Francisco and in Northern Europe*

it is often very foggy. You can't see. You must drive very slowly on the roads if there is fog. (windy) *If you live near the sea, it is often very windy. If you go sailing, you need a strong wind.*

Use temperatures to introduce the general adjectives: *hot, warm, cool, cold,* e.g.
It's 30°C (thirty degrees centigrade). *It's hot. It's 20°C. It's warm. It's 15°C. It's cool. It's 0°C* (nought degrees centigrade). *It's cold.* Then teach *wet* and *dry.* Say: *It's raining. It's wet. It's cloudy but it isn't raining. It's dry.* Write the adjectives as you say them next to the appropriate sentence on the board, e.g.

sun   *It's sunny.*   hot /warm/dry
cloud   *It's cloudy.*   cool

The picture frieze
Ask students to look at the weather frieze of sun, cloud, rain and snow at the top of pages 57 and 58 in the Students' Book. Point to each picture and say: *What's the weather like?* Elicit: *It's sunny.*

Exercise 1
Ask students where they can find out about the weather (the newspapers or TV). Ask students to look at the small weather map of Britain and the forecast. Students answer the question in the Students' Book by interpreting the symbols on the map and scanning the forecast for familiar words.

Exercise 2
Ask students to complete the list of weather words individually. Point out that you cannot say: ~~It's clouding/fogging/winding.~~

Exercise 3 LISTENING
Work through the words in the weather report and explain that *drizzle* is light rain.

TAPESCRIPT
Listen and circle the weather words and temperatures you hear.

Good afternoon from the Weather Centre. This is the report on the weather for today at 14.00 hours. It is cool and mainly dry but with some drizzle in places. There is a ground temperature of 4°Celsius. The outlook for tomorrow. Temperatures will fall to about 2°Celsius. The day will be mainly cloudy but with some sunny periods. Thank you for calling the weather line.

Exercise 4
Ask students to look at the photographs and say where the places are, e.g. *Where is Picture 1? It's Mexico City.* Select a student and practise an example exchange with Picture 1, e.g. *What's the weather like in Mexico City?* Elicit: *It's hot and sunny.* Do the exercise with the class as a whole, working S1 – S2, S2 – S3, etc.

KEY
Mexico City: *It's hot and sunny.*
Moscow: *It's snowy./It's snowing.*
London: *It's raining.*
Tokyo: *It's cloudy.* (You may like to introduce *It's dull* here).

SUGGESTED LESSON BREAK

PRESENTATION
Bring different photographs of other cities/places to the class, each showing a distinctive weather type. Ask students to look at the photographs. Ask: *What was the weather like in* (name of place) *yesterday?* Elicit: *It was ... (*weather). Write both the question and answer on the board.

Now ask students about each of the other cities in turn, e.g. *What was the weather like in Buenos Aires yesterday? It was hot and sunny.* etc.

GRAMMAR FOCUS
Students look at the Focus box and practise the question and answer forms chorally and individually. Encourage students to use the stressed form of *was* /wɒz/ in Yes/No questions and short answers: *Was it hot yesterday? Yes, it was,* and the unstressed form /wəz/ in statements and *Wh-* questions: *What was the weather like in Toronto? It was cold.*

(After the lesson students can refer to the full paradigm of the past simple of the verb *to be* in the Language review on page 137.)

Exercise 5

> BACKGROUND NOTE
> *Centigrade (Celsius) and Fahrenheit*: In Britain, both Centigrade and Fahrenheit scales are used to measure temperature. Freezing point is 0°C/32°F and boiling point is 100°C/212°F.

First ask students to write a vertical scale of centigrade (Celsius) temperatures from -5° to +25°. Ask them to grade the temperatures: *very cold, cold, quite cold, cool, warm, quite hot, hot, very hot.* This can be used for interpreting the temperatures in the World Weather chart. Point out that temperatures are given in both centigrade (Celsius) and Fahrenheit in the chart.

Ask students to look at the World Weather chart and find the four cities shown in the photographs. Explain how the letters have to be interpreted, i.e. *S = Sun = It was sunny.* (**not** It was sun or It was sunning.) Encourage students to use the past simple tense *it rained* and *it snowed* (**not** it was raining/snowing), but do not go into too much detail here. The past simple tense is introduced in greater depth in the next unit.

Ask the first question of the whole class: *According to the chart, what was the weather like in Mexico City yesterday?* Elicit: *It was warm and sunny.* Students then work in pairs. When students have asked and answered about the four cities in the photographs, they can go on to ask and answer about other cities on the chart.

Exercise 6
Ask students about the real weather conditions in the area, contrasting today and yesterday.

Exercise 7
Use a calendar to present the months in order. As you turn over each page, say the month and ask students to repeat it chorally. Students then work individually to reorder the list. It is important that they write the months out again to reinforce the spelling.

KEY
January, February, March, April, May, June, July, August, September, October, November, December

Exercise 8 SPEECHWORK
Play the tape, pausing if necessary for different students to repeat the months.

TAPESCRIPT AND KEY
Listen and say the months. Mark the stressed syllable or word each time.

<u>Ja</u>nuary <u>Feb</u>ruary <u>March</u> <u>A</u>pril <u>May</u> <u>June</u> July Au<u>gust</u> Sep<u>tem</u>ber Oc<u>to</u>ber No<u>vem</u>ber De<u>cem</u>ber

Exercise 9 READING

> BACKGROUND NOTES
> *Lord Byron* (1788-1824): An English romantic poet whose poetry was popular, but who was much criticised in his lifetime on moral grounds. He left England in 1816 to live in Southern Europe and never returned. He died of fever in Missolonghi in Greece at the age of thirty-six.

Say the names of the four seasons and write them on the board. Then ask: *Which months are winter/spring/summer/autumn months in this/your country?*

Students then read the first paragraph of the text. Ask them: *When does spring start in Britain? What about summer, autumn and winter?* Read the two middle paragraphs with the students and explain any new words and references as you go along. Ask the questions at the top of the page of the whole class.

Exercise 10

Students work in pairs discussing the questions. Draw the class together to hear some of the different answers for question 3. Write on the board:

EVENT	SEASON/MONTH
flowers	...
falling leaves	...
Carnival time	...
family gatherings	...

Now ask: *What about flowers? What season do you associate with flowers?* Elicit: *Spring.*
As you elicit answers from students, complete the right-hand column on the board.

Exercise 11 WRITING

Prepare the vocabulary for this by eliciting from the students different things to do in each season and writing them on the board, e.g.

T: What do you like doing in summer?
S: I like swimming.
T: What else do you do in summer?
S: Sunbathe, have meals on the patio/balcony, go to the country. (etc.)
T: Does everyone like summer?
S: No, I don't like summer.
T: Why not?
S2: I don't like the sun.

Write on the board:

SUMMER: *swim, sunbathe, have meals outside, go to the country*

Remind students to use the *ing* form after *like*. Give an example on the board of how to start the sentences, e.g. *I like summer because I like swimming and sunbathing. I also like ... and ... . I don't like winter because I don't like ...*

EXTRA ACTIVITIES
1 Weather game

Students draw two 4 x 4 lined squares. They then write the numbers 1, 2, 3, 4 above the squares and the letters A, B, C, D to the left (see diagram below). On the first set of squares the students write the following letters anywhere they like: C, FG, SN, R, S (These indicate weather conditions: cloud, fog, snow, rain and sun), and f (= fine) in all the remaining squares.

	1	2	3	4		1	2	3	4
A	C	f	f	f	A				
B	f	f	FG	f	B				
C	S	SN	f	f	C				
D	f	f	f	R	D				

The second set of squares is left blank, to record the position of the letters in their partner's squares. The object of the game is to discover and record the letters which the student's partner has in his/her squares. Players in turn choose squares and ask about the weather, e.g. *What's the weather like in C2?* (Players must ask complete questions, not just say *C2*). The other player must reply according to their diagram, e.g. *It's snowing.* The student who identifies the position of their partner's five main weather conditions first, is the winner.

2 Weather conversations

False beginners can practise some short conversations about the weather, e.g.

1
A: (It's) Not a very nice day, is it?
B: No, it's horrible!
2
A: (It's a) Lovely day, isn't it?
B: Yes, it's beautiful!

UNIT 20 Past events (1)

Suggested lesson break: after Exercise 2

PRESENTATION

Collect one or two travel brochures of Florida (or some other popular holiday destination) with pictures of some of the attractions there and a map to show where Florida is situated (on the south-east tip of the USA). Use the pictures and the map to illustrate your presentation of the past tense. Hold up the map and say: *Last summer I went to Florida for my holiday. I stayed in a hotel there for two weeks. I went to Disneyworld and I also visited Seaworld. I didn't go to Cape Canaveral because I didn't have time. The weather was marvellous and I enjoyed my holiday very much.* As you speak, write the past tense forms of the verbs you use on the board: *went, stayed, visited, didn't go, didn't have, was, enjoyed.*

Now ask the following questions of yourself (but don't answer them yet). As you do so, write the questions in a list on the board. Leave plenty of space beside each question to write the answers.

PAST TENSE QUESTIONS
Where did you go? (I went to Florida.)
Where did you stay?
How long did you stay?
What did you do?
Why didn't you go to Cape Canaveral?
What was the weather like?
Did you enjoy your holiday?

Practise the questions chorally and individually. Then get different students to ask you the questions. This time give the answers, and write them next to the questions on the board. Circle or underline all the examples of *did* and *didn't*.

Before you read

Still with books closed, ask students:
T: Where do people in your country like to go for their holidays?
S: To Sardinia, to Turkey, to Greece, to the USA.
T: Why do people like to visit Florida? What is nice about Florida?

As students give reasons, list them on the board, e.g. *Disneyworld, sun, good weather, warm in winter, Miami beach, Miami*. Now ask students to open their books and look at the photographs.

The photographs

BACKGROUND NOTES
The sphere: The photograph, taken at night, shows the geodesic dome at the entrance of the Florida Disneyworld EPCOT Centre (Experimental Prototype Community of Tomorrow). The dome houses 'Spaceship Earth' and is one of the landmarks of the EPCOT Centre, which opened in 1982. The ride in 'Spaceship Earth' is in the form of a journey through time from pre-history, forty thousand years ago, to the present day.
The castle: 'Cinderella Castle' is the central landmark in 'The Magic Kingdom'; the first area of Florida Disneyworld to be opened to the public in 1972. The castle, which is based on King Ludwig's castle at Neuschwanstein in Bavaria, is a feature of Disney theme parks throughout the world.
The boat: The 'Empress Lilly' in Disneyworld's 'Village' is a replica of a Mississippi paddle steamer. It is named after Walt Disney's wife and contains bars and restaurants.
The dolphin: Another of southern Florida's main tourist attractions is 'Seaworld', a theme park based on the sea.
The beach: Florida's Atlantic coast is an almost continuous white sandy beach and is the main tourist attraction.
Cape Canaveral: The picture shows the space shuttle at Cape Canaveral. Cape Canaveral is the headquarters of NASA (the National Aeronautics and Space Administration) near Orlando in southern Florida, and is the rocket launch base for space research and exploration.
The flying elephant: This is a 'flying chair' from one of the rides in Disneyworld. It is based on the Walt Disney film *Dumbo*, about a baby elephant which could fly.
Space Mountain (see postcard): This famous Disney roller coaster ride involves a terrifying

'drop' through darkness, interspersed with lighting effects to recreate a ride through space. As you queue for the ride, you can hear the screams of the people hurtling through the dark.

Ask students questions about each of the pictures. If they don't know what the pictures represent, use the background notes to describe them, e.g.
T: What's that animal?
S: It's an elephant.
T: What's its name?
S: Dumbo.
T: What's it doing in the picture?
S: It's flying.
T: Where can you see it?
S: In Disneyworld.

Ask students to read the introduction to Florida silently. When they have finished reading, ask: *How many people visited Florida last year?* (Over 42 million) *What is the temperature there in winter?* (Between 60 and 70°F) *What is the temperature in summer?* (In the 80s)

Exercise 1 READING

Refer to the postcard and ask the following questions:
Who is the postcard to? (Mrs Gibson)
Who sent it? (Caroline and her family)
Where is the postcard from? (Florida/Fort Myers)

Read the postcard aloud, explaining new words, e.g. *huge, pirate, seafood*. Then read aloud the True/False statements one by one for students to answer.

Exercise 2

Ask students to work individually finding the past tense forms of the verbs in the postcard. Then ask the two grammar questions of the whole class.

KEY
The regular past tense ending is *d/ed*. The regular verbs are: *visited* and *liked*.
The irregular verbs are: *had, was, saw, went, spent*.

SUGGESTED LESSON BREAK

GRAMMAR FOCUS

Write on the board the question: *Where did you go for your last summer holiday?* Ask students to study the Focus box. Now ask the question at the end of the box. (Answer *did*.) Remind students that *did* is used in all questions and negatives in the past simple tense. Now ask different students about their last summer holidays and elicit short answers, e.g.
T: Where did you go for your last summer holiday?
S: I went to Leningrad.
T: Did you visit the Hermitage museum?

s: Yes, I did.
t: Did you drink any vodka?
s: No, I didn't.

 Exercise 3 SPEECHWORK
Give extra practice of the past tense forms by stopping the tape and asking for choral and individual repetition. Make sure that students can hear the difference between the /t/ sound in *talked* /tɔ:kt/; the /d/ in *stayed* /steɪd/ and the /ɪd/ sound in *visited* /vɪzitɪd/

Exercise 4

> BACKGROUND NOTES
> *Brighton* /'braɪtən/: A large seaside town on the south coast of England, 75km south of London. It is famous for its elegant nineteenth-century terraced houses.
> *Bali* /'bɑ:li/: An island off the east coast of Java in Indonesia. It is famous for its preservation of the Hindu civilisation of ancient Indonesia and is a popular tourist destination.
> *Biarritz* /ˌbɪəˈrɪtz/: A fashionable seaside resort on the south-west coast of France on the Atlantic.
> *Barcelona* /ˌbɑ:səˈləʊnə/: An industrial city and large port on the northern Mediterranean coast of Spain. It is Spain's second largest city.

Ask students to look at the chart at the bottom of the page. Use the background notes to say where the places are. Practise pronunciation of the place names. Make sure that students understand how to interpret the ratings of ticks, crosses and signs, e.g. Ask: *What does ££ mean?* Elicit: *It means it was expensive.* etc.

Now work Teacher–Student through the questions and answers about the holiday in Brighton, e.g.
t: Where did you go for your holiday?
s: I went to Brighton.
t: How long did you stay?
s: I stayed (there) (for) two weeks.
t: What did you do there?
s: I went on an English course.
t: What was the weather like?
s: It wasn't very good.
t: And how was the hotel?
s: It was all right.
t: What was the food like?
s: It was expensive.
t: And how were the beaches?/
   What were the beaches like?
s: They were awful.

Ask students to work in pairs and to choose two places each to ask and answer about. Ask them to write their conversation about one of the places for homework.

Students can use the same questions to ask and answer about some of the places they went to for their last holidays. They can take notes and report back about their partner's holiday.

Exercise 5 WRITING
Ask students to choose any place they know, either in their own country or somewhere else, and 'send' a postcard from it. Explain that they should use Caroline's postcard from Florida as a model and add their own information and comments. Build up an example postcard on the board, e.g.

Dear Mark,
The weather is marvellous and I am having a great time here in Vancouver. It is a beautiful city. Yesterday we visited the 'Trade Fair'. It was very interesting. On Friday we went to Chinatown and had a wonderful Chinese meal.
Love,
Catherine

EXTRA ACTIVITIES
1 Memory game
In this version of the incremental memory game, each player must repeat the items which have gone before, and then add another item, choosing a word which begins with the next letter of the alphabet each time, e.g.
STUDENT A: I went shopping and bought some apples.
STUDENT B: I went shopping and bought some apples and some bananas.
STUDENT C: I went shopping and bought some apples, some bananas and a calendar.

Divide the class into groups. The list starts at one member of the group and continues until all the letters of the alphabet have been used. Anyone who cannot complete and add to the list must drop out of the game.

2 Guess my holiday
Divide students into groups. One student has to think of an imaginary holiday they took last week. Other students have to ask Yes/No questions starting with *Did you ...* to find out where the person went, how he/she travelled, where he/she stayed and what he/she did, e.g.
s1: Did you go to a hot country?
s2: Yes, I did.
s1: Did you fly?
s2: Yes, I did.
s1: Did you go to the USA?
s2: Yes, I did.
s1: Did you visit Seaworld?
s2: No, I didn't, etc.

FLUENCY Units 16–20

PRESENTATION
Use postcards or magazine pictures to introduce the topic of London and some of its more famous landmarks. Some students may have their own photos of London to bring to the class. Ask: *Who has been to London? Can you name some famous places buildings in London?* List the places on the board as they are mentioned, e.g. *Piccadilly Circus, Trafalgar Square*. If possible, show or pass round pictures of these as they are mentioned. Include St Paul's Cathedral, the Houses of Parliament, the Tower of London, the British Museum and Harrods (the department store in Knightsbridge) among the famous places. (See the background notes below for information about these.) Do some choral repetition of the place names.

Exercise 1

BACKGROUND NOTES
St Paul's Cathedral: The present building, a landmark in the City of London at the top of Ludgate Hill, is the fourth or even fifth religious building in the same place. After St Paul's Church was burnt down in the Great Fire of London, in 1666, Christopher Wren, an architect who also drew the plans for fifty-one other churches in London, designed a new cathedral. Work started on the new building in 1675, and thirty-three years later Wren's son finished it. Prince Charles and Princess Diana were married in St Paul's Cathedral in 1981.
The Houses of Parliament: These consist of the House of Commons, the House of Lords and Westminster Hall. The buildings are situated in central London overlooking the river. The present gothic buildings were designed in 1860 by Charles Barry and Augustus Pugin after the original Parliament Buildings were destroyed by fire. The House of Commons is the debating chamber for 635 elected representatives, or *MPs* (*Members of Parliament*).
The Tower of London: Situated on the Thames next to Tower Bridge, the Tower of London dates back to the Norman Conquest of England in 1066 by William the Conqueror (William I). It was built as a fortress, first of wood (1067) and then of stone (1077–1097), to show that William was indeed a 'conqueror'. Its size was gradually increased and throughout its history its many buildings have served as a treasury, an armoury, a mint, and a prison for important enemies of the state, as well as a place of execution. Two wives of Henry VIII were beheaded there. The Tower of London is now a museum which contains the Crown Jewels.

The shops: *Hamleys* is a well-known toy store in Regent Street. *Tower Records* is a large store which only sells recorded music and videos. *Selfridges* is a large department store in Oxford Street. All three stores are situated in the shopping and entertainment area known as London's 'West End'. Oxford Street advertises itself as 'the largest shopping street in Europe'.
The maps: All the stations marked are underground stations. *Liberty's* is an exclusive department store. *Marks and Spencer's* is a popular chain store selling clothes, food and household items.
The evening activities: *Miss Saigon* is a musical which tells the dramatic and tragic love story of an American and a Vietnamese bar girl at the time of the fall of Saigon during the last days of the Vietnam War. The story, but not the music, is based on Puccini's *Madame Butterfly*. *Stringfellows* is a fashionable nightclub and restaurant. *The Thames by Night* is a river cruise.

Ask students to open their books and look at the *Trip to London* page. To clarify the exercise, say: Imagine that you *went on a trip to London last week. What sightseeing did you do? Did you go to see St Paul's Cathedral or the Houses of Parliament or did you see the Tower of London? What was the weather like when you went? Was it sunny, cloudy or did it rain? What shops did you go to? Did you go to ... ? What did you do in the evening? Did you go to see ... ?* etc
Go through the chart in this way, pointing out the options in each category. Point out the example notes in Exercise 1 and say: *I went sightseeing. I went to the Tower of London. The weather was O.K. It was cloudy. Then I went shopping and I bought a Eurythmics CD.*

Now ask students to work individually and make similar notes about what they did in London. When they have finished, practise the names of the shops chorally and give some practice of reading the maps. Say:
T: Can you see Hamleys on the map?
S: Yes.
T: Hamleys is on Regent Street, quite near Liberty's and not far from Oxford Street underground station. What about Tower Records. Where is that?
S: It's on the corner of Regent Street and Piccadilly. It's next to Piccadilly Station.
T: Where is Selfridges?
S: It's on Oxford Street. It's quite near Marks and Spencer's and it's not far from Bond Street Station.

Exercise 2
Students work in pairs and ask each other about details of the trip, using the cues provided.

Practise the opening of the conversation working Teacher–Student, e.g.

T: Anna, did you have a nice time in London?

S: Yes, I did.

T: Did you go sightseeing?

S: Yes, I went to see ...

📼 Exercise 3 LISTENING

Explain that this is an authentic interview with a non-native speaker of English (an Italian woman) and that there are some grammatical mistakes. Explain also that her visit is spread over two days. Ask students to listen and note down five places the woman went to (the British Museum, lunch in Regent Street, the Tower of London, Tower Bridge, Harrods).

TAPESCRIPT

Listen to an Italian woman talking about how she spent some days in London. Did she do any of the things you did?

We didn't get up very early actually but, er, we tried to see as much as possible. We started from the British Museum and then we had our lunch in Regent Street in a steak house and immediately after I really wanted them to see the Tower of London. It took really three or four hours. At night we went to Tower Bridge when it's lighted up because it's really wonderful to see all the little lights. Then the next day we had planned to go and see a show, er, especially I wanted to see *Cats* but, really, we went there and there weren't any tickets – any available tickets. So it was really a pity and, er, so, we tried to make up for it by going to Harrods. You know you cannot go to London without visiting Harrods. And even though the stuff there is really expensive, we just bought some clothes with written 'Harrods' on it and just some souvenirs and that's all.

KEY

The thing she did which was the same as the students was to visit the Tower of London.

Exercise 4 PROJECT and ROLEPLAY

(If time is short, keep this activity for another lesson.)

Ask students to work in groups to make a chart of items, similar to those in the Students' Book, for their own capital city. Give an example by writing the headings on the board and eliciting different suggestions under each heading. Then give an example of a roleplay working Teacher–Student, e.g.

T: Did you enjoy your holiday in Rome?

S: Yes, I did.

T: What did you see when you were there?

S: I went to see the Coliseum and ...

Ask students to work in new pairs to do their roleplays. If there is time, they can move about the room as if at a party and roleplay different conversations with the people they meet.

Exercise 5 WRITING

Students can either write about a day in London or their own city. Ask a few students to read their postcards to the class, or to 'send' their postcard to another student, who can read it aloud.

CHECK Units 16–20

(For advice on handling this section, see the notes for Check Units 1–5.)

KEY

Ex. 1 1b 2a 3c 4a 5b (5 marks)

Ex. 2 1 a tube of toothpaste 2 a box of matches 3 a bottle of mineral water 4 a loaf of bread 5 a packet of crisps (5 marks)

Ex. 3 1 The red one. 2 The small one. 3 The chocolate ones. 4 The Italian ones. 5 The big one. (5 marks)

Ex. 4 1 spaghetti 2 bread 3 fish 4 bathroom 5 garden 6 rain 7 winter 8 Tuesday 9 milk (10 marks)

Ex. 5 1C 2UC 3C 4UC 5C 6UC 7C 8UC 9C 10UC (10 marks)

Ex. 6 1 any 2 no 3 any 4 any 5 some (5 marks)

Ex. 7 1 next to 2 between 3 in front of 4 behind 5 in front of (5 marks)

Ex. 8 1 in 2 on 3 in 4 in 5 at 6 in 7 in 8 on 9 at 10 in (10 marks)

Ex. 9 1 c) supermarket 2 f) post office 3 h) bus stop 4 e) taxi rank 5 a) swimming pool 6 i) car park 7 g) newsagent 8 d) bookshop 9 b) snack bar (10 marks)

Ex. 10 1 got up 2 went for 3 spent 4 had 5 swam and sunbathed 6 had 7 relaxed 8 had 9 went 10 went (10 marks)

CHECK YOUR PROGRESS

(See notes for Check Units 1–5.)

LEARNING TO LEARN 4

Ask students to have their vocabulary books ready at the last entries they made in them. Read each of the tips in the box aloud and, as you do so, ask students to do the following. Say: *Please look at number 1. What was the last word you wrote in your vocabulary book? Which unit was it from? Look at number 2. Choose a word you like from Unit 19 and say it aloud.* Ask several students to say their words aloud. *Now choose another word you like and whisper it several times.* Ask all the students to whisper their words at the same time. *Look at number 3. Choose one of the words from the list in Exercise 1 Unit 17 and draw it. Now show it to your partner. Number 4. I'm going to explain the word association chain game.* (See below.)

Word association game

One person chooses a word from Unit 20 and says it aloud, e.g. *beach.* The next person must say a word which comes immediately to mind. The next person continues with another word, and so on round the class, e.g.

s1: beach
s2: sunbathing
s3: brown
s4: bread

Find the meaning

Now ask students to complete the task at the end of the box. Ask them to tell you which way they want to learn the words. Then ask them to write each of the words in their vocabulary books together with a sentence, e.g.

opposite: Eleni is sitting opposite Karl.
petrol: Petrol is now very expensive.

PREVIEW Units 21–25

The photographs, dialogue and exercise

Ask students to look at the main photograph. Ask the first two comprehension questions in the Students' Book: *Who is Adam with?* (His brother Michael, and his brother's girlfriend) *Who is Laura with?* (Some friends – probably from the university) Then ask: *Where are they walking?* (Along/beside the river) *What's the weather like?* (It's warm and sunny.) *Is Adam pleased/happy to see Laura?* Students read the speech bubbles. Ask them the remaining comprehension questions.

🔲 The tape

Now play the tape while the students follow the conversation in their books.

TAPESCRIPT
Listen and follow the conversation in your Students' Book.

MICHAEL: Who's the girl with the dark hair?
ADAM: Which one?
MICHAEL: The one looking at you. She's wearing a white skirt.
ADAM: Oh ... it's Laura. She's an American student. She's studying English Literature at the university. I met her in the travel agent's. Hang on!

MICHAEL: What are you going to do?
ADAM: I'm going to say hello! Can you just wait a moment?
Hello, Laura!
LAURA: Adam, hi! I thought it was you.
ADAM: Why didn't you return my phone calls?
LAURA: I'm sorry Adam, I was really busy. I had six essays to write.
Is this your car? It's very nice.
ADAM: Er no ... It isn't mine. It's my brother's. Look, let's go for a coffee.
LAURA: Sure, fine.

The learning objectives

Go through the list of objectives in the box and ask students to find examples of each of the objectives in the dialogues.

Talk about personal property: *Is this your car? It isn't mine, it's my brother's.*
Describe clothes: *She's wearing a white skirt.*
Talk about future plans: *What are you going to do?*
Make suggestions: *Let's go for a coffee.*
Describe appearance: *Who's the girl with the dark hair?*
Talk about past events in sequence: *Why didn't you return my phone calls?*

UNIT 21 Personal property

Suggested lesson break: after Exercise 5

> BACKGROUND NOTE
> *Parking ticket*: Notification of an official fine for illegal parking. The fine is approximately £15. The ticket is usually put on the windscreen of the car, under the windscreen wipers. Other parking penalties include wheel clamps and having your car taken away, in which case the fine is about £75. The police in Britain do not have the right to ask for money for parking fines 'on the spot' where the car is parked.

PRESENTATION

Pick up a pen or pencil belonging to another student. Try not to let students see whose pen you have taken. Ask: *Whose pen is this?* Elicit: *It's mine.* Answer: *Yes, it's yours.* Point to another male student. Ask: *Is it his?* Elicit: *No, it isn't.* Point to a female student. Ask: *Is it hers?* Elicit: *No, it isn't.* Ask: *Is it mine?* (pointing to yourself). Elicit: *No, it isn't.* Ask: *Whose is it?* Elicit: *It's Selma's.* Write on the board:

Whose pen is this?
Whose is this pen?
It's mine./yours./his./hers./ours./theirs./Selma's.

Practise chorally and individually.

Exercise 1

Now ask students to look at the two photographs. Ask the questions in the Students' Book or the following more detailed questions.

PICTURE 1

What is the man holding? (A wallet)
Is it his? (No, it isn't.)
Whose is it? (It's the woman's.)
Where did she leave it? (In the bank)

Explain that *Heavens!* is an expression of surprise. Point out that the past tense of *leave* is *left*. Write this in a special past tense column on the board and add new verbs as they occur in the lesson.

PICTURE 2

Where are the people sitting? (Outside a café)
Who's the man standing next to the table? (A waiter)
Who owns the yellow car? (The man on the right)
Where is it? (On the other side of the road)
Why is the waiter pointing at the car? (It's got a parking ticket on it.)
What are his exact words? (Whose is the yellow car on the other side of the road?)

Say the waiter's lines yourself, making sure you say *well* conversationally. Explain that *I'm afraid = unfortunately.* Give some more examples of *I'm afraid,* e.g. *I must go, I'm afraid. I'm afraid the beer isn't very cold.* In a monolingual class, you can compare *well* with a similar sentence opener in the students' own language, e.g *Alors, ...* in French.

GRAMMAR FOCUS

Ask students to look at the Focus box. Say: *You can say 'Whose car is this?'. How else can you ask the same question?* Point out that *whose* is pronounced in the same way as *who's.* Students may need some practice in discriminating between *Whose is that?* and *Who's that?*

Ask students to look at the second section of the box and ask the question beneath it. Point out also:
– the absence of apostrophes in *ours, hers,* etc.
– that *his* and *its* are the same in both adjective and pronoun form
– that *its* must not be confused with *it's* (*it is*)

Refer to the note about *belong to* and give a few examples referring to objects in the classroom, e.g. *This book belongs to Martina. It's Martina's.*

Exercise 2

Either ask students to exchange possessions or walk round the class collecting some personal possessions from the students, e.g. a book/pen/bag/dictionary. For each item, you, or the students, ask in turn: *Whose is this/are these?* Students identify the item and respond: *It's mine./It's Julio's. /It belongs to Julio.*

Exercise 3

Identify all the objects in the pictures first and practise the pronunciation of the new words, e.g. *an electric drill, a watch, a fountain pen, a computer, a sewing machine, a gold bracelet, a personal stereo/Walkman, a razor, a football.* Give an example to show that in some cases several 'owners' are possible. Point to the car and ask:

T: Whose is the car?
s1: I think it's his.
T: Yes, or hers perhaps. What about the bracelet?
s1: I think it's the girl's.
T: Really?
s2: No, it isn't hers. I think it's the woman's.

Students now work in pairs, asking and answering about all the objects in the picture. Check the students' answers afterwards.

Exercise 4

Go through all the items in the questionnaire, explaining any new words. Change any items, e.g *the bible* to the *Koran,* as appropriate to the cultural background of the class. Ask students to copy the questionnaire into their notebooks, leaving space to write both their own answers *and* their partner's beside them.

Students first write in their own answers, using a tick or a cross (or Yes/No) and then interview their partner to find out his/her answers. Work Teacher–Student with one or two questions. Ask students to report back to the class on any surprising answers.

Exercise 5 SPEECHWORK

Students first complete the exercise silently, and then listen to the tape. Play the tape a second time. Ask students to repeat each word, noticing the spelling as they do so. Some of these words can be given as a spelling test in a later lesson.

KEY
1 ours 2 cat 3 win 4 how's 5 here

SUGGESTED LESSON BREAK

Exercise 6 LISTENING

Explain that a *leisure centre* is a place where you can do a number of different activities under one roof, e.g. swim, see films and play sports like volleyball. Explain the words in each category on the chart:
Item = object or thing
Description = what the item is like – if it is red, big, gold, etc.
Where left or lost = where the person left it or lost it. (Point out that *lost* is the past tense of *lose.*)
When = when the person left it there.

Add the past tense of *lose* (*lost*) and *find* (*found*) to your list on the board.

Write on the board the following words and ask the students to look them up in their dictionaries: *plastic (bag), changing room, essay.*
Ask them to copy the chart into their notebooks, leaving plenty of space to write the answers.

Play the tape while students listen and complete the information. Play at least once again afterwards for students to copy down the man's questions, pausing the tape where necessary. Check students' answers.

TAPESCRIPT
Listen to this conversation at a leisure centre and complete the information.

GIRL: Excuse me, I think I left a plastic bag here on Saturday.
MAN: We've got lots of lost property here and a lot of plastic bags. What's it like?
GIRL: It's black and white.
MAN: What's it got in it?
GIRL: A notepad, a book and some biscuits ... and a black pen.
MAN: Where did you leave it?
GIRL: In the café.
MAN: When did you leave it there?
GIRL: On Saturday, at about one o'clock.
MAN: I'll go and have a look. ... You're lucky, here it is!
GIRL: Great! It's got my essay in it!

Exercise 7 WRITING and 8 ROLEPLAY
Present the phrase: *gold, with a black strap* using a real watch if possible. Say: *This watch is gold and it's got a black strap.* Write on the board, underlining *with*: *It's gold, <u>with</u> a black strap.*
Ask: *What's your watch like, Mario?* Elicit: *It's silver, with a metal strap.* Ask: *What about yours, Anna?* etc.

Elicit other examples of sentences using *with,* e.g. *My bag's black, with a gold buckle.* Students copy another form like the one in Exercise 6 and then think of something to lose. They complete the form but do not write their name on it. Go round helping them with any new words or expressions. Do not insist that students write the date correctly as this will be taught in Unit 26. Tell students to memorise the details on their form. Collect the forms, mix them up and distribute them. If students get their own form they must choose another. In turn the students look at the form which they have been given and say what they have 'found'. Anyone who has 'lost' that item must call out: *I think (maybe) it's mine.* If it's a watch there may be several students who have written 'lost watch' notices. They must then answer the questions about it, e.g.

S1: I've found a watch. Whose is it?
S2: I think it's mine.
S1: What is it like?
S2: It's gold and it's got a leather strap.
S1: Where did you lose it?
S2: I lost it on the bus to school.
S1: When?
S2: Yesterday.
S1: O.K. It's yours./No, it isn't yours.

Draw attention to the skeleton conversation in the Students' Book to show students how to begin and end their conversations and demonstrate a conversation Teacher–Student first. Treat 'I've found' as a set phrase and avoid teaching the present perfect tense in detail here.

EXTRA ACTIVITY
Chinese whispers
Students form a chain. Whisper a sentence, e.g. *Whose is the orange car with the yellow wheels on the other side of the street?* to a student. This student whispers the sentence to the person on the left and so on, so that the whispered sentence passes round the whole class. The last person says the sentence aloud.

UNIT 22 Clothes

Suggested lesson break: after Exercise 5

Exercise 1
Use clothes which you and the students are wearing, magazine pictures, the photographs in the previous units of the Students' Book or your own sketches to illustrate the meaning of the clothes words listed. (Adam is wearing a blazer in Preview 1). Say:
T: What's this?
S: It's a skirt.
T: What's Adam wearing in this picture? (Preview 1)
S: It's a jacket.
T: Yes, it's a sort of jacket. It's a blazer. (etc.)

Write the words on the board as students (or you) mention them and practise their pronunciation. Then ask students to look at the picture of the people at the bottom of the page and to write down the clothes which the people are wearing. Ask them which clothes from the list are not in the picture. Point out that a suit may be worn by both men and women. In the case of women, it is usually a matching skirt and jacket.

KEY
Clothes listed which are not in the picture are: a hat, a dress (or a skirt), shorts, a coat, a blazer, a suit, a scarf, a vest, a tracksuit, a cardigan, a raincoat, a swimsuit.

Ask: *What are most people in the picture wearing?* (Trousers, jeans, jackets, sweaters, shirts, trainers, shoes)

Exercise 2

Present the patterns and shades. Say: T*his sweater is plain. It is plain blue. This blouse isn't plain. It's got flowers on it. It's flowery. It's a flowery blouse.* Repeat with *patterned, spotted, striped* and *checked*. Write the words on the board as you say them, e.g.

a blouse with	flowers on it	a flowery blouse
	a pattern	patterned
	spots	spotted
	stripes	striped
	checks	checked

Then ask about the students' own clothes. Ask: *Is your sweater plain?* Elicit: *No, it's patterned.* (etc.)
Ask students to work in pairs describing different people in the picture, e.g.
s1: What's that woman wearing?
s2: She's wearing a (black and white) checked jacket.

Exercise 3 SPEECHWORK

Give some initial practice of the two sounds. Say: *Say after me: /dʒ/... /dʒ/... John ... Jane ... /j/... /j/ ... you ... yes ...* . Then play the tape. Problems that may arise:
the use of /j/ instead of /dʒ/
the use of /tʃ/ instead of /dʒ/

Exercise 4

Pair each student with another student sitting across the room so that the exercise will not be too easy. Ask them to close their eyes or stand them back to back. The student who is being described can contradict during, or correct after the description, e.g.
s1: You're wearing a brown sweater.
s2: No, it isn't a sweater. It's a cardigan.

If the class is not too large, it may be more fun if each pair performs in turn so that the other students can watch and listen.

Exercise 5 About you

Finish the first part of the lesson with a general discussion conducted either as a whole class or in groups, depending on the size of the class.
Explain *casual* (opposite of *formal*). Make sure the students say *clothes* with an *s* /kləʊðz/. If they find the word difficult to pronounce, they could say /kləʊz/ instead, provided the vowel sound is long and the /z/ is voiced. Make a note of any tense mistakes, e.g. ~~I am buying my clothes at ...~~ or ~~I am reading ... magazines~~ and correct them generally at the end of the lesson.

SUGGESTED LESSON BREAK

Exercise 6 LISTENING

Before you listen, elicit phrases like: *jeans, casual clothes, cheap clothes,* etc. Point to the picture of the jeans jacket and ask students to describe it (it is decorated with patterned patches and it has red trimming/stripes). Explain that *customised* means *made to personal order* and that many people 'decorate' their clothes, particularly jeans and jeans jackets, so that they look different. Go through the headings in the chart. Explain *monthly clothes budget* = the money you spend on clothes each month. Say: *My niece has a monthly clothes budget of £20. She spends £20 on clothes every month.* Explain that *outfit* here means clothes. Students copy the headings into their notebooks and then listen as you play the tape once or twice. Check the answers and add the word *sweatshirt* to the list of clothes words on the board. Ask students who the sweatshirt and boots belong to (Henry's brother).

TAPESCRIPT
Listen to a British student talking about his clothes and complete the chart.

PRESENTER: Welcome to *The Clothes Show*. Today we are looking at students' clothes. Let's meet Henry Bourne. Henry is nineteen and in his first year at Swansea University in South Wales.

INTERVIEWER:	How much do you spend on clothes?
HENRY:	As little as possible! No, no, I suppose I spend on average about £20 a month.
INTERVIEWER:	Mm, £20 a month. What is your favourite style of clothes?
HENRY:	I like American-style clothes. This is my favourite outfit.
INTERVIEWER:	Well, as this is radio, let me tell you about Henry's clothes. Henry is wearing a customised denim jacket and jeans. So how are they different?
HENRY:	Well, I got them from the local jeans shop and I decorated them myself.
INTERVIEWER:	What about the rest of your clothes?
HENRY:	Well, I 'borrowed' the red sweatshirt and black boots from my brother. Most of the clothes I wear are his!

Exercise 7

Only do this exercise if you think it is appropriate to your group. Let students listen to the tape from Exercise 6 again. Then elicit the questions to use in the interview and write them on the board, e.g.

What do you do?
How much do you spend on clothes?
What's your favourite style of clothes?
What are you wearing today?

Some students may like to copy these questions into their notebooks to help them with their interviews. Students who say they buy clothes only once or twice a year can give an average figure per month.

Exercise 8 READING

BACKGROUND NOTE
TV-am: This is a TV company which broadcasts early morning television from 6 a.m. to 9.30 a.m.

Ask students to give you the names of any women TV news presenters (newsreaders) they know or like. Ask students to read the text silently and to guess the meaning of the following words: *bright, cheerful, blur, jewellery, allergic, distract.* Students can pair up to check the answers to the questions.

KEY
1c 2b 3a 4b

Exercise 9

Collect some magazine or newspaper photographs of famous people such as members of the British royal family, politicians, film stars, pop stars, musicians, sports personalities, etc. to display in the class. Different groups then compare their lists.

Exercise 10 WRITING

Students use the headings in the box in Exercise 6 to guide their paragraph but tell them to omit the last heading. Suggest instead that they elaborate on their favourite clothes and that they say what they usually wear at work or at school, what they like wearing at the weekend and what they like wearing for parties. Build up an example paragraph on the board:

SUGGESTED PARAGRAPH
My name is (Susanna). I'm (a student). I spend about (£50) a month on clothes. My favourite clothes are (casual). I usually wear (trousers) to (college). At the weekend I like wearing (jeans) and (a sweater) but at parties I usually wear (something smart – a dress or a miniskirt and lots of jewellery).

EXTRA ACTIVITIES
1 Clothes bingo

Students draw squares of 4 x 4 (sixteen squares) and write a different clothes word from the list in Exercise 1 in each square. The teacher then reads out the list in a different order. If the teacher reads a word which appears on a student's square, he/she crosses it out. The first student to complete a line horizontally, vertically or diagonally wins.

2 Clothes consequences

Students form groups of six to play this game of consequences. The framework is as follows:
Line 1: *X (famous male personality) met*
Line 2: *Y (famous female personality)*
Line 3: *He was wearing ...*
Line 4: *She was wearing ...*
Line 5: *And so they ... (activity, e.g. played tennis) together.*

Student 1 writes the first line, folds over the paper and passes it on to Student 2. Without looking at the previous line, Student 2 writes the second line, folds it over and passes it on to Student 3, etc. until all five lines have been completed. The last student (Student 6) opens up the paper and reads out the whole 'saga'. The game can be played several times with different students starting each time.

UNIT 23 Future plans

Suggested lesson break: after Exercise 5

PRESENTATION

Draw a man smoking a cigarette on the board and say: *This is my friend, Bob. Bob smokes twenty cigarettes a day. He says: 'Tomorrow I'm going to stop smoking.'* Now draw a woman on the board and say: *This is my friend, Carol. On Saturday evening she's going to a party. She says: 'I'm going to wear a black mini dress on Saturday.'* Elicit the following conversation:
T: What is Bob going to do?
S: He's going to stop smoking.
T: When is he going to stop?
S: Tomorrow.
T: When is Carol's party?
S: On Saturday evening.
T: What is she going to wear?
S: She's going to wear a black mini dress.

Write on the board the following table:

I'm			stop smoking	tomorrow.
He's		going to	wear a black	
She's			mini dress	on Saturday.

Leave the table on the board so that you can refer to it later.

Exercise 1

Ask students to look at the pictures in the left-hand column. Say:
T: Look at Picture 1. What's the girl on the left wearing?

s: A blue blouse and jeans.

T: What about the girl on the right?

s: She's wearing a yellow sweater and a grey skirt.

T: What are they doing?

s: They're listening to records.

Then ask two students to read the speech bubbles.

Repeat this procedure with the other two pictures. Then ask the questions in Exercise 1 and make sure the students use *going to* in their answers.

GRAMMAR FOCUS

Refer back to the table you wrote on the board during the presentation. Underline *going to* and put a bracket around the two words. Point out that *going to* should be seen as a fixed phrase: it is not possible to omit the *to*. Then ask students to look at the examples in the Focus box. Practise some of the questions and answers chorally, making sure that the students do not stress the word *to*. Ask the 'What's the difference' question.

KEY

1 I get up at 7 o'clock. = an everyday routine
2 I'm going to get up at 7 o'clock. = tomorrow or in the future

If they have already studied some English before, some students may ask if they can use *will*. Explain that you cannot use *will* to talk about future plans or intentions, i.e. you can't say: I̶ ̶w̶i̶l̶l̶ ̶h̶a̶v̶e̶ ̶a̶ ̶c̶u̶p̶ ̶o̶f̶ ̶c̶o̶f̶f̶e̶e̶ ̶a̶f̶t̶e̶r̶ ̶t̶h̶e̶ ̶l̶e̶s̶s̶o̶n̶. You may like to give some examples here of when you can use *will*, e.g. with predictions: *I think he'll be late/I think it'll rain tomorrow*. Explain that *going to* is the more useful future tense to learn at the beginning as it can be used for expressing plans, intention and prediction as well, e.g. *I think he's going to be late/I think it's going to rain*.

Exercise 2 SPEECHWORK

Ask students to copy the phrases into their notebooks. They can guess first where they think the stress will fall and then listen for confirmation. Encourage a steady rhythm by beating the stressed syllables at regular intervals on the desk.

TAPESCRIPT AND KEY

Listen and underline the stressed syllables.

What are you going to do?
What am I going to wear?
When are they going to leave?

Exercise 3

Give an example working Student–Teacher and then students work in pairs, e.g.

T: What are you going to do after the lesson, Pierre?

s1: I'm going to take a bus home.

T: Pierre, ask Antonio what he's going to do this evening.

s2: What are you going to do this evening, Antonio?

s3: I'm going to work at the restaurant.

Students now work in pairs. After the pairwork, ask each student to tell you some of his/her partner's plans so that they all get practice in using *she* and *he* as well as *I*. Ask: *Pierre, what is Antonio going to do after the lesson?* Elicit: *He's going to have a cup of coffee.*

As they tell you, write up the different plans under the four headings in Exercise 3. Then get students to practise short form answers by asking across the class: *Bernice, are you going to have a cup of coffee after the class?* Elicit: *Yes, I am./ No, I'm not.*

Extend this practice to include third person short form answers. Ask: *Lorenzo, is Bernice going to have a cup of coffee after the class?* Elicit: *Yes, she is./No, she isn't.* (Students can refer to the Language review on page 140 of their Students' Book for a full paradigm of the *going to* short form answers.)

Note

It is possible to omit *going to* if the main verb is also *go*, e.g. *I'm going home. I'm going to the shops.* However, encourage the full form *I'm going to go home. I'm going to go to the shops* at this stage so that students get used to the pattern.

Exercise 4

Conduct this as a class exercise, eliciting as many variants as possible.

SUGGESTED ANSWERS

1 I'm going to go to bed early tonight.
2 I'm going to stop smoking.
3 I'm going to change my job.
4 I'm going to buy a new suit.
5 I'm going to learn Spanish/take Spanish lessons.

Exercise 5

> BACKGROUND NOTE
> *Moscow*: The photograph shows Red Square in Moscow with the Kremlin and Lenin's mausoleum. Red Square is still the symbolic heart of Russia. The small groups of people around the umbrella are collecting around different foreign language guides in preparation for guided tours of the Kremlin.

Ask students to look at the photograph of Red Square in Moscow. Ask:
Where is it? (See background notes)
What season do you think it is? (Winter)
What's the weather like? (Cold but sunny)

How do you know? (People are wearing fur hats and heavy coats. There's snow on the ground.) *What do you think is happening behind the white umbrella?* (Perhaps somebody is selling something? See the background note for the correct explanation.)

Ask students to imagine that they are going on holiday to Moscow. Go through the instructions to the exercise and explain that *excluding underwear and socks* means that these are not counted in the fifteen items. At first, students work individually to make up their list. Remind them that three sweaters = three items. Go round helping with extra vocabulary, e.g. *woollen gloves, fur hat, fur (-lined) boots,* etc. Students compare their lists in pairs and then tell you something that was different on each of the lists, e.g. *Helena is going to take a leather jacket but I'm going to take an anorak.*

SUGGESTED LIST

a warm coat	2 sweaters
a hat	3 shirts/blouses
a pair of gloves	a pair of jeans
2 pairs of trousers	1 pair of boots
2 pairs of shoes	1 warm jacket

To buy: a fur hat, some Russian dolls

SUGGESTED LESSON BREAK

Exercise 6 LISTENING and COMMUNICATION FOCUS

In a monolingual class, ask students how they make suggestions in their own language. Then ask if they know how to do the same in English. Refer to the Communication Focus box. Write some more examples using *Let's* (*Let us*) on the board, e.g. *Let's have a party. Let's take the bus. Let's go by car. Let's buy some vodka.*

Now ask students how to say the same using *What about ... .* As they give the answers, write the sentences on the board next to the other sentences and point out the use of the *ing* form with *What about,* e.g. *Let's have a party. = What about having a party?*

Explain the rubric for the listening exercise: that some tourists are lost in Moscow and do not know what to do. Go through the list of suggestions and explain *passer-by.* Ask students which seems the best suggestion. Play the tape and check the answers afterwards. Point out that after *suggest,* they must use the *ing* form of the verb which follows.

TAPESCRIPT

Some tourists are lost in Moscow. They are discussing what to do. Which of these suggestions do they make? Do they suggest asking a policeman, asking a passer-by, asking a tourist, buying a map or going to the tourist office?

MAN:	What are we going to do?
WOMAN:	What about asking that woman?
MAN:	O.K. You ask.
WOMAN:	Excuse me, where is the Kremlin?
RUSSIAN:	('Sorry I don't speak English' in Russian)
WOMAN:	It's no good. She doesn't understand.
MAN:	Let's buy a map.
WOMAN:	O.K. but where? I can't see any book shops in this street.
MAN:	Look! There's someone over there with a map. He looks like a tourist. What about asking him?
WOMAN:	O.K. That's a good idea. You ask this time.

Exercise 7

Set the context for the exercise and go through the suggestions. Students work in groups. They can make their own suggestions as well as using those in the book. Go round the groups while they discuss, encouraging students to use *What about ...* and *Let's ...* where appropriate. With a class of false beginners, add *Why don't we ...* and/or *We could ... .* Allow a maximum of ten minutes for the discussion. Each group then selects one person to tell the other groups what their plans are, using the *going to* future, e.g. *We're going to have a small party with some food and drink. After that, Gianni is going to show some slides from his holiday in Rome. Then Sandra is going to play the guitar and we're going to sing some Italian songs. Then we're going to have some more wine ...*

The class can vote on what they think is going to be the best 'evening'.

Exercise 8 READING AND WRITING

Students use the handwritten note as a model to write a note to someone in the class. Ask one or two students to read aloud the notes they have received.

EXTRA ACTIVITIES

1 Suggestions: a chain game

One student suggests something to do in the evening or next weekend. The next student has to disagree with the suggestion and change it to something different using either *Let's ...* or *What about ...,* e.g.

S1: Let's go to the cinema.
S2: No, not the cinema. Let's go to the theatre.
S3: No, not the theatre. What about going to a nightclub?

Anyone who can't think of anything to do or gets the wrong verb form after *Let's* or *What about* has to drop out of the game.

2 Diaries

Students write a diary page for the next week by writing down what they are going to do on three evenings of the week. They then form groups of six and try to arrange an evening to meet when everyone is free. If they are unable to find an evening, one of the group must agree to move or give up one of their plans.

3 Resolutions

Explain that in Britain, it is customary at the end of the year for people to make resolutions for the next year, i.e. decisions about how they are going to improve their behaviour and lifestyle. Ask students to think of three resolutions which they would like to make, e.g. *I'm going to stop smoking. I'm going to give up (eating) sweets/chocolates. I'm going to learn Russian.*

UNIT 24 Personal appearance

Suggested lesson break: after Exercise 5

PRESENTATION

With Students' Books closed, present as many words as possible from the personal appearance vocabulary in the chart in Exercise 1, using the students in the class and magazine pictures, e.g. Say: *I'm medium height. I've got short, fair hair. I've got blue eyes.* Write on the board:

Size/Height	Hair	Eyes
medium height	fair	blue
	short	

Now point to another student and say: *Miguel is quite short. He's got dark wavy hair and brown eyes.* Write in the new words under the headings on the board. Now add the sentences:

I'm medium height.
He's short.
I've got short, fair hair.
He's got dark, wavy hair.
I've got blue eyes.
He's got brown eyes.

Ask different students to describe themselves, helping them with new words until most of the words in the chart have been introduced. Introduce any other words the students need or want to know, e.g. *fringe, bald, permed hair, thick hair, to wear your hair tied back/in a ponytail.*
Practise the pronunciation of the new words chorally and individually. Then ask students to open their Students' Books and look at the two photographs at the top of the page. Draw attention to the question in the first speech bubble and explain that *What's he like?* can refer to both appearance and personality. Explain that *really* means *very* in this case.

Exercise 1

Ask students to work in pairs, choosing words from the chart to describe Adam. They should look at each section in turn and select a suitable word or words, e.g.
(General appearance)
s1: He's fair and good-looking.
(Height)
s2: He's medium-height.

SUGGESTED CHOICE
He's fair, quite good-looking, medium-height and slim.
He's got short blond/fair, wavy hair, and blue eyes.

If you wish, ask students to describe other characters in the book, such as Chris, Laura and Sarah (Laura's friend on this page).

Exercise 2

Work Teacher–Student with another example of opposites from the chart, e.g. *fair – dark.* Demonstrate that some words have more than one opposite, e.g. *tall – short, long – short.* This can cause problems as some languages use the equivalent of *long* in both contexts. When students have finished, ask a few of them to come up to the front of the class and write their pairs on the board. When they have corrected their lists, students should write them in their vocabulary books, adding them to the previous list of adjectives made in Unit 10, Exercise 6.

KEY

fair – dark	fat – thin
pretty – plain	fat – slim
handsome/good-looking – ugly	long – short
tall – short	straight – curly
big – small	straight – wavy

 Exercise 3 LISTENING

> BACKGROUND NOTES
> *Whitney Houston* /ˌwɪtniˈhuːstən/: A black American soul singer, popular in the late 1980s, and one of the biggest-selling soul singers of all time.
> *Gloria Estefan* /ˈestəfɑːn/: A Latin American pop singer. Her first and most popular hit was *One-Two-Three.*
> *Rob Lowe* /ləʊ/: An American actor who appeared in several of the cult teenage American movies of the late 1980s.
> *Michael J. Fox:* An American actor who became famous for his role in the *Back to the Future* films. In the picture he is holding a 'Golden Globe' trophy which he won as best actor for his role in *Back to the Future.*

Before listening to the tape, ask students if they know the names of any songs by Whitney Houston or Gloria Estefan or know the names of any films starring Rob Lowe or Michael J. Fox.

Ask students to describe what the four people look like and what they are doing. Elicit: *to hold, microphone, bracelet, trophy, bow tie, dress, suit.* Play the tape and after each person is described, stop the tape and ask students to guess which one it is.

TAPESCRIPT

Listen and say which two people the speakers are describing.

She's standing up and she's singing. She's holding a microphone in her right hand. She's got brown, curly hair. Um, she's tall, she's slim and she's good-looking. She's wearing a bracelet on her right hand. She's wearing a long dress. She's wearing a blue dress.

Um, he's wearing a very smart black suit and he's got a bow tie on. He's got a white shirt. He's got short dark brown hair. He's very good-looking. He's not very tall. He's wearing glasses.

KEY

1 Whitney Houston 2 Rob Lowe

COMMUNICATION FOCUS
Ask students to look at the box silently for half a minute. Then say: *You want to ask about someone's appearance. You can say 'What's she like?' or you can say ...?* Elicit: *What does she look like?* Explain that *What sort of hair has she got?* can refer to the colour or the style. Also explain that you can say *Does she wear glasses?* or *Has she got glasses?*

To practise the questions and answers in the Focus box, ask students to look at the photographs of the singers and actors in Exercise 3. Ask:
T: What does Whitney Houston look like?
s1: She's tall ... (etc.)
T: Does she wear glasses?
s2: No, she doesn't.
T: Now, Roberto, ask Anna about Rob Lowe.
s3: What does Rob Lowe look like, Anna?

🔲 Exercise 4 SPEECHWORK
Some students find it difficult to make and hear the difference between *What's he like?* and *What's she like?* Write the two questions on the board and number them (1) and (2). Read a mixed set of these questions and ask students to say if they hear (1) or (2) e.g.
What's he like?... What's she like?... What's he like?... What's he like?... What's she like?... What's he like?... What's she like?...
Repeat the procedure with *What does he/she look like?* Then play the tape for students to repeat.

Exercise 5
Each student should first of all tell his/her partner which person he/she wishes to describe, e.g.

s1: I want to describe my brother.
s2: O.K. What's your brother like?

Students can use either *What's ... like?* or *What does ... look like?*

The second student should prompt the first student by asking questions such as: *Is he good-looking? What colour eyes has he got?*, etc. using the categories in the chart in Exercise 1.

SUGGESTED LESSON BREAK

Exercise 6 WRITING
Take the opportunity to practise the layout of letters. Refer back to the letter in Unit 9 of the Students' Book for comparison. Point out the use of the *ing* form in *Thank you for offering to meet me* and *Looking forward to seeing you.* Do not go into any detailed grammatical explanation of the use of the future continuous *I will be wearing.* You could say that *I'm going to wear* is all right, but *I'll be wearing* is better. Explain also that as this is a letter to someone older whom they have not met before, it is polite to sign off *Yours sincerely.* Give an example on the board of what to write in the middle paragraph, e.g.

I am quite tall. I've got long dark hair. I will be wearing a white jacket and blue jeans and I've got a red suitcase.

Ask students to write their own letter in their notebooks. Make sure students copy the complete letter into their books, putting their own address (but not name) at the top right-hand corner of the page.

Exercise 7 READING
Explain that some children were asked to describe their fathers for a magazine and this is what they wrote. Ask students to read the texts silently, making a list of unfamiliar words as they go along. At the end, they should see if they can guess the meaning of these words from the context or ask someone else in the class. As a last resort they can use a dictionary. New words: *the way, cough, plenty, stand up, clever, lift up, throw, air, once, catch, miss, bump, kind, wash, dry, dishes, let, cross, on my own.*

(Note that John-Paul has made an adverb from the adjective *grown-up* by adding -*ly* (*grown-uply*). In fact it is incorrect to apply this rule to hyphenated adjectives. Young children often generalise grammar rules like this, experimenting with language.)

When students have finished reading and have found out the meaning of the new words, draw a chart on the board like the one below (but without the ticks and crosses) and ask students to copy it and complete it with ticks or crosses as below. This will help them to answer which feature all the children notice about their fathers.

KEY

	eyes	hair	job	size/ height	age
John-Paul	✗	✓	✗	✓	✓
Camilla	✓	✓	✗	✓	✗
Hayley	✗	✓	✗	✓	✗
Aisling	✗	✓	✗	✗	✓

EXTRA ACTIVITY
Back to back

Find a large clear magazine picture of an 'ordinary' person, i.e. not a well-known figure. Divide students into pairs A and B. Ask all the A students to come to the front of the class and look at the picture for a count of fifteen seconds. Each A student then goes back to join B and proceeds to describe the person. B must prompt A with questions to get more details of the description. Then bring the class together and ask the B students to re-describe the person from what they have heard. There may be some disagreement between B students over details such as eyes, hair, size and age. Finally pass the picture round the class so that everyone can now see what the person looks like and the description can be revised.

UNIT 25 Past events (2)

Suggested lesson breaks: after Exercises 3 and 5

Exercise 1

Ask students to look at the pictures in their Students' Book in sequence. Write the words listed under Exercise 1 on the board to help prompt the answers. Ask:
What is the man carrying in Picture 1? (A suitcase)
What is he going to do? (Get on a train)
Is it a modern or an old-fashioned train? (An old-fashioned train)
Where is he in Picture 2? (In a sleeping compartment)
Is his journey going to be long or short? (Probably quite long)
What is he doing in Picture 3? (He's reading in bed.)
What is he wearing? (Pyjamas)
What time do you think it is in Picture 3? (Maybe 11, 11.30 or midnight)
What time is it in Picture 4? (Two o'clock in the morning)
Is he awake or asleep? (Awake)
Why do you think he wants to leave his compartment in Picture 5? (Because he wants a drink of water/wants to go to the toilet.)
Can he open the compartment door? (No, he can't.)
Why not? (It's locked/jammed.)

What does he do? (He shouts/knocks/bangs on the door.)
Who hears him? (The conductor)
What does this person do? (He unlocks the door.)
Ask students:
T: What do you think happens next?
   Do you think the conductor unlocks the door?
S1: Yes, I think he unlocks the door and the man goes to get some water.
S2: No, I think the conductor can't unlock the door because he hasn't got the right key. So the man waits in his compartment until morning.

Let students guess the ending but do not tell them if they are right or wrong.

Exercise 2 READING

Pre-teach the verbs *to work, to let somebody out,* to *fall asleep,* e.g.
(work) *How does this coffee machine work? This watch is no good. It doesn't work any more.*
(let out) *The man is locked inside his compartment. He wants the conductor to let him out.*
(fall asleep) *Last night I was very tired. I sat down in a chair in front of the television and fell asleep.*
Write the new verbs on the board. Students now work in pairs to arrange the order. Go round and help them with any new words. Check the final arrangement by asking different students to tell the story by reading out the correct sentence/paragraph in sequence.

KEY
C I had a ticket for the night train from London to Inverness, in Scotland.
F I got on the train and went straight to my compartment.
B I locked the door, got undressed and got into bed. I read a little and then fell asleep.
E I woke up at two in the morning because I wanted a drink of water.
A When I tried to open the door, I couldn't. I banged and shouted. Soon a conductor heard me and opened the door with a special key.
D I said: 'There's something wrong with the lock.' He said: 'No, there isn't. I'll show you.' He came inside and locked the door. 'This is how it works,' he said.
G We both spent the next three hours locked inside the compartment waiting for someone to let us out.

Ask a few questions to check comprehension of new verbs, e.g. *What did the man do before he fell asleep?* (He read) *What happened at 2 a.m?* (The man woke up) *How long did they spend in the compartment before someone let them out?* (Three hours)

GRAMMAR FOCUS

Ask students to go back and write down all the examples of past tense verbs from the story. Ask them in pairs to sort the verbs into regular and irregular. Students then compare their list of irregular verbs with the one in the Focus box (*had* appears in the story but not in the Focus box as this verb was introduced in Unit 20). Tell students that it is important that they learn this list for homework and that they should add to the list any other irregular verbs that they have already met, e.g. *have – had, is – was, see – saw, lose – lost, buy – bought, find – found, leave – left*. Ask the questions at the bottom of the Focus box.

KEY

The irregular verb which has the same spelling in the past tense is *read*.
Regular past tense endings: *walked, opened, closed, locked, banged, shouted, tried, washed*

Ask students to repeat all the past tense endings in chorus after you, first the regular and then the irregular. Ask students to cover the list and give a spot-check on the irregular verbs, e.g.
T: What's the past tense of 'hear'?
S: Heard. (etc.)

Exercise 3

See if students can tell the story sentence by sentence in a chain with their books closed. Write on the board the following linking words for them to use: *and then, but, so, because*.

Start the story off by saying the first sentence:
The man had a ticket for the night train from London to Scotland.

SUGGESTED LESSON BREAK

Exercise 4

Remind students how to form past tense questions. Say: *Last year I went on holiday to the USA.*
Oh? Where did you go?
How long did you stay?
What did you see?
Who did you go with?

Write the questions on the board in the form of a table. Circle the word *did* in each question. Now ask students to look at the question cues in Exercise 4. Ask complete beginners to write down the full form of each question in their notebooks. Point out the use of *last* in *When did you last make a long journey? When did you last have a cup of coffee/go to the cinema?* etc.

Students now ask and answer the questions in pairs. They should take notes of their partner's answers for use in the next writing exercise.

Exercise 5 WRITING

Students can write about their partner's or their own journey. Write on the board some helpful sentences and phrases, e.g.

*I arrived **at** the airport/station/the hotel.*
*I arrived **in** Venice/England.*
*I got **to** the airport/Venice.*
*We left **after** breakfast/lunch.*
*We had breakfast and **after that** we left.*

Ask students to divide the composition into three paragraphs and to note down some ideas, e.g.

PARAGRAPH 1 *Leaving*
– got up 6 a.m.
– breakfast – only coffee
– taxi to station

Give an example of possible first and last sentences for the students to use:
On the day of their departure, John and his family got up at ...
Finally they arrived at .... at ... o'clock ... . They were very pleased that the journey was over.

SUGGESTED LESSON BREAK

Exercise 6 LISTENING

Explain that students are going to hear a story about a Danish businessman who travelled to a strange city. Make sure the students know where Denmark is. Ask what the capital city is (Copenhagen). Pre-teach *taxi-driver, give a tip, look out of the window*. Play the tape a couple of times and see if the students get the point, i.e. that the businessman's hotel was opposite the station and the taxi-driver had cheated him by driving him around for half an hour. Ask students if they know any similar 'taxi-driver' stories.

TAPESCRIPT

Listen to a story about a traveller and say why it's amusing.

MAN: Did you ever hear the story about the Danish businessman who arrived late at night at a railway station in a strange city?

WOMAN: No, what happened?

MAN: Well, he got straight into a taxi and he gave the taxi-driver the address of his hotel.

WOMAN: Yes...

MAN: Well, the journey took about half an hour and when they arrived the man gave the taxi-driver a big tip, and went into the hotel and went straight to bed. When he woke up the next morning and looked out of his hotel window, he saw that the hotel was exactly opposite the railway station!

WOMAN: Now, that reminds me of a time when I was in ...

Exercise 7 READING

> BACKGROUND NOTES
> *Sir Alec Guinness* (born 1914): A famous
> British stage and screen actor who made his
> first appearance in films in 1934 and from
> there went on to star in many films, including:
> *Kind Hearts and Coronets, The Lavender Hill
> Mob, The Ladykillers* and *The Bridge over the
> River Kwai*. More recently he played the role
> of Smiley in the television adaptations of some
> of John Le Carré's spy novels.
> *James Dean*: A young Hollywood actor who
> was tipped to be Marlon Brando's successor.
> He only made three films (see the reading
> passage) but because of his talent and his early
> and sudden death he became a youth cult
> figure. His 'rebel image' still lives on.

See if students can answer any of the *Before you
read* questions. If they can't, tell them that they
will find the answers when they read the text.
Explain that, in this case, *legend* means someone
very famous for something particular, i.e. acting.

Ask: *Do you know Sir Alec Guinness? Who is
he?* (An actor/film star) *Is he old or young?* (Old)
Say: *Sir Alec Guinness met James Dean a long
time ago. He tells the story here. It's a strange (=
funny) story and it's true.*

Ask students to read the text to find out why the
story was strange. Give students plenty of time to
read and ask them to note down any new words.
They should try to guess their meaning before
looking them up in a dictionary. Alternatively,
they can ask you for help. Students answer the
questions printed in the book or, alternatively,
they ask and answer them in pairs.

Check that students understand and can use the
following new words from the text: *tired, full,
fast, laugh, apologise, hungry*. If there is time,
use the text to ask additional questions using the
past simple tense, e.g. *How did Sir Alec Guinness
feel after his journey? Why couldn't he get a
table in the restaurant? What did James Dean
look like? What was his new car like? What did
Sir Alec Guinness say to him? How did Sir Alec
Guinness apologise?*

Ask students if they have any personal experience
of premonitions and if they believe in them.

For homework, ask students to note from the text
any new past tense forms of verbs and to add
them to their list of regular and irregular verbs,
e.g.

IRREGULAR	REGULAR
meet – met	turn – turned
speak – spoke	ask – asked
	reply – replied
	laugh – laughed
	apologise – apologised
	crash – crashed
	die – died

EXTRA ACTIVITIES

1 Past tense bingo

Students draw squares of 4 x 4 (sixteen squares).
Write a list of between twenty-five and thirty
irregular past tense forms on the board (but not
the base forms). Ask students to choose sixteen
of these and write them in the squares. When
they are ready, you call out the base forms of all
the verbs in random order. Students must cross
off the right past tense verb as soon as they
recognise it on their square. The first person who
crosses off all the words in their squares wins.

2 My weekend

Ask students to draw three or four large pictures
to illustrate how they spent their weekend. Assure
them that these need not be artistic drawings. One
student volunteers to come to the front of the
class with her/his pictures and to describe the
weekend using the pictures as visual aids. This
activity can also be done in groups. If you prefer,
students can illustrate an important event in their
past.

FLUENCY Units 21–25

> BACKGROUND NOTES
> *Interpol*: An international police organisation
> for helping national police forces to catch
> criminals.
> *Louvain*: A university city, not far (24 km)
> from Brussels, the capital of Belgium.
> *Dutch*: People from the country of Holland.
> *Montpellier*: A large university town in the
> south of France.
> *Le Havre*: The second largest French port on
> the north coast of France, on the English
> Channel. Le Havre – Portsmouth (on the south
> coast of England) is one of several sea routes
> between France and England.
> *Hampshire*: An English county in southern
> England. Portsmouth is in Hampshire.

Exercise 1 READING

Refer students to the page and ask:
Where does this come from? Is it from a book?
(No, it's from a newspaper.)
What is 'Interpol'? (See background note)

What does 'to murder' mean? (To kill someone illegally or intentionally.)
What is a murder hunt? (When the police are looking for a person after a murder.)

Ask students to read the questions before they read the article. Point out on a map Portsmouth, Le Havre, Louvain and Montpellier. Ask students to work out the meaning of *officers* and *camping site*. Check the answers to the questions across the class. Point out the past tense *caught* from *catch*.

Exercise 2

Ask students the questions:
T: What does Jean-Michel Bellingcourt look like?
S: He's about one point eight-five metres tall, and thin. He's got wavy black hair and a moustache.
T: What's he wearing?
S: He's wearing jeans, a red T-shirt and a black anorak.

Now ask students to look at the pictures of the three men. Ask different students to describe each man and to say what he is wearing. Teach the word *bald* when describing the first man. Then ask different students to explain why the first two pictures are not Jean-Michel Bellingcourt, e.g.
S1: It's not the first man because he's wearing glasses and he hasn't got wavy black hair.
S2: It isn't the second man because ...

KEY
It's the third man because he's thin. He's got wavy black hair. He's wearing a black anorak and a T-shirt.

Exercise 3 ROLEPLAY

Divide the class into two groups of equal numbers of As and Bs. Say to all the A students: *You are going to be 'the caller', someone who telephones the police with some information. Read your Student A role and prepare what you are going to say to the police.* Some students might like to write out what they are going to say, or to make notes. Say to all the B students: *You are going to be a police officer. You answer the telephone at the police station. This is your form. You must ask questions to complete it.*

Ask B students to copy the form into their notebooks and work in pairs or groups to think of questions to ask Student A, using the cues to help them. Students can also think of additional questions to ask. Give a few examples on the board, e.g. *How tall is the man? Is he big or small/fat or thin? How old is he? What does he look like? What colour's his hair?* Explain that *Circumstances* here means 'what the person is doing'.

Ask students to look at the opening conversation in the Students' Book just below the police form and work Teacher–Student to give an example of how to start the conversation, e.g.
T: Hello, Hampshire Police. Can I help you?
S: Yes, I'm staying ...

As students prepare their roleplays, go round and assist with any new vocabulary. Help the B students to interpret the form, reminding them what the categories refer to.

When students are ready, ask A students to close their books. Tell B students to keep their books open and to complete the information on the form in their notebook as they talk. Students now start their roleplay.

SUGGESTED CONVERSATION
B: Hello, Hampshire Police. Can I help you?
A: Yes, I'm staying in a hotel in Portsmouth and I think I can see the man who Interpol are looking for.
B: Can you describe him?
A: Yes, he's quite tall – about 1.85 metres.
B: Is he fat or thin?
A: He's medium build.
B: About how old is he?
A: I think he's about forty.
B: Right, and what sort of hair has he got?
A: He's got dark, wavy hair and a moustache.
B: A moustache?
A: Yes.
B: And what is he wearing?
A: He's wearing jeans, a red T-shirt and a black anorak.
B: And where is he at the moment?
A: He's in the car park at the Seaview Hotel in Portsmouth. I'm staying at the hotel and I can see him from my window. He's in the car park now.
B: I see. What is he doing?
A: He's looking inside a car. I think he's going to steal it.
B: Right. What is your name and address, please?
A: My name is ... and I live at ...

Exercise 4 LISTENING

Play the tape once for gist. Then play it again and ask the following questions:
What time was this news report?
When did the murder happen?
When did the police get the phone call?
Did the man in the car park look like Mr Bellingcourt? Was it him? Who was it?

TAPESCRIPT
Listen to a news report. Was the man in the car park Mr Bellingcourt?

NEWSREADER:
This is the news at ten thirty. Interpol are still looking for Jean-Louis Bellingcourt, who is wanted in connection with the murder of the

Dutch couple last week in France. Last night, after a phone call from a member of the public, Hampshire police questioned a man in a hotel in Portsmouth. The man, who police say looked exactly like M Bellingcourt, was in fact a salesman from Manchester ... Police are now…

For homework ask students to rewrite the third paragraph of the newspaper article to describe one of the other two men in the pictures in Exercise 2. They will have to imagine the man's height and the rest of his clothes.

CHECK Units 21–25

(For advice on handling this section, see the notes for Check Units 1–5.)

KEY

Ex. 1 1 Who 2 When 3 How 4 Where 5 What
6 Whose 7 Why 8 How 9 What 10 When
(10 marks)

Ex. 2 1 yours 2 mine 3 hers 4 his 5 theirs
(5 marks)

Ex. 3 1 got 2 read 3 fell 4 heard   could
6 spent 7 woke 8 came 9 said 10 went
(10 marks)

Ex. 4 1 What did you watch?
        2 What did you see?
        3 What did you read?
        4 Where did you go?
        5 What did you buy?
        (10 marks)

Ex. 5 1 are you going to
        2 I'm not going to
        3 Are you going to
        4 They're (They are) going to
        5 He's not (He isn't) going to
        6 We're (We are) going to
        7 are you going to
        8 is she going to
        9 I'm not (I am not) going to
        10 Are you going to
        (10 marks)

Ex. 6 1b 2b 3b 4a 5b (5 marks)

Ex. 7 1 The weather wasn't very nice for our holiday.
        2 What's the name of John's doctor?
        3 Who's going to sit next to Pam?
        4 I didn't see the last James Bond film.
        5 Let's ask the boy with the dark hair.
        6 Why didn't you answer my letter?
        7 Could you sit down? I can't see.
        8 That isn't yours. It's mine.
        9 She doesn't like wearing dresses.
        (10 marks)

Ex. 8 ACROSS: sweater jeans cardigan suit
jacket blouse DOWN: boots vest tie dress
tights raincoat (12 marks)

CHECK YOUR PROGRESS
(See notes for Check Units 1–5.)

LEARNING TO LEARN 5
Write on the board:

The comparative form of adjectives
tall – taller
old – older
white – whiter

Now say:
T: How do you make the comparative?
S: You add *er*.
T: What about *white – whiter?*
S: You only add *r*.
T: Why?
S: Because the word ends in *e* already.
T: Now look at some more examples.

Write on the board:

big – bigger
interesting – more interesting
beautiful – more beautiful

Ask:
T: Do you want to change the rule? Do you add *er* to all adjectives?
S: No, with long adjectives, you use the word *more*.
T: What about *bigger?*
S: It has two *g*s.

Write a few more examples on the board so they can test their rule, e.g. *darker, more famous, larger, thinner*. Do not go into more detail over the comparatives now. They are taught and practised in depth in Units 28 and 29.

PREVIEW Units 26–30

BACKGROUND NOTE
Goldsmith: Oliver Goldsmith (1730-1774) was an English poet, playwright and essayist, and a contemporary of Samuel Johnson. He wrote a number of comedies, of which the most successful was *She Stoops to Conquer* which was first performed in Covent Garden in 1773. The play is still regularly performed today.

The photographs and the dialogue
Ask students about the photographs. Ask:
Picture 1
Where's Laura? (At home/In the sitting room)
What is she doing? (Washing/Drying her hair)

Picture 2
What has Adam got tickets for? (For the theatre/
For the play *She Stoops to Conquer*)
The tickets
When is it on? (Friday 4th August)
The programme
Is it a serious or a funny play? (It's funny/a
comedy.)
Picture 3
Is the theatre old or modern? (It's modern.)
*What is Laura studying at university? Can you
remember from Preview 6-10 tape?* (English
literature)

🔲 The tape and the exercise
Play the tape and then read the True/False
sentences aloud. Ask students to correct the
sentences that are false.

TAPESCRIPT
Listen and follow the conversation in your
Students' Book.

LAURA: Hello, Laura speaking.
ADAM: Oh, hello, Laura. It's Adam here.
LAURA: Oh, hi, Adam. Nice to hear you.
ADAM: Listen, would you like to go to the theatre
on Friday?
LAURA: Yes, I'd love to. What's on?
ADAM: *She Stoops to Conquer* by Goldsmith.
It's on at the Theatre Royal.
LAURA: Oh, great.
ADAM: They say this is Goldsmith's funniest
play.
LAURA: Actually, we're reading one of
Goldsmith's plays in our drama group at
the moment.
ADAM: Are you? Well I hope you like this one.

ADAM: Well, did you enjoy it?
LAURA: Yes, it was really good. Very funny.
Thanks for inviting me.
ADAM: Well, I enjoyed it too. Now what about
something to eat?

The learning objectives box
Ask students to read the objectives in the box and
to find examples of the language in the dialogue.

Talk about dates: *Friday August 4th.*
Invite people to do things: *Would you like to go
to the theatre on Friday?*
Talk about definite arrangements: (no example in
the dialogue but invite suggestions from
students, e.g. *I'm going to the theatre on
Saturday.*)
Talk on the telephone: *Hello, Laura speaking.*
Compare people and places: *The funniest play in
years.*
Talk about temporary activities: *We're reading
one of his plays at the moment.*

UNIT 26 Dates and arrangements
Suggested lesson break: after Exercise 5

🔲 Exercise 1
Write on the board: *Today is (Monday 6th May).
Yesterday was (Sunday 5th May). Tomorrow is
(Tuesday 7th May).* Practise these dates chorally
with the class, ensuring that when they speak
they say: *Monday the sixth of May.* Present the
rest of the ordinal numbers and practise them
chorally.

Then ask students to study the ordinal numbers in
their Students' Books and to tell you what is
usually added to numbers to make them ordinals
(*th*). Play the tape, pausing for students to repeat
the numbers. To check, dictate a few ordinal
numbers to give students practise in writing the
abbreviated form.

Present and practise the rest of the months of the
year, using choral and individual repetition.
Write the months on the board and point out that
they are written with an initial capital letter. Go
through the notes in Exercise 1. Point out again
that although we say *January the second* this
should not be written.

Elicit from students the full spoken forms of the
dates which are written in the notes. Point out
that the spoken form can be: *January **the** second,
nineteen ninety-one* or ***the** second **of** January
1991.* Also point out that when the date is written
in numerals only, e.g. *2/1/91,* the order is always
day, month, year. This differs from the practice in
some other countries.

Exercise 3
Go through the exercise with the whole class.

Exercise 4
Ask: *What's the date today?* Elicit: *It's (Monday)
the (sixth) of (May).* Also ask: *What was the date
yesterday?* and *What's the date tomorrow?*
Students work in pairs asking and answering
about the dates in Exercise 4. Check and then ask
about other important and topical dates.

KEY
Bastille Day, which celebrates the storming of the
hated Bastille prison in Paris during the French
Revolution (1789), is on July 14th.
May Day, celebrating International Labour Day
and the coming of spring, is on May 1st.
Christmas Day, celebrating the birth of Christ in
the Christian calendar, is on December 25th.
New Year's Eve, the last day of the year in the
Roman calendar, is on December 31st.

Exercise 2

BACKGROUND NOTES
The South Bank Centre: A complex of concert halls, art galleries and open-air exhibition sites on the south bank of the River Thames in central London. One of these open-air sites is Jubilee Gardens. The 'Gran Fiesta' was a festival of Latin American culture which took place there.
Waterloo: A mainline and underground station in London, near the South Bank Centre.
Embankment: The underground station immediately opposite the Centre on the other side of the River Thames. There is a pedestrian bridge over the river at this point.

Ask students to look at the poster. Then ask:
What's the poster for? (A 'Gran Fiesta'/A Latin American Fiesta)
What are the people on the poster doing? (They're dancing.)
What is a 'Gran Fiesta'? (A big party/A big dance/A big celebration)
What things can you do at the Fiesta? (You can listen to music, dance, eat and drink.)
How much are the tickets? (£6)
Would you like to go?
Now ask: *Where's it on?* Elicit: *It's on at the South Bank Centre.* Ask: *When's it on?* Elicit: *It's on from the sixth to the sixteenth of July.*

To provide further practice of dates, ask: *What date does the Fiesta start?* Elicit: *It starts on the sixth of July.* Get one student to ask another: *What date does it finish? It finishes on the sixteenth of July.*

GRAMMAR FOCUS
Write on the board a week from your next weeks' diary, e.g.

MAY
Monday 17th – free

Tuesday 18th – have dinner with John

Wednesday 19th – cinema

Thursday 20th –- free

Friday 21st – play tennis with Susan

Saturday 22nd – Simon's party

Sunday 23rd – free

Now ask and answer yourself about your arrangements for next week: *What are you doing on Monday? I'm not doing anything. What are you doing on Tuesday? I'm having dinner with John.*

Get a student to ask you about Wednesday:
s1: What are you doing on Wednesday?
T: I'm going to the cinema.

Now students ask each other about your arrangements.
s1: What's he/she doing on Thursday?
s2: He's/She's not doing anything.

Ask students to look at the Grammar Focus box and to say if the sentences are about present or future time. (They're about future time.)

Refer students to the note, and point out that the present continuous tense is often used for definite arrangements in the future, particularly if a time expression is used.

Exercise 5
Students now interview three other students in the class, asking them what they are doing on specific days in the future. They can use the question form: *What are you doing on Monday/ on 20th May?* or if they prefer: *Are you doing anything on Monday?* They then tell the class about the other students' future arrangements.

SUGGESTED LESSON BREAK

 Exercise 6 LISTENING

BACKGROUND NOTES
Heathrow: London's biggest airport. The other major airport serving London is Gatwick.
BA: British Airways, the national airline.
Terminal: The building from which the flight leaves. At Heathrow Airport there are four terminals. Most British Airways European flights (except for Paris flights) leave from Terminal 1.

Remind students that Adam works in a travel agent's and ask them to copy the chart from the Students' Book into their notebooks.

Play the tape and ask students to record the information, paying special attention to the writing of the date. Explain also that most of Europe is one hour ahead of British time. Play the tape several times if necessary. Check that all students have the right answers since they will need the information to write the letter in Exercise 7.

TAPESCRIPT
Listen to a conversation between Adam and a customer about a trip to Germany. Note down the travel details.

MISS THOMPSON: Hello.
ADAM: Hello? Is that Miss Thompson?
MISS THOMPSON: Yes, speaking.

ADAM:	This is Adam from Hogg Robinson travel agent's. I've got your ticket for Frankfurt on 4th March.
MISS THOMPSON:	Oh, good. Could you give me the details again?
ADAM:	Yes, you're travelling on a British Airways flight, and you're leaving London Heathrow, Terminal 1, on 4th March at 7.50 – that's 07.50 hours and you're on Flight BA 902.
MISS THOMPSON:	Hang on, I'm just writing it down. So that's flight BA 902 at 7.50 from Heathrow Airport.
ADAM:	That's right. And the arrival time at Frankfurt Airport is 10.20 local time. They're one hour ahead of us.
MISS THOMPSON:	Fine ... 10.20 arrival at Frankfurt. Good.
ADAM:	When can you come and collect the ticket, or shall I post it?
MISS THOMPSON:	No, I'm coming into town tomorrow. I'll collect it then.
ADAM:	Fine. See you tomorrow. Bye.
MISS THOMPSON:	Goodbye.

Exercise 7 WRITING

Ask students to look at the letter in their Students' Book. Remind them how to lay out a letter (see Units 9 and 24). Refer to the address in the top right-hand corner of the letter in Exercise 7 and explain that nowadays it is quite common to omit the commas in the punctuation of addresses in letters. Remind students of the closing phrases. Explain that they are writing a letter from the woman on the tape in Exercise 6 (Carole Thompson) to a friend of hers called Hanna. The friend, Hanna, lives in Frankfurt and is going to meet Carole when she arrives at the airport. Students can begin their letters in class and finish them for homework. As they begin their letters in class, monitor their work and help with any phrases or vocabulary which they may need.

SUGGESTED LETTER

23 Park Street
York YO1 5AT
(*Date*)

Dear Hanna,
I have now got the details of my trip to Frankfurt. I'm leaving from London Heathrow at 7.50 a.m. on March 4th on flight number BA 902 and I'm arriving at Frankfurt at 10.20 a.m.
Thank you for offering to meet me. I'm looking forward to seeing you and Stefan.
Love,
Carole

COMMUNICATION FOCUS

Get two students to read out the speech bubbles at the top of page 83. Point out that *Would you like to ...* is a polite form of invitation. Get students to act out similar conversations, e.g.
S1: Are you doing anything on June 6th?
S2: No, why?
S1: There's a good film on at the Odeon. Would you like to go?
S2: What is it?
S1: *Back to the Future III.*
S2: Yes, I'd love to./
Yes, that would be great./
Oh, I'm sorry, I can't. I'm doing a typing exam that evening.

Refer students to the Communication Focus box and get them to practise the pronunciation of the sentences chorally. Remind students that *I'd* is a short form of *I would* (see Unit 16: *I'd like a box of chocolates, please*).

Exercise 8 ROLEPLAY

> BACKGROUND NOTES
> *Lenny Henry*: An English comedian.
> *The Hackney Empire*: A variety theatre in the East End of London.
> *Concessions*: This means that cheaper tickets are available for special groups of people such as students, unemployed people and old age pensioners.

Refer students to the advertisement for Lenny Henry's concert and the open diary. Explain who Lenny Henry is. Practise some of the concert dates, e.g. *the twenty-second of January* and then ask questions about the dates in the diary. Say: *Look at Student B's diary. What is he/she doing on January 22nd/Monday?* Elicit: *He's/She's meeting friends from Sweden.* Help students with the other responses (*going to the cinema/keep fit class/Rick's party*).

Divide the class into As and Bs and ask them to read their roles. Help with any problems and then draw attention to the opening and closing of the conversation as given in the model exchange under the diary. Play the part of A yourself first, with a student playing the part of B. Then ask all students to work through the roleplay once, after which they change parts. Go round and make a note of any errors that students are making and allow time to go over these afterwards.

SUGGESTED CONVERSATION
A: Lenny Henry is doing a show next week. Would you like to come?
B: I'd love to, but I'm quite busy next week.
A: Well, what about Saturday the 27th? Are you doing anything that evening?
B: Yes, I'm going to Rick's party.
A: What about Friday?

B: No, I'm going to my keep fit class.
A: O.K. What about Wednesday?
B: I'm sorry I can't. I'm going to the cinema with Laura. But I'm free on Tuesday.
A: Yes but I'm not free on Tuesday. What about Thursday?
B: Yes, Thursday is O.K.
A: O.K. I'll get tickets for Thursday and I'll meet you outside the theatre at 7.30.

EXTRA ACTIVITIES

1 Send a note

Students select someone in the class to write an invitation to. That person must then reply to the note, e.g.

INVITATION
Dear Dana,
Are you doing anything on Saturday 5th May? If not, would you like to come to a concert with me?
Georgio

REPLY
Dear Georgio,
Thanks for your invitation. I'm afraid I'm going to the theatre on Saturday 5th May. What about Wednesday 9th?
Dana

In principle, the notes can go backwards and forwards until a conclusion is reached.

2 Date it

Set a time limit of two minutes and ask students to write down three personally important dates for them in the past. These should preferably include a month, but year dates will do. They then show these dates to their partner who asks about them, e.g. *What happened on May 6th 1985?* (*I got married.*) or *What happened in 1989?* (*I left university.*).

UNIT 27 Telephoning

Suggested lesson break: after Exercise 3

PRESENTATION

Draw on the board, or use pictures to show, two people talking to each other on the telephone. Then act out a series of mini phone conversations with yourself taking both parts.
A: Hello, 69077 (six-nine-oh-double seven).
B: Hello, it's (Susan Roberts) here. Can I speak to John, please?
A: Speaking.

Practise this conversation Student–Teacher, writing different phone numbers on the board, then practise Student–Student. As you practise, point out that the British often answer the phone

with the number. The phone number is usually expressed as individual digits (with the exception of double numbers like *double seven*) and that *0* is said as *oh*, **not** ~~zero~~. Present and practise other mini conversations in the same way, e.g.
A: Hello, 33601.
B: Hello, this is (Susan). Is (John) there, please?
A: I'm afraid he's out. Can I take a message?
B: No, thank you. I'll call back later.

A: Hello.
B: Hello. Can I speak to (John)?
A: Who's speaking?
B: It's (Susan). Can I leave a message?
A: Yes, certainly.

With students who are false beginners, you might like to teach additional phrases such as, e.g. *Hold on./Hang on. I'll go and get him/her.*

Exercise 1 LISTENING

Tell students to look at the skeleton conversation in their books and think about what words and phrases are missing. Explain *that's a nuisance.* Now ask students to listen to the tape and complete the conversation. Play the tape a second time for them to check to give them time to complete all the missing parts. Check the final version and then play again getting students to shadow the conversation as they hear it.

TAPESCRIPT AND KEY
Listen and complete the conversation.

MRS GIBSON: Hello. 33467.
ADAM: Oh, hello, Mrs Gibson. It's Adam here. Can I speak to Laura?
MRS GIBSON: I'm afraid she's out.
ADAM: Oh, that's a nuisance.
MRS GIBSON: Can I take a message?
ADAM: No, thanks. Just tell her I phoned and I'll call back later.
MRS GIBSON: O.K. I'll do that. Bye for now.
ADAM: Bye.

COMMUNICATION FOCUS

Remind students that *I'll call back* means *I will call back*. Practise all the sentences chorally. Then get students to practise phone conversations in pairs, using the phrases in the Focus box.

Exercise 2 SPEECHWORK

This type of exercise can be quite difficult for some students. You may need to pause the tape after each phrase and repeat it again yourself with the same intonation before asking the students to judge if it is a rising or falling intonation.

KEY
Hello? (Up) This is Helen speaking. (Down) I'm afraid he's out. (Down). It's Laura here. (Up) I'll call back later. (Down) Who's speaking? (Up)

Exercise 3

Students work in pairs. They should read the instructions carefully first, think about what they are going to say and then close their books before roleplaying. Check by asking different students to 'telephone' each other across the class. (Model telephones which are passed from person to person might be useful here.)

SUGGESTED CONVERSATIONS

CALL 1
A: Hello, 22856 (double two-eight-five-six).
B: Oh, hello. Can I speak to John, please?
A: I'm afraid he's out.
B: Oh, that's a nuisance.
A: Can I take a message?
B: No, it's all right, thank you. I'll call back later. Bye!

CALL 2
A: Hello, 99273.
B: Oh, hello, Jorge. It's Anna here.
A: Oh, hello, Anna.
B: Are you doing anything on Saturday morning?
A: No, I'm not. Why?
B: Well, would you like to come swimming with me?
A: Yes, I'd love to.
B: Great. Let's meet outside the swimming pool at 11 o'clock.
A: O.K. See you there at eleven o'clock on Saturday. Bye!
B: Bye!

SUGGESTED LESSON BREAK

Exercise 4 READING

BACKGROUND NOTE
The telephones: Starting from the top left clockwise, these show a telephone with piano keys for the number buttons, a phone in the shape of 'Garfield' a comic strip cat, a cellular phone which is linked to a special telephone communications network and a cordless telephone linked to a telephone connection in a house.

Ask the *Before you read* question to the whole class and encourage students to describe the telephones. Introduce expressions like *a cordless telephone, an unusual shape, in the shape of a ...* and *a mobile telephone*. Ask students if any of them have similar telephones in the office or at home. Then read the four questions aloud and ask if anyone has an answerphone at home. Find out if they have any difficulties with it. Ask students if they like answerphones.

Then ask students to read the text and answer the questions individually. Check by asking the questions to the whole group.

Exercise 5 About you

Ask the questions to the whole class or divide the class into groups. False beginners may like to list the advantages and disadvantages of cordless telephones, car phones and answerphones and then report back and compare their answers. Monitor and help with any new vocabulary which students might need, such as *convenient, useful, easy to use, difficult to use, dangerous*, etc.

Exercise 6 LISTENING AND WRITING

Explain that students are going to hear an answerphone, and somebody leaving a message on it. Ask them to copy the chart into their notebooks. Play the tape once for students to listen. Then play the tape again, pausing for them to note the correct details.

TAPESCRIPT
Listen to the answerphone and write down the details of Paul's message.

RECORDED MESSAGE:
Hello. This is Jane and Dave Wells' answerphone. I'm afraid Jane and Dave can't come to the phone right now but if you'd like to leave a message we'll call you back as soon as possible. Please speak after the tone. /BLEEP/

PAUL:
Oh, hi ... er... this is Paul wanting to talk to Dave. Um, the time is 6.30 on Monday evening. I just wanted to ask ... are you free on Friday lunchtime? Can you come to lunch? My number is 62213. Bye!

Exercise 7

Allow time for students to prepare their messages. If time is short, ask them to prepare their messages at home.

SUGGESTED MESSAGE 1
Hello. Jane, it's Gerry here. I want to talk to you about the weekend. I'll phone back later.

SUGGESTED MESSAGE 2
Hello, Dave. This is Tina. Can you meet me for a coffee at 11 o'clock tomorrow? Can you call me back? My number is 227889. Thanks, bye.

The cartoon

BACKGROUND NOTE
The cartoon: This is by James Thurber (1894-1961), an American cartoonist and humorist whose works such as *The Thurber Carnival, Thurber's Dogs* and *The Thurber Album* are regarded as classics. Much of his work was published in *The New Yorker,* an American magazine.

See if any students can explain why the cartoon is funny. Ask if students know of any other cartoons by James Thurber and what they know about him. Use the notes above to explain who he was. Ask students when they think the cartoon was drawn. Say: *When did he draw the cartoon? How do you know?* (He probably drew it in the 1920s or the 1930s because the telephone is very old-fashioned.)

EXTRA ACTIVITIES

1 Answerphone message
Ask students to prepare a permanent answerphone message to record on their own answerphone. This can be funny if they wish and they can choose a famous person to imitate, e.g. Marilyn Monroe or Crocodile Dundee.

2 Research a cartoon
Ask students to find other cartoons in their own language which feature the telephone as part of the joke.

UNIT 28 Comparison (1)

Suggested lesson break: after Exercise 5

The comparison of adjectives is divided into two lessons, one based on shorter adjectives which add *er* and the other based on longer adjectives which form the comparative with *more*. If the need for longer adjectives arises, e.g. *more expensive* in Exercise 3, show briefly how *more* and *most* are used to make comparisons of longer adjectives.

PRESENTATION
With books closed, write on the board a chart with information about four people, e.g.

Name	Ann	John	Lisa	Robert
Height	1m 66	1m 70	1m 78	1m 82
Weight	62 kilos	66 kilos	69 kilos	70 kilos
Age	18	21	22	34

Say: *John's taller than Ann. Lisa's taller than John. Lisa's shorter than Robert. Robert's heavier than Lisa. John's lighter than Lisa. Ann's younger than John. Robert's older than Lisa.*

Practise the sentences chorally and individually and get students to make similar sentences from the chart. Then get them to ask and answer comparing the information, e.g. *Is Lisa older than John? Yes, she is. Is Ann older than Lisa? No, she isn't.*

Write example sentences on the board. Refer back to the chart and say: *Robert's the tallest of the four. Ann's the shortest of the four.* Ask

students to make similar sentences from the chart about the weight and age of the people. Students then ask each other questions and answers about the people in the chart, e.g. *Who's the tallest? (Robert (is).)* Write example sentences on the board.

Exercise 1

> BACKGROUND NOTES
> *Christopher Reeve*: An American actor who played the part of Superman in the series of films based on the American comic-book hero.
> *Princess Diana*: Diana, Princess of Wales is the wife of Prince Charles. Prince Charles is the eldest son of Queen Elizabeth II and therefore heir to the British throne.
> *John Cleese*: A British television comedian and film actor, who became internationally famous with the film *A Fish Called Wanda*.

Now ask students to look at the people in their Students' Book. Ask questions to see if students know who the people are and what they do. Refer students to the questions about the heights and get them to speculate. They can look up the answers in the back of the Students' Book on page 141 to see if they were right.

GRAMMAR FOCUS
Work through the list of adjectives explaining and giving examples for each one. Use diagrams and pin figures to explain their meaning. Get students to make example sentences. Ask the question about the comparative endings to the whole class.

KEY
In adjectives which form the comparative and superlative with *er* and *est*, if the adjective ends in a vowel + a consonant the final consonant doubles: *big – bigger, thin – thinner*. If the adjective ends in a consonant + *y*, the *y* changes to *i*: *dry – drier, dirty – dirtier*.

Exercise 2
Do this exercise with the whole class and ask different students to write the comparative and superlative forms on the board. Other students should point out if there are any spelling errors.

Exercise 3
Ask students to look at the list of topics in the chart and ask different students to give an example for each category, e.g. *I am taller than Martina. Milan is hotter than London.* Then ask Students to work in pairs making different sentences with the adjectives. Help them with names of cities and sports. Bring the whole class together and check by asking students to provide sentences.

Exercise 4

Appoint a different student to be the questioner for each category. The appointed student asks various students in the class for their opinions, e.g.

s1: Who is the tallest student in the class?
s2: I think Manuel is the tallest.
s3: No, I think Juan is the tallest. He's taller than Manuel.

(In the case of the geographical features, monolingual classes can discuss their country, whilst multilingual classes can discuss an agreed geographical area, e.g. Latin America, Europe, the Middle East, the Far East, etc.)

The 'questioner' writes all the suggestions for each category on the board and students then decide which are the right answers, if necessary by voting.

Exercise 5 SPEECHWORK

Ask students to copy the sentences into their notebooks. Practise the sentences chorally before playing the tape. Students then underline the stressed syllables and repeat the sentences at the same time.

KEY

He's <u>tall</u>er than me.
He's <u>thin</u>ner than her.
She's <u>young</u>er than you.
I'm <u>old</u>er than him.
It's <u>bet</u>ter than that.
It's <u>cheap</u>er than this.

SUGGESTED LESSON BREAK

Exercise 6 READING

Before the students read, ask them to name some of their favourite holiday resorts and to list their attractions. Say: *What's your favourite holiday resort? Why do you like it?* Get students to talk about the beach, the sea, the food, the nightlife and the countryside. Then ask them to open their books and read why the British like to go abroad. Check by asking questions, e.g. *What do the British think of the weather abroad? Why do they like foreign food? What do they think of the people abroad?* etc.

Explain that *fishier* and *meatier* come from the adjectives *fishy* and *meaty* which in turn come from the nouns *fish* and *meat*. This illustrates how language can be generated from a rule, but point out also that these particular adjectives are not commonly used. Ask students to give the base adjective form of all the comparatives in the text and write a chart on the board, e.g.

ADJECTIVE	COMPARATIVE
good	*better*
(fishy)	*(fishier)*

Students then write sentences saying what features of other countries are better than their own country.

Exercise 7

Ask the class to form groups and choose a 'secretary' whose job it is to report back to the rest of the class later. Students discuss what aspects of their own country/countries are different, attractive and unusual to a visitor from another country.

Exercise 8 WRITING

Ask round the class for a few suggestions of places to write about and generate a discussion by listing the places in a top ten list on the board. Students can either choose a place from the list or choose a place of their own. Begin an example advertisement on the board to show students what to do. They then start their writing in class. Go around the class helping students with adjectives or phrases they may need. Students finish the writing for homework.

SUGGESTED ADVERTISEMENT

COME TO SUNNY CORFU
where the sea is warmer
where the beaches are cleaner and the people are friendlier
Relax on the terrace of your hotel in the warm summer sun.
Enjoy the beautiful scenery.
Make all your dreams come true in Corfu.
The best place in the world for your summer holiday.
You know you deserve it!

EXTRA ACTIVITIES
1 Comparison dictation

Students draw a picture containing simple visual information from a description which you dictate.

THE DICTATION:

'Draw a big mountain in the middle of the picture. There are some other high mountains behind the big mountain. There is a house at the bottom of the mountain. Next to the house is a tree. Outside the house there is a woman. The woman is wearing a very large hat, a white blouse and a long spotted skirt. She is carrying a bag. Next to her is a big dog.'

The students' finished picture will probably be something like this:

Ask students to exchange their finished drawings in pairs and to compare them, e.g. *My tree is taller than yours. The woman's hat is bigger in my picture.* Select pairs of students to show their drawings to the class and to talk about them.

2 Visual comparison

Collect about ten large magazine pictures similar in theme to the topics listed in Exercise 3: a picture of a city, e.g. Hong Kong, Dallas; a picture of a sport, e.g. an ice-hockey match. Display the pictures in the classroom. The pictures are designed to stimulate students to make sentences of comparison. Set a time limit and ask students to walk round writing sentences of comparison about each picture. Collect the pictures and show each picture to the class asking for different sentences.

UNIT 29 Comparison (2)

Suggested lesson break: after Exercise 4

PRESENTATION

If possible, take a world map into the class. With Students' Books closed, ask students to look at the map and to name some of the major cities of the world. Write them on the board. When you have written at least ten cities, say: *Which five cities do you think are expensive?* As students suggest names which differ, introduce comparative sentences: *I think (New York) is more expensive than (Geneva)./less expensive than (Milan).* Then ask a student: *Which is the most expensive city?* Elicit: *I think (Paris) is the most expensive city.* Write example sentences on the board and practise them chorally.

Exercise 1 and GRAMMAR FOCUS

Ask students to open their books and find out if their suggestions were right. As they scan the chart of the cities ask questions, e.g. *Which is the least expensive city?* (Caracas) *Is Teheran less expensive than Geneva?* (No, it isn't. It's more expensive.) *Where is Dakar?* (In Senegal)

Read aloud the paragraphs at the bottom of the chart. Check comprehension by asking questions, e.g. Is *New York more expensive than Oslo?* (No, it isn't, it's less expensive.) *Which is the most expensive European city?* (Oslo) Then ask students to list some of the items which they think are included in 'a shopping basket of food and household items'.

Finally, refer to the Focus box and point out that the comparative and superlative of adjectives is formed using *more* and *most* when the adjectives contain three or more syllables. Exceptionally, some two-syllable adjectives may take *more* and *most* to form the comparative and superlative.

Exercise 2 About you

Do the three questions with the whole class.

Exercise 3

Practise the long adjectives chorally, making sure that students place the stress on the correct syllable, e.g. <u>beau</u>tiful <u>in</u>teresting <u>live</u>ly <u>noi</u>sy pol<u>lu</u>ted <u>dan</u>gerous fa<u>shion</u>able ex<u>pen</u>sive

Ask students to name cities to which the adjectives apply, e.g. *Bologna is a beautiful city.* List on the board some cities which can be compared sensibly, including those which may be in the news at the moment, e.g. the city where the Olympic Games are being held or a city where an important meeting is taking place. Remind students that shorter adjectives such as *lively* and *noisy* form the comparative with *er*. Practise the example sentences in the Students' Book chorally. Students then do the exercise in pairs.

Exercise 4 WRITING

Explain *multinational company* (a company which has branches in a lot of different countries) and find out if anyone in the class can name an example of one, e.g. *Exxon.* Ask the whole class for some ideas for the letter and assemble these under headings on the board, e.g.

Advantages of living in centre	*Advantages of living in suburbs*
easier to get to work	*quieter*
better shops and schools	*cleaner*
cultural life more interesting	*safer*
more for children to do	*cheaper*

The letter can be started in class and finished at home.

EXAMPLE LETTER
You asked me if it is better to live in the centre or the suburbs. I think it is better to live in the centre of the city because it is easier for you to get to work. Also, the shops and the schools are better and the cultural life is more interesting. There are more things for the children to do too. In our city the suburbs are a long way from the centre. They are quieter than the city but life is more boring there. Also the shopping is not very good and everything is more expensive. Believe me, living in the centre is definitely better!

SUGGESTED LESSON BREAK

Exercise 5 READING

Ask students to look at the photographs in the reading text and the *Before you read* questions. Use the photographs to discuss with the students their answers to the questions, and find out what else they know about Japan. List the information in categories under headings on the board, e.g. *Japanese cities, Japan's nearest neighbours,*

Japanese products, Japanese companies, Japanese culture. Make a distinction between facts and any opinions students may have. Draw out their knowledge of Hiroshima and Nagasaki.

POSSIBLE QUESTIONS TO ASK STUDENTS
What's the capital of Japan? (Tokyo)
What other Japanese cities do you know? (Osaka, Kyoto, Hiroshima, Nagasaki)
Do you know what happened to Hiroshima and Nagasaki in 1945? (The allies dropped atomic bombs on them.)
Which countries are nearest to Japan? (The People's Republic of China and the USSR)
What products does Japan make? (High technology goods, cars, motorbikes, televisions, radios, videos, stereo equipment, cameras)
Do you know the names of any Japanese companies? (Sony, Sanyo, Samsung, Sansui, Honda, Mitsubishi, Suzuki, etc.)
Do you know anything about Japanese culture? (Facts: They practise martial arts like Judo and Karate. Japan is a rich country. Their prices are very high, etc. Opinions: They work very hard. Japanese companies are very organised, etc.)

Now ask students to read the text and note three of Japan's achievements. As they read, they should guess the meaning of the following words: *achievements, economic miracle, adaptable, in ruins, impressive, to be proud of.*

📼 Exercise 6 LISTENING
Ask students to look at the picture of the car and to read the explanation in their Students' Book. They then say what they think is inside it. Ask: *What sort of car do you think it is?* (It's a Cadillac.) *What do you think is inside it? What do you think is on the roof?* Elicit some of the vocabulary which occurs on the tape. Students listen to the tape and see if they were right. Play the tape a second time, pausing at intervals to explain any new words. Remind students of the word *customised* from Unit 22 and find out if they know of any more unusual customised vehicles.

TAPESCRIPT
Look at the picture of the world's longest and most luxurious car. It's owned by a Japanese businessman. What do you think there is inside the car? Listen and find out.

NARRATOR:
Now here's an interesting report. Our motoring correspondent, Julie Parsons, went to Japan to do a survey on the Japanese car industry. But in Osaka, at Kenji Kawamuda's Sports Centre she found something really different. Julie, over to you.

JULIE:
Thanks, Martin. Let me tell you about the most extraordinary car in the world. Kenji Kawamuda, a Japanese businessman, owns a Cadillac. So,

what's so unusual about that? Well, it's sixty-seven feet long and that's over twenty metres. It's got twenty-two wheels. There's space for fifty passengers and there are six car phones. As I said, it must be the world's most extraordinary car. Inside there's a cinema and a television lounge, a cocktail bar, and a bedroom for four people. On the roof there's a mini-golf range, a mini-swimming pool and a hot tub.

If you visit Osaka you can see the world's longest and most luxurious car on permanent display at Kenji's Sports Centre.

NARRATOR:
Thanks, Julie. And now back to the Motor Show at Earls Court, London. Back to you, Barry ...

EXTRA ACTIVITY
Class survey
Ask students to carry out a survey of the class to find out the most popular:
– pizza topping
– soft drink
– ice cream flavour
– Sunday afternoon activity
– first name (male and female)

Students work in groups to prepare and fill in a questionnaire for all the members of the group. A 'secretary' from each group then reports the results back to the teacher and the whole class, and the teacher collates the results on the board to arrive at the final figures.

UNIT 30 Temporary activities
Suggested lesson break: after Exercise 2

BACKGROUND NOTES
Scuba dive: Swimming under water with tanks of air attached to your back so that you can breathe.
Primary school: The first school for children. In Britain children usually start primary school at five and leave to go to secondary school at eleven.
Bungalow: A single-storey house.
Queensland: One of the states of Australia. The others are New South Wales, Victoria, South Australia, Western Australia and Northern Territory.
The Great Barrier Reef: A huge coral reef, 1,250 miles long, off the east coast of Queensland, Australia. The reef is teeming with rare specimens of tropical fish.

Exercise 1 READING
Ask the two *Before you read* questions to the class as a whole. Find out if students in their countries take a year off after leaving school and

before going to university. Now ask students to look at the photographs on the opposite page. Ask: *What are the people doing and where are they?* (The man is herding sheep. He's riding a horse. He's probably somewhere hot because the grass is brown. The woman is teaching. Perhaps not in England because the children all look quite dark.) *What sort of jobs can young people do in other countries? What are some of the problems of working in another country? What are some of the advantages?*
Try to elicit some of the vocabulary that will occur in the texts, e.g. *to settle down, to have a good time, spare time, tough, remote, lonely.*

Read the introductory paragraph aloud and explain *straight.* Ask students to skim read the two fact summaries and to tell you where Annabel and Julien are spending their year abroad. Use a map or globe to point out Honduras in Central America, Bordeaux in France, Queensland in Australia and the Great Barrier Reef, and discuss what the climate is like. Now ask students to read the texts silently. Encourage them to guess the meaning of the following words or to look them up in a dictionary: *outback, flies, light aircraft,* plus any other words which didn't arise in the earlier discussion.

Ask students to work in pairs asking and answering the comprehension questions. Check the answers with the whole class.

GRAMMAR FOCUS

Explain *temporary* and *permanent* by giving examples, e.g. Say: *My sister is a student. She's at university. In the holidays she works in a café. It's a temporary job. It isn't a permanent job. It's only for six weeks.* Read the two sentences in the Focus box aloud and ask students the question.

KEY
1 = Temporary   2 = Permanent

Ask students if a similar distinction is made in their own language. If so, how?

Go back to the texts and ask the class to give examples of the present continuous for talking about temporary situations.

Exercise 2

Divide students into As and Bs. Ask Bs to reread the text about Annabel and As to reread the text about Julien. They are going to play the part of the person they read about. When they have finished reading, get students to suggest possible questions to ask their partner. Write them on the board, e.g.

Where do you come from? What are you doing at the moment? Where are you working? Where is that exactly? What's it like in ... ? What's the

work like? Where are you living? What are you doing in your free time? What are you going to do when you finish?

Students now close their books and interview each other with A as Julien and B as Annabel.

SUGGESTED LESSON BREAK

 Exercise 3 SPEECHWORK
Special practice is given to the discrimination between *leave* /li:v/ and *live* /lɪv/ as this is a very common area of confusion for students and very frequently causes misunderstandings. Practise the sounds before playing the tape. After checking the sentences, practise them chorally with the whole class.

TAPESCRIPT AND KEY
Which do you hear, sound one, or two?
One: /ɪ/ as in *live.* Two: /i:/ as in *leave.*
A Where do they live? (1)
B When do you leave? (2)
C When did she live? (1)
D I'm living here. (1)
E He's leaving with his parents. (2)
F Did they leave together? (2)

Exercise 4 LISTENING
Ask students if they have any friends or relations who are working temporarily in Britain or the USA. If so, write a chart on the board similar to the one in the book and ask students questions to complete it. Ask: *Do you know anyone who has got a temporary job in Britain/the USA? Where's he/she from? What's he/she doing in Britain/the USA? What does he/she do normally? Has he/she been to any other countries for his/her job?*
When you have completed the chart, it can serve as a model for the students for the listening exercise. Students now copy the headings of the chart into their notebooks. Play the tape once and ask students to listen without writing. Play the tape a second time for them to complete the information in their charts. Have a map of the world to hand to show the countries which Jean Pierre travelled to. Discuss any points of interest the interview might arouse.

TAPESCRIPT
Listen to someone who is living and working in Britain and complete the information in the chart.

INTERVIEWER: Jean-Pierre, where do you come from?
JEAN-PIERRE: I'm from France, in the south-east, in Grenoble.
INTERVIEWER: And what are you doing here in London?
JEAN-PIERRE: I'm studying English but also I'm working in Paddington College as a laboratory assistant.
INTERVIEWER: As a laboratory assistant?

JEAN-PIERRE: Yes.

INTERVIEWER: And what sort of college is that?

JEAN-PIERRE: It's a technical college.

INTERVIEWER: And how long are you here for?

JEAN-PIERRE: I'm here for a year.

INTERVIEWER: A year. What else are you doing here?

JEAN-PIERRE: I'm studying by correspondence with a French university.

INTERVIEWER: So you're doing a correspondence course.

JEAN-PIERRE: Yes.

INTERVIEWER: What subjects are you doing?

JEAN-PIERRE: Public health.

INTERVIEWER: Public health. So what do you do back in France then? What's your job?

JEAN-PIERRE: I'm a nurse in France.

INTERVIEWER: Do you work in a hospital in Grenoble, or what?

JEAN-PIERRE: I worked for one year in a university hospital. After I went to developing countries for four years.

INTERVIEWER: Which countries did you go to?

JEAN-PIERRE: I went to Uganda. I went to the Sudan, to Ethiopia and I went to El Salvador.

INTERVIEWER: El Salvador? Gosh, was that interesting?

JEAN-PIERRE: Yes, very interesting.

INTERVIEWER: So what are you going to do when you go back to France?

JEAN-PIERRE: When I go back to France I want to continue this kind of work or maybe I'm going to Vietnam or Cambodia.

INTERVIEWER: Good luck, Jean-Pierre.

JEAN-PIERRE: Thank you very much.

Exercise 5 WRITING

Discuss the girl in the photograph and ask questions, e.g. *What's her job?* (She's a chambermaid.) *Where's she working?* (In a hotel) *Where do you think she's living?* (Perhaps in the same hotel) *Do you think she's earning a lot?* (Probably not) *What do you think she's doing in her spare time?*

Students then read the advertisement to see if they were right. Ask further questions: *Where's the hotel?* (In central London) *What does a chambermaid do in her job?* (She serves breakfast and cleans the hotel bedrooms.) *What can she do in her free time?* (She can go to language classes/study English.)

EXAMPLE LETTER

By the way, I forgot to tell you about Carmen. Did you know she's in London? She's working as a chambermaid in a hotel in Oxford Street. She's serving breakfasts and cleaning hotel bedrooms!

She's living in the hotel and earning about £70 a week. Not bad! She's also learning English in her spare time because she has a lot of free time in the afternoons. She's says she's having a wonderful time.
What about you? What are you doing now?
Do write and tell me.
Love,
....

Students then write a similar letter about someone they know.

EXTRA ACTIVITIES
1 Lucky dip
Prepare three sets of cards. Each set should have at least ten cards in it, preferably more.

SET 1 PLACE CARDS
These cards consist of names of different places in the world.

SET 2 ACTIVITY CARDS
These cards consist of activities, e.g *working in a factory, studying Russian, staying with a family,* etc.

SET 3 ENJOYMENT CARDS
These cards consist of enjoyment rating in the form of stars. There are only three possible ones:
* = not having a good time/not enjoying it
** = having quite a good time
*** = having a wonderful time.

Ask a student to select a card from each set and to tell the class about his/her temporary activities. The selected cards are returned to the correct sets and shuffled. Other students do the same thing.

2 Jigsaw letter
Compose a letter similar to the example letter about the chambermaid in Exercise 5. Copy it so that there is one for each group of students. Then cut each letter up into pieces of about a sentence length. Each group receives an envelope with all the pieces of the letter jumbled up for them to reconstruct. Make sure that the cuts occur in mid-sentence so that the students have to use their knowledge of English sentence structure, as well as meaning, to piece the letter together.

FLUENCY Units 26–30

Exercise 1 DIAL A CONVERSATION

BACKGROUND NOTES
La Scala: A famous opera house in Milan, Italy.
Carmen: A popular opera by Bizet.
Camper van: A type of caravan.

> *Mini-marathon*: A short road race. A full marathon is over 26 miles; a half-marathon about 13 miles and a mini-marathon anything from 5 to 13 miles.

The object of the activity is to give students as much practice in handling conversations as possible in an information-gap situation. To make the activity more enjoyable, students should divide themselves into As and Bs before looking at the page. They should then only look at their own bubbles. The conversations are numbered 1 to 9 in a jumbled order to increase the surprise element. Students need not do all the conversations.

Before students begin the exercise, demonstrate how it works with one of the students. Take the part of A yourself. The student takes the part of B. Ask the student to select a number, e.g. number one. Study your instructions for a minute and get the student to do the same then demonstrate the conversation to the class.

EXAMPLE CONVERSATION
A: I've got two tickets to see *Carmen* at La Scala. Would you like to come?
B: I'd love to. When's it on?
A: Next Thursday.
B: I'm sorry, I'm afraid I can't. I'm going to a meeting/doing an exam that evening.
A: Never mind. Another time perhaps.

When students are confident that they know what to do, ask As and Bs to form pairs. One of them 'dials a number', in other words chooses a number at random. Both of them must find the conversation which corresponds to that number. They read their instructions silently, asking you if there are any problems, and then conduct the conversation. After approximately twenty minutes, draw the class together and check on a few conversations. Make notes of any language difficulties as you listen and spend some time discussing these afterwards.

Exercise 2 NOUGHTS AND CROSSES

Draw a similar set of squares on the board but write different adjectives. You can then give an example of how the game works without giving away correct sentences for the students' own game. When you are sure that students know what to do, ask them to play the game, first copying the word square from their books into their notebooks. You must be available as arbiter of the sentences. If they prefer, students can copy a blank version of the squares into their notebooks and play with this, whilst referring to the Students' Book for the adjectives.

The same idea can be used to practise other points of grammar, e.g. irregular past or perfect tense forms, or pronouns like *every, all, none, each,* etc.

CHECK Units 26–30

(For advice on handling this section, see the notes for Check Units 1–5.)

KEY
Ex. 1 1b 2a 3b 4a 5c 6c 7c 8a 9c 10b
(10 marks)

Ex. 2 1 cheaper 2 more expensive 3 harder
4 longer 5 more comfortable 6 more interesting
7 better 8 bigger (8 marks)

Ex. 3 1 hottest 2 wettest 3 most exciting
4 tallest 5 longest 6 most polluted 7 worst
8 most beautiful 9 best (9 marks)

Ex. 4 1 an 2 a an 3 a 4 the 5 the 6 the 7 the
8 (–) (–) (10 marks)

Ex. 5 1 6th March 1991
2 24th November 1989
3 12th April 1999
4 31st July 1964
5 22nd February 1975
6 3rd September 1939
7 15th August 1988
8 9th October 1949
9 23rd January 1972
(9 marks)

Ex. 6 1b 2a 3c 4b 5b (5 marks)

Ex. 7
Dear Tom,
I'm arriving on Monday, October 4th and taking the train to Leeds. I'll call you and arrange a time to meet. How was your summer?
Yours,
Sam
(15 marks)

CHECK YOUR PROGRESS
(See notes for Units 1–5.)

LEARNING TO LEARN 6
The purpose of this section is to help students become more aware of their mistakes and to see them as a positive part of the learning process.
Ask students to look at the two pictures. Ask:
T: Why is Picture 1 wrong?
S: Because the student doesn't repeat the correct word.
T: Why is Picture 2 different?
S: Because he repeats the correct word.
T: Does this help him?
S: Yes.

Ask different students to tell you how they come to class. Correct any mistakes, making sure they repeat the correct form in a sentence. This method of correcting is most appropriate when you are practising specific points of language.

Write on the board the sentence: *I went to England for to learn English.* Mark it with a cross and ask: *Why is this sentence wrong?* When a student gives you the correct version, cross out the word *for* on the board. Explain that oral repetition is not the best way to correct a mistake in written work and that a better way is to write the sentence again (though obviously this is not necessary for spelling mistakes).

Now write on the board: *The museum was very intresting.* Write *sp* beside the sentence to indicate the nature of the mistake. Ask: *What is the mistake? Is it a grammar or spelling mistake? What is the correct spelling of 'interesting'?*

For homework, ask students to go back over their written work for the last three weeks and to see if similar mistakes recur, e.g. not putting capital letters for nationalities, forgetting the third person *s*, getting past tense forms wrong, etc. Tell students to make a note of these recurrring mistakes and to give them special attention when they next do some written work.

PREVIEW Units 31–35

The photographs and the dialogue
Ask students about the photographs. Ask:
Picture 1
What's Laura doing? (She's riding her bike/bicycle.)
Where's she going? (Into town)
Who's the other girl? (Laura's friend Sarah)
Where's she going? (To lunch)
Picture 2
What hits Laura's bike? (A white car/van)
or:
What knocks Laura off her bike?/Why does Laura fall off her bike? (A white car hits her/knocks her off.)
Picture 3
What happens? (She hurts her arm. Her books fall out of the bike basket/onto the ground.)
Who helps her? (A man with a beard and glasses)
Picture 4
Who is the man? (Professor Morgan)
What does he do with the bike? (He picks it up.)
Picture 5
Where are Laura and Professor Morgan? (In the medical centre at the university)
Picture 6
What's the nurse doing? (She's putting Laura's arm in a sling.)
Picture 7
Where are Laura and Professor Morgan? (In the car park)

What's Professor Morgan going to do? (He's going to take Laura home in his car.)

Write any new vocabulary on the board, e.g. *to hit, to knock off, to fall off, to hurt, to fall out of, to pick up, medical centre, a sling, to take somebody home.*

🔲 The tape and the exercise
Play the tape and then ask the comprehension questions.

TAPESCRIPT
Listen and follow the conversation in your Students' Book.

SARAH:	Are you coming to lunch, Laura?
LAURA:	No, I've got to go into town. See you later.
SARAH:	O.K. See you.
LAURA:	Watch out! Hey road hog! Ow!
PROF. MORGAN:	Are you all right?
LAURA:	I'm O.K. but I think I've hurt my arm.
PROF. MORGAN:	You're Laura Martinelli, aren't you?
LAURA:	That's right. Oh, it's Professor Morgan.
PROF. MORGAN:	Are you sure you're O.K? The driver didn't stop, I'm afraid. Look, let me take you to the Medical Centre. Do you think you can walk?
LAURA:	Yes, thanks.
PROF. MORGAN:	Would you like a cup of tea?
LAURA:	Yes, please. With lots of sugar.
NURSE:	How do you feel now?
LAURA:	A bit dizzy but not too bad.
PROF. MORGAN:	Everything O.K?
LAURA:	Yes, thanks for the help. I've never had an accident on my bike before.
PROF. MORGAN:	Come on. Let's leave the bicycle here and I'll take you home in my car.

The learning objectives box
Ask students to read the objectives in the box and to find examples of the language in the dialogue.

Offer and order food and drink: *Would you like a cup of tea?*
Ask and talk about recent events: *I've hurt my arm.*
Ask and talk about experiences: *I've never had an accident before.*
Talk about illness and discomfort: *How do you feel?/A bit dizzy.*
Talk about things you've got to do: *I've got to go into town.*

UNIT 31 Eating out

Suggested lesson break: after Exercise 3

PRESENTATION

From magazine pictures, or from drawings on the board, teach or elicit from the students basic food vocabulary. Practise the vocabulary chorally and individually and write it on the board in categories, e.g.

Meat	*Fish*	*Fruit*	*Drinks*
pork	cod	apple	orange juice
lamb	trout	orange	apple juice
beef/steak	salmon	banana	mineral water
chicken		melon	lager
		grapefruit	beer
		strawberry	wine
			(red/white/rosé)

Vegetables	*Salad*
potatoes	tomatoes
carrots	lettuce
peas	cucumber
beans	
onions	
cabbage	
cauliflower	
mushrooms	

Exercise 1

> BACKGROUND NOTES
> *Chicken Kiev*: Chicken breasts stuffed with butter, herbs and garlic.
> *Chicken Oscar*: Breast of chicken in a prawn and broccoli sauce.
> *Onion rings*: Onion sliced into rings and then fried.
> *Credit card*: The most widely used credit cards in Britain are Access, Visa (Barclaycard) and American Express.

Ask students to look at the plate at the top of the page in their Students' Book. Ask what there is on the plate (a restaurant bill, some coins/change/ money, a credit card and a credit card receipt). Ask if they can read any of the items on the bill, e.g. *Ch(icken) Kiev, Ch(icken) Oscar, Continental salad, Onion rings, Extra mushrooms, half a litre of Heineken (lager), a glass of white (wine), a coffee.*

Read aloud the jumbled sentences in Exercise 1 and get students to practise them chorally and individually.

Now ask students to look at the four pictures and the blank speech bubbles. Students work in pairs with the jumbled sentences to try to match them with the pictures and the bubbles. (There are two sentences to each picture.) Explain that a *dessert*

is a sweet course. Check students' answers with the whole class, and then write the correct dialogue on the board for students to copy.

KEY
1
WAITER: Are you ready to order now?
WOMAN: Yes. I think I'll have the chicken.
2
WAITER: What would you like to drink?
MAN: Could we have a lager and a glass of white wine, please?
3
WAITER: Would you like a dessert?
WOMAN: No, thank you. No desserts. Just coffee.
4
WAITER: Here are your coffees.
MAN: Thank you. And can we have the bill too, please?

Exercise 2 LISTENING

Students refer to their written version of the dialogue when they listen. The recorded dialogue is identical except for the three differences (steak not chicken, glass of red wine not white wine, tea not coffee)

TAPESCRIPT
Look at your completed conversations for Exercise 1. Now listen to the dialogue and note three differences.

WAITER: Are you ready to order now?
WOMAN: Yes. I think I'll have the steak.
MAN: And I'll have ...
WAITER: What would you like to drink?
MAN: Could we have a lager and a glass of red wine, please?
WAITER: Would you like a dessert?
WOMAN: No, thank you. No desserts. Just tea.
WAITER: Here are your teas.
MAN: Thank you. And can we have the bill too, please?
WAITER: Yes, certainly.

Exercise 4

> BACKGROUND NOTES
> *Fresh leaf tea*: Not powdered instant tea.
> *Oxtail soup*: A type of thick, beef-flavoured soup.
> *Still*: Without gas.
> *Sparkling*: With gas.
> *Chilled*: Cooled.

Refer students to the picture of the drinks machine and go through the possible choice of drinks which can be obtained from it. Explain the new vocabulary. Set up a substitution drill to practise *I think I'll have/I'd like ... , please*. Call out an item, e.g. *oxtail soup, chilled orange, chilled blackcurrant, water, chocolate,* etc. and point to a different student each time to provide the complete sentence, e.g.

T: Oxtail soup.
S1: I think I'll have oxtail soup, please.
T: Chilled orange.
S2: I'd like chilled orange, please.

Now practise dialogues Teacher–Student, e.g.
T: Would you like something to drink?
S: Yes, please.
T: What would you like?
S: I think I'll have chilled orange, please.
T: Still or sparkling?
S: Sparkling, please.

Students now work in pairs, changing parts after each conversation. Go round the class and check that students are asking *What would you like?* not *What do you like?*, and *I'd like ...,/ I'll have ...* not *I like ...* or *I have ....*

 Exercise 3 SPEECHWORK.

This exercise emphasises some of the common difficulties which students have in hearing and producing contracted forms. Play the tape several times if students find it difficult to hear the differences. Students then listen and repeat the sentences.

TAPESCRIPT AND KEY
Look at the alternatives in your Students' Book, then listen and say which words you hear.

1 I like chicken.   4 She'd like coffee.
2 I'll have steak.   5 His fish is nice.
3 I'm having a dessert. 6 I'll have the fish.

Now listen and repeat the sentences. (Sentences repeated with pauses.)

SUGGESTED LESSON BREAK

COMMUNICATION FOCUS
Ask students to study the Focus box silently. Point out especially:
– The use of *I'll* not *I* in *I think I'll have the chicken* (a form which the students have already practised in Exercise 4).
– The use of *the. I think I'll have the chicken* refers to the chicken which is described on the menu. *I think I'll have chicken* means chicken in general or chicken as opposed to fish. Both are possible.
– The indefinite article *a/an/some* is common but not necessary in orders like *I'd like orange juice/lager.* (but you cannot say: ~~I'd like the lager.~~)
– All three types of requests are acceptable: *I'd like, Can I have* and *Could I have.*

Practise the offers chorally and give special practice in saying *I'll have* and *I'd like.*

Exercise 5 ROLEPLAY

> BACKGROUND NOTES
> *Prawn cocktail*: Prawns served with mayonnaise on a bed of green salad.
> *Lamb kebab*: Small pieces of lamb grilled on a skewer.
> *Chicken Kiev*: (See the background note in Exercise 1.)
> *Risotto*: Rice cooked with onion and other ingredients such as mushrooms or chicken.
> *Chocolate mousse*: A rich dessert made with chocolate, sugar, eggs and cream.

Ask students to look at the menu in their Students' Book. Explain that there are usually three *courses* to a meal: *a starter, a main course* and *a dessert.* Explain that there are several *dishes* in each course, e.g. *Fillet steak* and *Chicken Kiev.* Go through the menu explaining any new food words. Alternatively, elicit and write on the board suggestions for another menu. This can be more tailored to local food. It is important, however, that students know the new food words on the menu in the book.

Refer students back to the pictures and bubbles in Exercise 1 and ask a pair of students to act out the dialogue. Then ask another pair of students to act out a similar dialogue, but to choose different items from the menu in their books.

Students now form groups of four to six, choose one person to act as waiter and begin the roleplay. If possible, try to record one of the roleplays to play back later for correction and feedback.

Exercise 6 READING
Start a general discussion about restaurants and the sort of food the students like to eat, using the *Before you read* questions. Introduce the phrases *take-away foods* and *fast food.* Then ask students to look at the two reading comprehension questions. See if they can answer these before reading the text. Students read the text and note the answers.

EXTRA ACTIVITIES
1 Visitors' menu
In groups, students work out a menu to offer a visitor to their country, which shows a range of their national dishes. The main dish should be accompanied by a list of ingredients.

2 Class survey: most popular food
Students conduct a survey in their class to find out the names of five popular, and fairly cheap, dishes to eat in local restaurants.

UNIT 32 Recent events

Presentation

With books closed, walk around the class, performing different actions and then commenting on them using the present perfect with *just*, e.g. *I've just dropped my pen/opened the door/closed my book/cleaned the board/ written my name/sat down/stood up.* Ask students to do the same. Introduce the question: *What've you (just) done?* Then get students to ask each other about a third student, e.g.

s1: What's Francesca just done?
s2: She's just opened her book.

Write example sentences on the board and practise them chorally and individually.

Exercise 1 LISTENING

Ask students to look at the photograph of Mr and Mrs Gibson in their Students' Book. Ask:
Who can you see? (Mrs Gibson)
What has she got in her hand? (A magazine or a brochure and a letter)
Does she look happy or sad? (She looks happy.)
Why? (She's just heard/received some good news.)
What do you think has happened?

Now ask students to read the three *Before you listen* statements in their books and say which they think is true. Explain comp*etition, exam* and *receive.* Play the tape and ask students to listen and say why Mrs Gibson is happy. Play the tape twice if necessary.

TAPESCRIPT
Listen and find out why Mrs Gibson is so happy.

MRS GIBSON:	Oh no! I can't believe it!
MR GIBSON:	What is it?
MRS GIBSON:	You remember I entered a car competition last November?
MR GIBSON:	No?
MRS GIBSON:	Well, it was a quiz all about cars. Anyway, I've won! Look!
MR GIBSON:	What have you won?
MRS GIBSON:	A new car!
MR GIBSON:	I don't believe you! Let's have a look. Yes, you're right! You've won a Metro.
MRS GIBSON:	It's fantastic! I can't believe it.

Play the tape again, stopping at the lines *Anyway, I've won! What have you won?* and get students to tell you what they heard. Write on the board:
I've won. What have you won?
Then move on to the Grammar Focus.

GRAMMAR FOCUS

Explain that one of the uses of the present perfect is to talk about events which have just happened, often when we can still see the result of the event. We do not use the present perfect to talk about an event when we mention a specific time in the past. Compare the two sentences:
I've just had a letter from Sue. (Present perfect)
I had a letter from Sue yesterday. (Simple past with a specific time reference: *yesterday*)

It is important to spend time at the early stages establishing the concept of this tense, and to show how it differs from the past simple. Point out that the present perfect tense is formed with the present tense of the verb *to have* and the past participle. Give examples with verbs whose forms are different in the past and past participle, e.g.
do – did – done, write – wrote – written, take – took – taken.
Start to build lists on the board of regular and irregular verbs in columns showing their base, past tense and participle forms. These can be added to in the next exercise.

Exercise 2

Ask students to describe what is happening in each picture, e.g.
T: Where is the man in Picture 1?
s: He's in the kitchen.
T: What has he done?
s: He's dropped/broken a cup.

Students must select a suitable verb from the list. Not all the verbs will be used in this exercise. The exercise can be repeated using *just*. Explain that using *just* emphasises that the action happened very recently.

Exercise 3 SPEECHWORK

Practise the sound first, making sure the students do not exaggerate the h sound too much or allow the back of the tongue to touch the roof of the mouth. Then play the tape for students to listen and repeat.

Exercise 4

This exercise is a simple guessing game to practise questions and short form answers. It also practises the word *something* in a useful context. Have a list of ideas to give students if they cannot think of anything, e.g.
You've just lost your passport/child/suitcase/air ticket.
You've just dropped your wallet into the swimming pool/sea/river.
You've just left your purse/handbag in the bank/ supermarket.
You've just broken your bracelet/favourite teapot/ Walkman.
You've just seen a bad car accident/a ghost/your ex-boyfriend/girlfriend.

Draw students' attention to the example exchange and demonstrate how the exercise works by taking the part of A yourself and asking a good student to take the part of B.

Exercise 5 Caribbean cruise

Bring as many dice as possible to the class so that students will get more practice if the game is played in pairs or small groups. Quickly go through the items on the board with the class to explain any new vocabulary such as *roulette* and *lottery*. Demonstrate how the game works first by playing two rounds in front of the class with two or three other students, e.g.

T: (Throws a 5 and moves the button to square 5.) I've just dropped my wallet in the sea. It says 'Move back 3'. (T moves button back to square 3.)

S1: (Throws a 3 and moves his/her button to square 3.) I've just seen a dolphin. It says 'Move on 1'. (S1 moves button on to square 4.) etc.

It is important to establish that players must not simply read the information in the square but that they should change the verbs into the present perfect tense, according to the example. Explain *move* and point out its pronunciation.

EXTRA ACTIVITIES

1 Guess the context

Copy the following short conversations so that each pair of students has a copy. Ask them to try and work out the context for each conversation and say what has just happened in each case.

1
A: Oh no! I'm sorry!
B: Don't worry. It's not new.
2
A: Can you move it?
B: No.
A: Does it hurt a lot?
B: Yes, it does. I can't walk.
3
A: What's the matter?
B: It's cold.
A: I'll ask for another one.
4
A: I don't want to go.
B: But Hong Kong is a very exciting place.
A: Maybe, for a holiday.

2 Observation game

Two students leave the room. The rest make some simple change in the classroom such as open a cupboard, move a desk, put a pencil on the floor, clean the board, etc. The two people are called back and have ten Yes/No questions using the present perfect tense to find out what the change is. All the answers must be short forms, e.g. *Have you opened the window? No, we haven't.*

UNIT 33 Experiences

Suggested lesson break: after Exercise 3

Exercise 1

BACKGROUND NOTES
The Taj Mahal: The magnificent white marble mausoleum built between 1632 and 1643 in Agra, India, by the Mogul Emperor Shah Jahan in memory of his favourite wife, Mumtaz Mahal. It is in a garden with pools and fountains.
The Sugar Loaf mountain: A famous landmark of Rio de Janeiro, *Pao de Acucar* (1,296ft) is a steep granite mountain towering over Copacabana and Ipanema beaches.
The temples of Kyoto: Kyoto is the ancient capital of Japan. It is a centre of Buddhism and has a famous 59ft statue of Buddha as well as many beautiful temples built over the water.
The Colosseum: An amphitheatre in Rome, begun in AD72 under the Emperor Vespasian. It had a capacity of 80,000 spectators. Public sport included the killing of early Christians by lions and gladiators. The building is now a ruin in the centre of Rome. It is still remarkably well-preserved.
The Great Barrier Reef: (See note in Unit 30.)
The Floating Market: Bangkok, the capital of Thailand, on the river Chao Phray, is built on *klongs* or canals and it was once known as 'the Venice of the East'. Boats still play a major part in the city's life and the Thonburi Floating Market on *Klong Dao Kanong* early in the morning (see picture) is one of many fascinating spectacles for visitors to Thailand.
The Great Wall of China: A defensive fortification about 1,500 miles long, running from the coast of north-east Hopei to west Hansu. It was built in 246–209 BC to defend China's northern frontier, and substantially rebuilt under the Ming dynasty (1368–1644).

Point out the names of the places listed in the Students' Book and practise them chorally with the students. Then ask students to work in pairs and match the names with the photographs.

PRESENTATION and Exercise 2

Get students to look at the photographs and talk about what they can see in them. Teach or elicit some of the vocabulary from the background notes. When you have talked about all the photographs, (or if you prefer, while you are discussing the photographs) say to a student: *Have you ever seen the Taj Mahal?* Elicit: *Yes, I have.* or *No, I haven't.* Then get a student to ask you the same question, and say: *No, I haven't. I've never been to India.*

Get students to ask each other individually about one or two of the other pictures and then ask them to work in pairs, asking and answering *Have you ever ...* questions about each picture in their Students' Book. Select one or two students to report back to the class about their partners, e.g. *Maoro has seen the Colosseum but he hasn't seen Sugar Loaf mountain. He's never been to Brazil.*

Now draw students' attention to the example exchange in Exercise 2. Ask students to write down the names of five places of interest which they have seen. (These do not have to be the places in the Students' Book.) In pairs, students then tell their partners and ask their partners if they have seen the same places, as in the example exchange

GRAMMAR FOCUS

Ask students to study the Focus box silently, then ask the question about the position of *ever* and *never*. (*Ever* and *never* are positioned before the main verb, i.e. before the past participle.)

Draw students' attention to the question and answer forms with *How many times ...* and practise them chorally and individually. Then ask other questions Teacher–Student, e.g.

T: What's your favourite film?
S: *Gone with the Wind.*
T: How many times have you seen it?
S: I've seen it four times.

Follow this with questions and answers Student–Student across the class. Make sure that students use the words *once* and *twice*.

Now draw students' attention to the note about the difference between *been to ...* and *gone to ...* . Point out that *been to* means to go and to come back, whereas *gone to* means that the person is still at the other place. Draw two explanatory diagrams on the board:

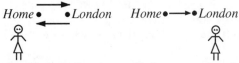

She's been to London.   She's gone to London.

🔲 Exercise 3 SPEECHWORK

Ask students to write the sentences in their notebooks, and then to guess where the stress is going to fall before they listen. Play the tape and then check their answers.

TAPESCRIPT AND KEY
Listen and underline the stressed syllables.

<u>Have</u> you ever <u>seen</u> it? <u>Have</u> you ever <u>read</u> it? <u>Have</u> you ever <u>been</u> there? <u>Have</u> you ever <u>tried</u> it?

Students then listen again and repeat the phrases.

SUGGESTED LESSON BREAK

Exercise 4
Show how the words *something* and *somewhere* are formed, and point out that in questions we use the words *anything* and *anywhere*.

Read out the questions in the Students' Book and ask students to make notes in their notebooks. When they have completed their notes, explain that each student now has to ask several other students if they have done similar things. Draw students' attention to the example exchange and demonstrate how it works first, with a student taking the part of A and the teacher taking the part of B, e.g.

S: Have you ever read *Madame Bovary* by Balzac?
T: No, I haven't.
S: Have you ever read *David Copperfield* by Charles Dickens?
T: Yes, I have.
S: Did you enjoy it?
T: Yes, I did. I thought it was a very good story.
S: I enjoyed it too.

Students now refer to their notes and ask questions of other students in order to find others who have read, seen, eaten and done the same things which they have done.

When students have finished, get several of them to act out their conversations. Write two or three of these on the board as examples. Point out the tense change from the present perfect to the past simple. The present perfect is used in this case for a general question about the past, with no specific time reference. The past simple is then used when referring to the particular event or time in the past when the experience took place (*Did you enjoy it?*). It would be wrong to ask: ~~Have you enjoyed it?~~

🔲 Exercise 5 LISTENING

BACKGROUND NOTES
The Jorvik Centre: The Jorvik Viking Centre recreates life in York at the time of the Viking invasion in AD 867. It is on the site of the original settlement. Visitors travel in 'time cars' past tableaux, complete with sounds and smells, of a market, houses and a wharf, until they reach the archeological excavations of the present day.
The Railway Museum: York has always been an important railway centre. This museum tells the story of railways in Britain and includes the carriage used by Queen Victoria.
The Castle Museum: Inside the museum, are reconstructions of cobbled stone streets, with buildings and shops, to show what life was like in York from the 16th to the 19th century. The museum was once a prison.

Howard's End: Laura is confused. *Howard's End* is the title of a novel by E. M. Forster. She may be thinking of Castle Howard, a stately home set in beautiful grounds in the countryside not far from York. It is open to the public during the summer.

York Minster: The word *minster* is Anglo-Saxon for *a large central church,* in this case a cathedral. The present building, the fourth cathedral to stand on the site, was begun in 1220 and took more than 250 years to build. It has more than 100 stained glass windows, some of which are more than 700 years old.

Clifford's Tower: A stone tower situated opposite the Castle Museum. It was built in the 13th century on the site of William the Conqueror's original wooden castle.

If you wish, use the background notes to give more information about the places. Ask students to try to guess the answers to the questions before listening. Then play the tape for students to see if their guesses were right.

TAPESCRIPT

Listen to a conversation between Adam and Laura and answer the questions. Use the list of famous places in York to help you.

LAURA: I've got a free afternoon.
ADAM: That's nice. What are you going to do?
LAURA: I'm going to visit the Castle Museum.
ADAM: Oh, good idea.
LAURA: Have you ever been there?
ADAM: No, I haven't, actually.
LAURA: So how do you know it's good?
ADAM: Well, people say it's good.
LAURA: I thought you'd seen all the famous places in York.
ADAM: Er …
LAURA: So what have you seen? What about the Jorvik Centre?
ADAM: Er … no.
LAURA: Have you seen the Museum Gardens?
ADAM: No.
LAURA: Have you been to Howard's End?
ADAM: Er … no.
LAURA: Well, what HAVE you seen?
ADAM: I've seen the cathedral – York Minster!
LAURA: That's not very much! One of these days, Adam, I'll take you sightseeing in York!

Exercise 6 About you

BACKGROUND NOTES
Mombasa: The second largest city in Kenya, after Nairobi, and the main port for Uganda and Rwanda, as well as Kenya.

Mount Kilimanjaro: The highest mountain in Africa (19,317 ft). It is in north-east Tanzania near the Kenyan border.

Victoria Falls: A waterfall on the Zambesi river, 350–400ft high, broken by islands into four parts.

Serengeti National Park: A game park situated in Tanzania in Africa.

Start a general discussion about sightseeing in one's local area. Make a note of any mistakes in tenses and point these out when the discussion is over.

Exercise 7 WRITING

Before students start the exercise, ask them where Kenya, Mombasa, Kilimanjaro, Zimbabwe and the Victoria Falls are situated. Use the background notes for extra detail if necessary. Explain *mosquito net, scorpion* and *sleeping bag*. Students work individually to copy and complete the letter. Check by asking students to read a sentence each, or asking them to exchange each other's work to correct while you read out the completed letter. Ask if any students have ever slept in a sleeping bag/tent/under a mosquito net.

KEY
haven't written   've been   've read   've done   've been   've climbed   've flown   've just seen   have you ever slept   's found

For additional practice of the present perfect, comprehension questions can be asked on the letter. For homework, students should copy all the verbs in the unit into their notebooks, and add the past simple and past participle forms, e g.

be – was – been	*read – read – read*
come – came – come	*see – saw – seen*
do – did – done	*sleep – slept – slept*
find – found – found	*think – thought – thought*
fly – flew – flown	*try – tried – tried*
go – went – gone	*write – wrote – written*

Tell students that you will give a spot check on these in the next lesson.

EXTRA ACTIVITY
Discussion: Have you ever?

Ask students to form groups to discuss other personal experiences. Make a list of questions for each group to discuss, e.g.

Have you ever walked in your sleep?
Have you ever missed a plane?
Have you ever fainted?
Have you ever met anyone famous?
Have you ever won a competition?

If the answer is *yes*, students then ask questions in the simple past, e.g. *When/Where did it happen?*

Suggested lesson break: after Exercise 3

PRESENTATION and Exercise 5

With books closed, use yourself to present the parts of the body. Say each word as you point to the part and get students to practise chorally. Ask: *What's this?* Elicit: *It's your head*, etc. Then ask students to use the picture of the tennis player (Michael Chang) in their Students' Book to practise naming the parts of the body. Students copy the vocabulary into their notebooks.

Exercise 1

Ask students to look at the photograph at the top of page 105 in their Students' Book and to tell you what they can see pictured around it. Elicit or teach: *thermometer, pills, tablets, capsules, a bandage, a plaster, a safety pin, antiseptic cream.* List the words on the board. Now ask students what they think is the matter with the woman lying down. Ask: *Who is she?* (An athlete) *Why is she lying down? What is the matter with her?* (She's probably hurt her leg/knee/ankle.) Some students may suggest: *She's broken/sprained/ twisted her leg/ankle/knee.*

Exercise 2

With books closed, present a range of ailments to the students. Mime the ailments yourself, or draw pictures on the board. Ask: *What's the matter (with him/her/me)?* Provide or elicit the following answers: *He's/She's got a headache/a cold/a sore throat/a cough/a temperature/a stomachache. He/ She feels sick/ill/very hot/dizzy/tired. He's/She's hurt his/her arm/leg*, etc. *He/She doesn't feel well.*

Practise the pronunciation chorally and individually and then practise questions and answers Teacher–Student, followed by Student–Student.

Ask students to open their books and do the exercise in pairs, e.g.
A: What's the matter with him in Picture 1?
B: He's got a cold.

Practise the short forms by asking:
T: Has he got a stomachache in Picture 1?
S: No, he hasn't. He's got a cold.

End by asking if anyone in the class has got a cold, a cough or a headache.

Exercise 3 LISTENING

Pre-teach the word *remedy*. Play the tape once only for gist.

TAPESCRIPT
Listen to the advertisement. What is it for?

Are there days when you get headaches – headaches so bad you want to scream? Now, when a headache strikes, take Soludin. Soludin stops headaches fast. Soludin is today's fast but gentle remedy for headaches and stress. Don't let a headache spoil your day. Soludin stops the headache in your day.

SUGGESTED LESSON BREAK

Exercise 4

With books closed, write on the board prompt words for offers of help: *glass of water, tissue, aspirin, cough medicine, sit, lie, home, bed, doctor.* Then present an ailment and an offer of help. Say to a student: *Alain, you've got a headache ... What's the matter?* Elicit: *I've got a headache.* Respond: *Would you like an aspirin?* Give other ailments to different students and demonstrate the other possible offers, e.g. *Would you like to see a doctor?* Practise Student– Student across the class, then get students to each write a list of at least five things which are wrong with them. In pairs, students practise talking about ailments and offering help, using different ailments from their lists and offers from the prompts on the board, e.g.
A: What's the matter?
B: I feel very tired.
A: Would you like to lie down?

COMMUNICATION FOCUS

Ask students to study the items in the Focus box silently. If you wish ask them to copy the items into their notebooks.

Exercise 6 ROLEPLAY

Draw students' attention to the explanation and the skeleton dialogue. Remind students of the invitation form: *Would you like to ...* from Unit 26. If necessary, build up an example dialogue on the board from students' suggestions. Students then work in pairs to write their own dialogue. They should both have copies of their finished dialogue. Ask them to try to memorise it as far as possible and to close their books as they roleplay.

SUGGESTED CONVERSATION
A: Hello. Is that Miguel?
B: Yes, it is.
A: It's Paco here. Would you like to play football this afternoon?
B: I'm afraid I can't.
A: Oh, what's the matter?
B: I've hurt my leg.
A: Oh, how did it happen?
B: I fell off my bike.
A: Oh, I'm sorry.
B: It's O.K. Maybe we can play next week.
A: Sure. Bye!

Exercise 7 SPEECHWORK

Ask students to copy the words into their notebooks. Then get them to guess where the stress is going to fall. Play the tape once for them to see if they were correct. Check their answers. Then play the tape again and ask students to circle the reduced syllables.

TAPESCRIPT AND KEY
Stressed syllables are underlined.
Vowels in reduced syllables are circled.

<u>tem</u>perature <u>me</u>dicine <u>diff</u>erent <u>res</u>taurant
<u>dic</u>tionary <u>in</u>teresting

Exercise 8 WRITING

Remind students again of the invitation form: *Would you like to ...* . Also remind them of the *ing* form after: *Thank you for ...* , e.g. *Thank you for inviting me ...* . Build up an invitation note together with the students on the board, followed by a written reply. Then ask students to write their own invitations and replies. Encourage them to suggest other types of invitation. Ask a few pairs of students to read aloud the notes they received and sent.

SUGGESTED NOTES
Dear Danielle,
Would you like to come to the cinema with me tomorrow evening to see 'Police Academy 5'? It's on at the Plaza Cinema and it starts at 9.15.
Yours,
Anna

Dear Anna,
Thanks for inviting me to the cinema tomorrow evening. I'd like to see 'Police Academy 5' but I'm afraid I can't come because I've got a sore throat and a temperature and I'm in bed!
Yours,
Danielle

Exercise 9 About you

Students can ask the questions in pairs or small groups and report back to the class any unusual remedies from the answers to question 2.

Exercise 10 READING

> BACKGROUND NOTE
> *Flu*: *influenza*, a type of viral infection.

Ask students to read the questions first and then to scan the instructions for the information. Explain *flu* and *dose* before they read. Tell them not to worry about any other words they do not know.

EXTRA ACTIVITIES
1 Goal: A spelling game

One student thinks of a word from Unit 34 and other students must try to guess the word. See Unit 4 Extra activity 2 for detailed instructions.

2 A cure for hiccoughs

Students form groups to think of the five best ways to cure hiccoughs. Bring the class together and collate all the remedies on the board, e.g. *The best way to cure hiccoughs is to put a big key down your back.*

UNIT 35 Things to do

Suggested lesson break: after Exercise 4

Exercise 1

> BACKGROUND NOTES
> *Chemist*: In Britain, a chemist is licensed to dispense and sell medical drugs as well as selling minor medicines, soap, perfume, make up, etc. It is also possible in most chemist's to get films processed, although there are now an increasing number of separate photoshops or photolabs (laboratories) offering a rapid processing service.
> *Prescription*: In order to give a patient drugs such as antibiotics, a doctor will write a prescription, which the patient then takes to the chemist's to be dispensed.
> *Newsagents*: It is becoming quite common nowadays for the apostrophe *s* to be omitted in names on signs, e.g. chemists, newsagents, Lloyds, Harrods. However, it is advisable for students to retain the apostrophe for shops as many examination boards still consider its omission to be a mistake.
> *Videotech*: There are many video shops like this in Britain. They usually hire out video cassettes for a small charge which people take home to watch. They sometimes also sell video cassettes. In this case, Adam has hired a video and has to take it back to the shop.

Ask students to look at the shop and place signs in their Students' Book and to tell you what each of them represent. Ask: *What's Lloyds?* Elicit: *It's a bank.* etc. Suggest *video shop* for *Videotech*. Ask a student to read the sub text under *Healthways Chemist* (*prescriptions, cosmetics, perfumes, photography*) and explain to the students what these mean. (See the background note above.)

Direct students to Adam's list of things to do. Explain: *to cash a cheque, to collect* and *to return* (in this case, *to give back*.) Point out that the items on the list are in note form and so articles are omitted. Ask individual students to read the list inserting *a* or *some* where necessary. Then ask students to do the matching exercise in pairs. Check students' answers with the class.

PRESENTATION and Exercise 2

Show students your empty wallet. Say: *I haven't got any money. I've got to go to the bank.* Ask a student: *Where have I got to go?* Elicit: *You've got to go to the bank.* Ask: *Why have I got to go to the bank?* Answer your own question: *To get some money./To cash a cheque.* Practise the phrases chorally and individually and then build up the following exchange in which students ask each other about you, e.g.

s1: What's (Mr/Mrs Wright) got to do this morning?

s2: He's/She's got to go to the bank.

s1: Why's he/she got to go to the bank?

s2: To cash a cheque.

If you wish, get students to continue the practice asking and answering about going to the post office to get some stamps.

Do Exercise 2 with the whole class.

GRAMMAR FOCUS

Ask students to read the Focus box silently. If students ask if they can use *must* instead of *have got to,* explain that it is possible but that *I've got to* is stronger. It implies that there is some external reason for you to do something. Compare *I must go to bed now* which is more of a personal, internal decision about what seems important to the speaker at the time. If you wish, point out also that *have got to* is not used when referring to routine obligations. Give some more examples of the infinitive of purpose and point out you cannot say: She's going to Britain for to learn English.

Exercise 3

To give extra practice of the infinitive of purpose, try to elicit as many suggestions as possible for each place, e.g.

BANK
to get/change travellers' cheques
to change money
to cash a cheque
to pay a bill
to order a cheque book/statement
to transfer money

CHEMIST
to buy some aspirin
to buy a film
to collect some photos
to leave a prescription
to get some medicine

NEWSAGENT
to buy sweets/cigarettes/a magazine/newspaper, etc.
to order a magazine
to pay a paper bill

Exercise 4

Students can build the list on their suggestions in Exercise 3, or they can suggest other places and things to do, e.g. *go to the travel agent's/library/supermarket/bus station/town hall,* etc.

SUGGESTED LESSON BREAK

▶ Exercise 5 LISTENING

Remind students that Mrs Gibson is Laura's landlady and that Adam works in a travel agent's. Go through the rubric with the students to ensure that they understand the situation and task. Ask students to copy the chart into their notebooks. Play the tape pausing at intervals for students to complete the information. Afterwards you can ask two students to reconstruct and roleplay the same conversation from their notes.

TAPESCRIPT

Mrs Gibson wants Adam to give her some advice about her holiday. Laura telephones Adam to arrange a time when he can come and talk to Mrs Gibson. Listen and complete the information with a tick for 'Yes' and a cross for 'No'.

ADAM: Hello. 776351.

LAURA: Hi, Adam. Laura here.

ADAM: Oh, hi Laura.

LAURA: Listen, could you come and talk to Mrs Gibson about her holiday?

ADAM: Sure. What about this evening?

LAURA: No, I think Mrs Gibson's got to visit her sister this evening.

ADAM: Well, I can't come tomorrow evening. My aunt's coming to stay and I've got to take her out to dinner. What about the day after tomorrow. Friday?

LAURA: Yes, Friday is fine. Let's say Friday, at, er, half past seven?

ADAM: Fine.

LAURA: See you then. Bye.

ADAM: Bye.

Exercise 6 ROLEPLAY

Ask students to look at the flight timetable for London – Madrid – London. Check that students understand how the timetable works by asking questions, e.g. *What time does the first flight leave London?* (Eight thirty) *What time does it arrive in Madrid?* (Eleven fifty) *What time does the second flight leave Madrid?* (Twenty thirty-five. *What time must you check in for the seventeen oh five flight from Madrid to London?* (Fifteen thirty-five) etc.

Divide Students into As and Bs and ask them to study their roles and prepare what they are going to say. A students should practise saying the times to themselves, B students should study the times they need to arrive in London and Madrid and practise a few sentences starting with *I've got to ... .* Demonstrate an example roleplay first with you taking the part of the person in the travel agent's. Then ask students to work in pairs, starting with the model conversation. Ask a couple of students to perform for the rest of the class later. If you think that students will find this very demanding, write a skeleton dialogue on the board to help them, and gradually rub it out while they practise.

SUGGESTED CONVERSATION

A: Can I help you?

B: Yes, I'd like to book a flight to Madrid next Friday.

A: Yes, what time of day do you want to travel?

B: Well, I've got to be in Madrid at half past twelve in the morning.

A: I see. Well, there's a flight leaving London at eight thirty and arriving in Madrid at eleven fifty.

B: Yes, that's fine.

A: And when would you like to travel back to London?

B: I've got to be back at half past ten in the evening.

A: The same day?

B: Yes.

A: Well, there's a flight from Madrid at twenty thirty-five arriving in London at twenty-one fifty.

B: That's fine. What time have I got to check-in at London Airport?

A: Check-in time is one and a half hours before departure time. That's seven a.m. at London Airport.

B: O.K. Thank you.

Exercise 7 WRITING

Explain that the letter should be fairly formal and polite. Go through the paragraph guide and elicit suitable sentences for each paragraph, particularly Paragraph 3, e.g. *Would you like to ...? What about ...?* Write these last two on the board. Students can then use the framework in their Students' Book to write their own letter.

SUGGESTED LETTER

Dear Mr and Mrs Roberts,

Thank you very much for inviting me to lunch next Saturday. I'm afraid I can't come because I've got to go to my cousin's wedding. Would you like to come and have tea with me next week some time? What about Wednesday?

Best wishes,

Cristina

EXTRA ACTIVITIES

1 Things to do: a chain game

One student starts by saying: *I've got to cash a cheque.* The next person in line says: *I've got to cash a cheque and I've got to buy some stamps.* Students continue round the class until somebody makes a mistake or forgets what to say.

2 Excuses

Tell students that somebody they do not like has invited them to dinner the following Saturday. In groups, they must think of five convincing excuses for refusing the invitation without sounding rude. Each group then joins another group to see if they can agree on the three best excuses.

FLUENCY Units 31–35

Exercise 1 READING

Ask students to look at the main picture. Then ask: *Where is this? Can you find it on a map of the world? How long does it take to fly there from your country? Where does the plane stop on the way? Would any of you like to go to Hong Kong? Why/Why not?*

Explain that from Britain it is possible to stop in Amsterdam on the way to Hong Kong. Ask students: *What country is Amsterdam the capital of?* (Holland). *What nationality are people who come from Holland?* (Dutch). Ask: *Have any students ever been to Amsterdam?* and what it is famous for (Canals). Students then read the four comprehension questions and scan the letter for the answers. Ask additional questions to elicit Dave's plans.

Exercise 2

Ask students to tell you what they already know about Hong Kong. Ask: *Who governs Hong Kong?* (The British Governor General) *What is the currency?* (Hong Kong dollar) *What's the capital city?* (Victoria) *What's the climate like?* (It's subtropical.) If students do not know the answers, do not tell them, since they will find the answers in their Students' Book. Students then read *Hong Kong at a glance.* Explain any new vocabulary. Students then prepare six questions to ask someone in the class, e.g.

Where is Hong Kong situated? How many people live in Hong Kong? What is the capital? What currency do they use? What languages do they speak? Who governs them? What is the weather/ climate like? What do they export? Students then use these questions to interview someone in the class.

Exercise 3 ROLEPLAY

> BACKGROUND NOTES
> *Vegetable lasagne*: A vegetable sauce in between layers of flat sheets of pasta.

The roleplays can be done simultaneously with students working in pairs on each conversation. Alternatively, you can select different pairs to perform each conversation and ask other students to observe and note down any mistakes they hear. Students should have time to read their roles before each roleplay and to ask for any assistance, but they should try not to look at their books while they speak.

📼 Exercise 4 LISTENING

Play the tape twice, pausing for students to note down the information.

TAPESCRIPT

You are soon going to land in Hong Kong. Listen to the information about your arrival. Note the time of arrival in Hong Kong, the weather, the temperature what you can see from the left-hand side of the plane as you come in to land.

Hello, this is Captain Norton speaking. We have just begun our descent into Kai Tak airport. We are due to land in twenty minutes – on schedule at 9.40. The weather in Hong Kong is warm and sunny with a temperature of thirty-five degrees Celsius.
If you look out of the left-hand side of the aircraft as we come in to land, you'll get a wonderful view of Hong Kong Island. We hope you have enjoyed the flight. Have a good stay in Hong Kong!

EXERCISE 5 WRITING

Ask students to read the information about *Things to do and see in Hong Kong*. Explain *harbour, cruise, fabulous, bargains*. (The inset picture shows the night market.) Students should use this information in their letter. Tell students to use Dave's letter as a model. They must use their imagination to describe what the hotel is like. Ask students to write the letter for homework.

SUGGESTED LETTER

The Peninsula Hotel,
Hong Kong
(*Date*)

Dear ...,
I am now here in Hong Kong and I'm staying in the Peninsula Hotel. It's a big hotel and there's a wonderful view from my window.

The flight was very long. It took twenty-two hours and I was very tired when I arrived. I met an interesting man on the plane. He was from Hong Kong and he told me a lot about the city. In fact, we're meeting this evening to go to an open-air night market.

Hong Kong is an exciting city. The streets are always crowded. I've been on a tour of Hong Kong Island, I've been on a cruise around the harbour and I've had a Chinese dinner on a floating restaurant. The weather's very hot at the moment. It's over 30°C! Tomorrow I'm going to visit a watch factory.
Life is good! See you soon.
Best wishes,
...

CHECK Units 31–35

(For advice on handling this section, see the notes for Check Units 1–5.)

KEY

Ex. 1 1 Have you ever been 2 did you go
3 I went 4 I've been 5 I've got
6 Have you ever read 7 I read 8 did you think
9 I thought 10 it was 11 Did you like
12 I haven't read 13 Have you hurt
14 haven't broken   15 did you do (15 marks)

Ex. 2 1 gone 2 fallen 3 lost 4 dropped
5 broken 6 seen 7 find 8 won 9 had 10 hurt
11 eaten 12 read (12 marks)

Ex. 3 1 back 2 stomach 3 body 4 mouth 5 foot
(5 marks)

Ex. 4 1 a 2 a 3 my 4 an 5 your 6 an 7 her
8 his 9 the 10 – (10 marks)

Ex. 5 1c 2a 3d 4b 5e (5 marks)

Ex. 6 1c 2b 3a 4a 5a (5 marks)

Ex. 7 1b 2a 3a 4b 5b (5 marks)

Ex. 8 1g 2i 3b 4f 5j 6h 7d 8e 9a 10c
(10 marks)

CHECK YOUR PROGRESS
(See notes for Units 1–5.)

LEARNING TO LEARN 7

Ask students what they usually do when they see a new word which they do not understand. Explain that it is not always necessary to know the exact meaning of a word and that there are very few words whose general meaning cannot be guessed from the context. Write on the board examples of words that the students should be able to guess from context and word formation, e.g. *thoughtful, hopeless, furious.*

*1 She was a **thoughtful** sort of person. (think/ thought + full)*
*2 The situation was **hopeless**. (hope + less)*
*3 When he arrived home at midnight, his wife was **furious**. (upset? angry?)*

Ask students first what sort of word it is (e.g. a noun, verb, etc.), and then ask them to guess what the word means from its parts or from the general context of the sentence. Ask students to read the 'Learning to learn' section in their Students' Book silently and to do the task at the end. Check their answers.

PREVIEW Units 36–40

The photographs and the dialogue

Ask students to look at the photographs and to say who and where the people are and what is happening. Elicit or teach the relevant new vocabulary:

The invitation: *invitation, ball*

Picture 1: *clothes shop, shop assistant, evening dress/ball dress*

Picture 3: *to try on, mirror*

Picture 4: *evening dress, dinner jacket, bow tie, to get into (a car), (open-topped) sports car*

Picture 6: *angry, annoyed, to give advice, to suggest*

Read the bubble sentences aloud and explain or demonstrate new vocabulary, e.g. *size 12, someone else, arrange, too tight, slam, shut, gently.* Get students to guess what the other person is saying in each picture, i.e. the shop assistant in Picture 1, Adam on the other end of the phone in Picture 2, Mrs Gibson in Picture 3, Laura in Picture 4 and Adam in Picture 5. Write students' suggestions for each picture on the board.

📼 The tape and the exercise

Play the tape for students to see if they were right and to answer the comprehension questions. Check these with the whole class.

TAPESCRIPT

Listen and follow the conversation in your Students' Book.

MRS GIBSON:	There's one for you.
LAURA:	Oh, it's my ticket for the Summer Ball. 'Grand Summer Ball, Friday June 21st, at The Assembly Rooms, York.'
MRS GIBSON:	Are you going with Adam?
LAURA:	No, with David. You remember, the one who drove me home after my bicycle accident.
MRS GIBSON:	Oh yes, the professor.
LAURA:	Mmm.
ASSISTANT:	Can I help you?
LAURA:	I like this very much but have you got it in size 12?
ASSISTANT:	I'm afraid not, we've only got size 10 and size 14.
LAURA:	Mm, I think I'll leave it.
LAURA:	I'm sorry, Adam but I'm going with someone else. I arranged it weeks ago.
ADAM:	Who are you going with?
LAURA:	David Morgan. My professor.

ADAM:	Oh, he's David now, is he? O.K. Well, that's fine by me, just fine!
LAURA:	Adam, wait a minute. Adam, I can explain.
LAURA:	Do you think it's too tight?
MRS GIBSON:	No, it's fine. It's a lovely dress.
DAVID:	Remember don't slam the door. Just shut it gently.
LAURA:	I remember.
ADAM:	I'm really fed up!
MICHAEL:	Well, if you feel so angry, why don't you do something about it?

The learning objectives box

Ask students to read the objectives in the box and to find examples of the language in the dialogues.

Go shopping for clothes: *Have you got it in size 12?*
Give instructions: *Just shut it gently.*
Talk about rules: *Don't slam the door.*
Talk about feelings and emotions: *If you feel so angry why don't you do something about it?*
Talk about past events in people's lives: *I arranged it weeks ago.*

If there is time, discuss the pictures further by asking more questions, e.g. *Why is Professor Morgan worried about the car door? What do you think Adam is going to do? Have you ever been to a ball?*

UNIT 36 Shopping for clothes

Suggested lesson break: after Exercise 6

Exercise 1 About you

Introduce the topic of shopping with books closed, by asking the three questions to the whole class. Encourage a free-ranging discussion and don't stop the students mid-sentence. Make a note of any mistakes to comment on at the end of the discussion. Before students open their books, find out if any of them work, or have ever worked, in a shop. Ask them if they think different nationalities have different shopping habits, and if so, what they are. Introduce the vocabulary: *to compare prices, to look for a bargain.*

Exercise 2 READING

Ask students to open their books and to look at the cartoon. Ask: *What's the customer wearing?* (A striped shirt and a large spotted tie). Practise the expression *It suits you/doesn't suit you* by giving examples about yourself. Say, e.g. *Black doesn't suit me. Tight skirts/trousers don't suit me.* Get students to give you examples of colours and clothes which do/don't suit them. Ask why the cartoon is funny and introduce the expression *to tell a lie.* Then ask students to read the text individually and to identify the different kinds of shoppers. Check the answers with the whole class and find out if they agree with the conclusions drawn in the article.

Ask students to work in pairs and to list all the words and phrases in the text that are to do with shopping, e.g. *shopping, shops, comparing prices, cheaper, how much it costs, shoppers, shopping for clothes, shop assistant, It suits you perfectly, madam.* List these on the board and get individual students to provide you with example sentences for each word or phrase.

Exercise 3
Bring the whole class together to answer the questions about the picture. Remind students of Laura's question to Mrs Gibson in the Preview section when she was trying on her evening dress (Do you think it's too tight?) If you wish, introduce the vocabulary *(shirt) cuffs* and *sleeves.*

COMMUNICATION FOCUS
At this point, do not aim for students to completely memorise all the shopping expressions. They will have the opportunity for freer roleplay in the next lesson of the unit. Concentrate more on pronunciation and understanding at this stage. Practise all the sentences chorally, substituting other items of clothing and accessories for those given. Remind students that the word *suit* in this case is a verb, and should not be confused with the noun *suit,* meaning a jacket and trousers/skirt made of the same material. Also remind students that *I'll* is the contracted form of *I will* and that they should think of both sentences in the *Making decisions* section as set expressions.

Exercise 4
Ask students to work in pairs to complete the conversation.

KEY
ASSISTANT: Can I help you?
CUSTOMER: Yes, I'm looking for a suit.
ASSISTANT: All the suits are over there on the left.
CUSTOMER: Thanks.
(Later)
CUSTOMER: Can I try this one on?
ASSISTANT: Yes, sure. The changing rooms are over there.
CUSTOMER: Thanks.
(Later)
ASSISTANT: Is it any good?
CUSTOMER: No, not really. The skirt's too long and anyway the colour's wrong. Have you got it in a size 10 in black?
ASSISTANT: No, I'm sorry, we haven't. That's all we've got.
CUSTOMER: O.K. Then I'll leave it.

 Exercise 5 LISTENING
Play the tape and ask students to check their conversations. Then ask them to read their corrected conversation in pairs and to change parts. Ask one pair to read their conversation for the whole class to hear and comment on.

TAPESCRIPT
As in the key to Exercise 4 above.

Exercise 6 SPEECHWORK
Ask the whole class to say which words have the /u:/ sound before playing the tape. Then play the tape for students to see if they were right.

KEY
boot, fruit, juice, do, noon

SUGGESTED LESSON BREAK

Exercise 7
Remind students of what was wrong with the man's jacket in Exercise 3. (It was too small.)

Then ask students to look at the cartoons in their Students' Book and to describe what each person is wearing. If you wish, write the words on the board as they give them to you. Get them to look at the first picture and the example answer and then say to a student: *What's wrong with the trousers in Picture 1?* Elicit the answer: *They're too short.* Get students to ask similar questions and give similar answers Student–Student across the class about the other pictures. Note that some of the students may also be familiar with the parallel structure *not* + adjective + *enough,* e.g. *It's not big enough.* If so, let them use this when they describe the pictures, but do not introduce it unless prompted by the students.

Exercise 8
Practise the conversation with several individual students first. Then ask all students to roleplay the conversations in pairs. Monitor their work, making sure that they change parts.

Exercise 9 ROLEPLAY
Ask students to look at their completed dialogues from Exercise 4, and at the Focus box again. Practise the expressions *over there, on the left* and *on the right.* Then, with books closed, practise the first three lines of the roleplay with different students:
S1: Can I help you?
S2: Yes, I'm looking for a (jacket).
S1: All the (jackets) are over there (on the right).

Now practise the last part of the roleplay with several students:
S2: Have you got one in black/a bigger one/a longer pair/a size 14?

S1: No, I'm sorry, we haven't. That's all we've got.

S2: O.K. Then I'll leave it.

Finally, practise a complete dialogue with a student. Take the part of the shop assistant yourself.

If you wish, get students to roleplay their shopping situations in pairs first, while you monitor. Then select a pair of good students to act their roleplay in front of the class.

Exercise 10 LISTENING

As students offer explanations about what they think the programme is going to be about, explain the words and phrases in the *Before you listen* section. Find out if any students have credit cards and what they use them for. Ask if they have any opinions about the use of credit cards, i.e. if they think that they are a good thing. Explain the title of the programme, *Your Mind and Body* and the words: *pay for, purchases* and *solve*. Play the tape once for students to listen, again for them to answer the questions and a third time to encourage fluent listening. After you have played the tape, see if students have any experience of this kind of problem amongst their friends or neighbours.

TAPESCRIPT

Listen to part of a radio programme, *Your Mind and Body*, and answer the questions in your Students' Book.

NARRATOR:

For some people shopping can become a disease. They can become addicted to shopping in the same way that people can become addicted to alcohol or dangerous drugs. They are called 'shopaholics'.

PATTI:

My name's Patti. I'm twenty-four. I was a shopaholic. It started when I went shopping one morning and bought ten pairs of shoes. It was very exciting. Then I did it again – and again. I couldn't stop buying shoes and I had hundreds of pairs of shoes. I always paid for the shoes with credit cards. I had nine credit cards altogether and I got terribly into debt. I didn't wear the shoes. I just hid them all over the house.

NARRATOR:

Patti decided to get help from a doctor.

PATTI:

When I understood that I had a problem I went to the doctor and things got better. Now when I go shopping for shoes, I never go shopping alone.

NARRATOR:

So if you think you have a problem ...

EXTRA ACTIVITY
Discussion: Worst or best?

In groups, students can discuss their worst item of clothing and their best (i.e. favourite) item. Write example sentences on the board:

The worst item of clothing I have ever bought was a pink suit with purple spots on it. I have never worn it.
My best item of clothing is a brown leather jacket.
I bought it in Spain. I wear it all the time.

UNIT 37 Instructions

Suggested lesson break: after Exercise 3

PRESENTATION and Exercise 1

Ask students to look at the photograph and answer these questions:
What's Adam doing? (He's learning to drive.)
How do you know? (There's a letter 'L' attached to the bumper of the car.)
What does the letter 'L' stand for? (Learner)
Who is with Adam? (His brother Michael)
What's he doing? (He's teaching Adam to drive.)
Where is this happening? In the town or in the country? (Probably in the country)
How do you know? (There's a tree and some grass behind them.)
What sort of a car is it? (A jeep)

Get students to ask and answer the two questions in Exercise 1. Then draw students' attention to the speech bubble and say: *What does Michael say exactly?* Point out how the adverb *slowly* is formed from the adjective *slow* plus *ly*. Demonstrate and practise other adverbs by miming activities and asking students: *What am I doing?* Elicit: *You're walking quickly. You're singing happily. You're writing slowly,* etc. Teach or elicit the irregular adverbs which are listed in the Grammar Focus box. Practise the examples chorally and individually.

Now give students instructions using the imperative positive and negative, e.g. *Stand up, please. Sit down, please. Don't talk, please. Don't smile, please* and then give further instructions using the imperative and adverbs, e.g. *Open your book slowly, please,* etc. Practise the sentences chorally and individually, then get individual students to give other students similar instructions.

GRAMMAR FOCUS

Ask students to study the Grammar Focus box quietly for a short time and then go through it with them. Ask students to do the first task and write the adverb forms of the listed adjectives. Then ask them to look at the sentences in the

105

Focus box, and the example sentences which they have copied from the board, and to answer the questions about the position of adverbs of manner in the sentence.

KEY

quickly   angrily   simply   easily   beautifully
firmly   politely

Adverbs of manner come after the main verb. If there is a noun after the main verb, the adverb of manner comes after the noun.

Remind students of the spelling rules in English involving the following:
– change of *y* to *i*, e.g. *happy – happily*
– omission of the final *e*, e.g. *simple – simply*
– the doubling of the final consonant with *ful* endings, e.g. *beautiful – beautifully*

COMMUNICATION FOCUS
Ask students to study the instructions in the Communication Focus box.

Exercise 4
Students all write an instruction on a piece of paper and fold it. Ask them to pass the pieces of paper round the class until you tell them to stop. Each student then carries out the instruction which is written on the piece of paper which they have received.

Exercise 2
Go through all the instructions. Say them aloud and ask students to make a suitable gesture or facial expression for each one. Ask students to give equivalents from their own cultural background and in their own body language. Discuss any gestures which are rude or impolite or culturally offensive.

Exercise 3 LISTENING
Make sure that students understand what the conversations are going to be about before playing the tape. Play the tape twice and check the answers. Ask students if they think the advice about examinations is good advice or not.

TAPESCRIPT
Listen and say which conversation is about how to make a cake, which is about how to play a video cassette, which is about how to act a scene in a play and which is about how to answer examination questions. Listen.
1
LECTURER: Now, remember the most important thing about the examinations is always read the questions carefully. Right, now let's look quickly at some possible exam questions.
2
WOMAN: Let me show you. Put the video in, gently. That's right. Now press the button which says 'play'. You need to press it firmly, like this. That's it. Now if you want to stop it you just ...

3
WOMAN: Adrian, walk slowly towards Diana. Diana, turn and look into Adrian's eyes and ask: 'What is your pleasure?'
DIANA: How do I say it?
WOMAN: Say it quietly. Almost in a whisper.
DIANA: 'What is your pleasure?'
WOMAN: Good.
4
MAN: Now, Emma, take the milk and pour it carefully into the bowl. I said carefully!
EMMA: Sorry, Daddy.
MAN: Oh no, it's all over the floor! Come on, let's wipe it up immediately.

Now look at your Students' Book, listen again and tick the adverbs as you hear them. Which adverb is used most often and which is not used at all?

KEY
Carefully is used most often.
Angrily isn't used at all.

SUGGESTED LESSON BREAK

Exercise 5 READING
Use the *Before you read* questions as the basis for a general class discussion. Ask for suggestions from students and write up a list of things that people do wrong at interviews on the board, e.g. *They talk a lot. They don't talk at all. They smoke. They don't answer the questions,* etc. Ask students what is happening in the cartoon. (An interviewee in a leather jacket and a crash helmet is arm-wrestling with the interviewer.) Use the cartoon to explain the meaning of *motorcycle clothes, leather jacket, crash helmet, arm-wrestling competition* and *interviewer.*

Read through the two comprehension questions and then ask students to read the text individually to find the answers. Ask them to guess the meaning of the following words and expressions: *the most obvious mistakes, prepare, show interest, the whole time, fall asleep* and *snore.*

Exercise 6 WRITING
Go through each of the adverbs, practising their pronunciation and illustrating their meaning. Students can begin the writing in class and finish it at home. Ask them to find another adverb in the set of instructions (*honestly*) and an adjective for a facial expression (*cheerful*). When students have completed the writing activity, discuss each of the pieces of advice and find out whether they agree with it or not. List those instructions which they think are not appropriate behaviour in their country.

EXTRA ACTIVITY
1 Write a note
Students write a note to a friend. Say to students: *A friend is going to use your home while you are away. Think of a piece of equipment you have, such as a video-recorder, a hi-fi set or a food processor, and write a note with instructions about how to use it.*

UNIT 38 Rules

Suggested lesson break: after Exercise 4

Exercise 1

> BACKGROUND NOTE
> *Access for disabled*: People are asked not to park because disabled people have to be able to use that area of a street to get in or out of a building.

Ask students to look at the photographs of the signs and notices in their Students' Book and ask what the students can see in each photograph. Explain any new vocabulary, e.g. *sign, lake, rowing boat, grass, lawn, access for disabled, seatbelt, lay-by, keep off, caravan (park)*.

Point out the use of prepositions, e.g. *in, on* and *by* and then ask students to do the exercise in pairs. If they wish, students can also suggest other locations to add to the ones listed in the Students' Book.

(The notice about smoking and cockroaches in the top right-hand corner of page 120 is not part of the exercise but if students ask, it is an American notice sometimes found in bars.)

COMMUNICATION FOCUS

Present *must, mustn't* and *can't* by giving examples from the school, or other environments with which students are familiar. Say: *You mustn't/can't smoke in the classroom, but you can smoke in the coffee lounge/bar.* Get students to tell you where you can smoke in their countries (e.g. in restaurants) and where you mustn't smoke (e.g. on buses). Write examples on the board and ask students to repeat them chorally and individually.

Draw students together and ask them to look at the Focus box. Read the sentences aloud and refer at the same time to the appropriate notices for the first two sentences. Point out the spelling of *mustn't*.

Exercise 2

Point to the first notice and say or elicit: *This means that you mustn't drive down that road/ street.* Mention that 'No entry' signs may also

occur on doors. In this case they mean: *You mustn't go through that door*. Elicit sentences from the students for all the other notices.

Exercise 3 About you
If students are studying in Britain, relate these questions to the local area. Students work first in pairs making suggestions of places and then come together for a general class discussion. Ask them also to name some places where you *can't* fish, swim or ride a bike.

Exercise 4
Ask students to close their books. Ask if any of them are members of a gym or health/sports club. If they are, ask what sort of rules they know about and write these in note form on the board. Now ask them to open their books and to work on the exercise as instructed, using a dictionary if necessary. If time is short, the exercise can be finished for homework.

SUGGESTED LESSON BREAK

 Exercise 5 LISTENING
Remind students of Unit 20 and the Disneyworld theme parks. Ask students who have been there if they noticed anything special about the Disney employees. Ask them to look at the list and guess what rules might exist concerning, e.g. moustaches/beards. Ask them to make a list in their notebooks in preparation for the listening. Play the tape and ask students to tick or cross against the list as appropriate.

TAPESCRIPT
A young American is talking about some of the rules for people who work for the Disney Corporation in Disneyworld. Look at your Students' Book, listen, and tick the things which the employees can do and put a cross against the things which they mustn't do.

INTERVIEWER:
Tell me Julie about some of your dress rules.
JULIE:
Well, the rules about personal appearance and hygiene are very detailed and very strict. The Disney Corporation want all their employees to have an all-American, clean look. So, for example, men mustn't have a beard or a moustache. And women mustn't wear heavy make-up. They can wear lipstick, but it must be light and very natural-looking.
INTERVIEWER:
What about perfume?
JULIE:
Yes, that's O.K. and aftershave too. But it mustn't be too strong. They want you to smell fresh because you're meeting the public all the time. And no smoking of course. That's obvious.

107

Oh, and workers mustn't wear hats if they work in Disneyland and I don't know why. But you can wear Mickey Mouse ears ...

Exercise 6 READING

Ask the students to work in pairs asking the first *Before you read* question to each other. Then find out from a show of hands how many students smoke and how many smoked in the past but don't now. Use this to lead into a general class discussion based on the remaining questions. Do not expect more than approximate guesses for the last question.

Ask students to read the text individually making a note of the answers to the questions. Check the answers with the whole class. Ask if any information in the chart surprised them. Check that they have understood the meaning of *ago, since then, health organisations, still, forbidden, warning, seriously damage, even, figures.*

EXTRA ACTIVITY
Make a notice

Tell students to write a notice about bar rules for the noticeboard in a club. Copy the following list of problems to help students make their notice.

PROBLEMS
Some members are forgetting to show their membership cards.
Some are taking glasses from the bar out to the swimming pool.
The juke box often doesn't work because some members are putting foreign coins in it.
Some people are wearing their swimming costumes and shorts in the bar.

UNIT 39 Feelings and emotions

 ## Exercise 1 LISTENING

BACKGROUND NOTES
The three paintings represent:
Claude Monet's 'The Water-Lily Pond': Monet (1840-1926) was one of the school of French impressionists. This painting shows the bridge and lily pond in the artist's garden in Giverny.
Edvard Munch's, 'The Scream': Munch (1863-1944) was a Norwegian painter and graphic artist. 'The Scream' is one of his best-known works.
Franz Hals's 'The Laughing Cavalier': Hals (1582-1666) was a celebrated Dutch portraitist.

Ask students to look at the pictures and to describe each of them. Introduce or revise the vocabulary: *bridge, river, lake, stream, trees, water lilies, to scream, frightened (He looks*

frightened.), happy. Ask if any students can identify the pictures (see the background notes). Then play the tape and ask students to choose a piece of music for each picture.

TAPESCRIPT
Short extracts from the following:
1 Vivaldi's *Four Seasons* (*Allegro* from *Autumn*)
2 Michael O'Rourke's *Field Nocturne Number 5*
3 *Storm* from Benjamin Britten's *Four Sea Interludes*

SUGGESTED ANSWERS
Monet – Piece 2 (*Nocturne*)
Munch – Piece 3 (*Storm*)
Hals – Piece 1 (*Autumn*)

Exercise 2

Ask students if they know any of the pieces of music and can name them. If you wish, introduce the vocabulary: *classical music* and *pop music*. Go through the list of adjectives in the exercise and illustrate their meaning by facial expressions and miming. Students repeat the words after you. Then play the music again and ask: *How do you feel when you listen to the (first) piece of music?*

Exercise 3

Ask individual students: *What colour do you think of when you hear the word (sad)?* etc. Do not insist that every student joins in. Point out that there are no right answers. Accept that some words may suggest completely different colours to different students.

Exercise 4

Go through the questionnaire with the students and explain any new vocabulary, e.g. *dark street, a telephone that doesn't work, valuable, take off.* Draw students' attention to the example exchange. Point out that the two parts of the answer sentences are reversible. Demonstrate how the exchange works by taking the part of A and asking a few students different questions from the questionnaire. Then get students to ask and answer the questions in pairs. They can write four or five answer sentences for homework. Avoid other ways of expressing these ideas that you may know, e.g. *Going to the dentist makes me (feel) frightened. Going to the dentist frightens me. I'm frightened of/nervous about going to the dentist.*

Exercise 5 READING

Ask students to look at the photographs. Ask the *Before you read* questions. Introduce the vocabulary: *police officer, suitcase, doll, label, paper bag, war, evacuee.* Ask students to read the first paragraph of the text. Write the following questions on the board.
When did this happen?

Where did it happen?
How many children left their homes?
Where did they go? Why did they go?
Now ask students to read the other three paragraphs and ask these questions:
How old was the little girl?
Who did she go to the railway station with?
Did her dad go? What did she have with her?
Did the girl want to go?
What could the girl see when the train moved away?
Help students with new vocabulary, e.g. *Second World War, upset, to get on, to cry, to sniff, to wave, to move.*
Discuss the reading comprehension questions in Exercise 5 with the whole class. If you wish, introduce further adjectives such as *miserable.* Explain *homesick* and *lonely.*

Exercise 6 About you
Introduce the questions by asking all students the question: *When did you last cry?* Find out their attitudes towards crying. Then ask them to work in pairs and discuss the five questions, bearing in mind students' sensitivities. Obviously some students may not wish to answer some questions, and should not be pressed to do so. Draw the whole class's attention to any interesting answers, which are not unduly personal.

EXTRA ACTIVITIES
1 A question of emotion
Write the following list of questions on the board and ask students to form groups to discuss them.

Where, when and why did you last:
– lose your temper?
– scream with laughter?
– scream with fear?
– hug somebody?
– sing aloud in public?

2 Draw an emotion
Give a large piece of drawing paper to each student and some coloured felt tip pens. Ask them to draw either: anger, fear, happiness, or sadness. Set a time limit of two minutes and then in turn ask each student to present his/her drawing and to explain it.

UNIT 40 Biography

Suggested lesson break: after Exercise 6

Exercise 1 READING
In groups, students look at the map at the top of page 123, the picture of the immigrants arriving at Ellis Island and the words in the *Before you read* section. They discuss what they think the article is going to be about. Get students to come

together as a class to report. Do not correct any versions that are incorrect at this stage.

Now ask students to read the article silently and see if they were right. Tell them to make a note of any new words and to try and guess their meaning as they read. Help them with any words which they can't guess.

Exercise 2
Remind students of how to form questions in the past tense. Present *When was she born?* as a static question but do not go into any detail about the passive at this stage. Let students work individually preparing their questions. Go round and monitor, making sure that students are not concentrating on only one or two question words, and that their questions are grammatically correct.

Students then ask questions of each other in turn across the class.

EXAMPLE QUESTIONS
1   When was Assunta born?
2   Where was she born?
3   Where is Melfi?
4   What were her parents' names?
5   Why did the family emigrate/go/escape to New York?
6   When did they arrive in New York?
7   Where did they go to/settle?
8   What did Assunta do/Where did she work for several years?
9   When did she marry?
10 Who did she marry?
11 Why did she begin to make spaghetti sauce?
12 Where did she make the sauce?
13 Why did they move to a factory?
14 What did they call the sauce?
15 Where did they sell the sauce?
16 What did an American food company pay for the recipe?
17 When did they buy it?

Exercise 3
Ask students to form groups to try and retell the story. Go round and monitor. As you listen, make notes of any mistakes in verb tenses or prepositions.

GRAMMAR FOCUS
Use the notes in the Focus box to highlight the use of *ago* and *for.* Give and elicit more examples using the students' own lives and backgrounds, e.g. *The lesson began half an hour ago. Last year I went on holiday for two weeks.*

Exercise 4
Explain *over* (in this case – *more than*) and *a few.* If appropriate, point out the distinction between *few* (*not many*) and *a few* (*some*). Go through all

the events in the list and elicit suggestions.
Expect disagreements over the years. If you wish,
set the exercise as a project for homework.

KEY

1 Over two hundred years ago. (1789)
2 A few years ago. (1985)
3 About twenty years ago. (1969)
4 About seventy-five years ago. (1917)
5 About fifty years ago. (1939)

Exercise 5

Students prepare some questions using the cues
and then form pairs to ask each other the
questions.

Exercise 6

Draw attention to the last sentence and give some
more examples from your own life using *before*
and *after* + the *ing* form, e.g. *I went to university
ten years ago. I stayed there for three years.
After leaving university I got a job in a school in
London.* Students report what their partners said
using *in, for* and *ago, before* and *after.*

SUGGESTED LESSON BREAK

📼 Exercise 7 LISTENING

Remind students of the article in Unit 22 about
Lisa Aziz. Ask students to look at the words in
the *Before you listen* section and to look them up
in a dictionary. Ask them to imagine, without
looking at the skeleton schedule, what her
morning routine is for a television programme
that starts at 6 a.m. Students then copy the
skeleton schedule into their notebooks. Explain
pick up and *rehearsal.* Ask what students think
she does for the rest of the day.

PART 1

Play the first part of the interview on the tape for
students to complete the schedule.

PART 2

Ask students to copy the biographical chart into
their notebooks leaving plenty of space to write.
They can fill in Lisa's name and date of birth. If
you wish, pre-teach some vocabulary, e.g.
*newsreader, career, art history, religion,
journalism, local radio.* Play the tape once
through for students to get the feel of the whole
interview and to note that the information does
not come in the order of the headings in the
chart. Play the tape a second time, pausing at
intervals for students to note the information
required. Check the information and then play the
tape a third time for students to note down what
Lisa thinks about her present job and why she
thinks it's challenging.

TAPESCRIPT

PART 1

Listen to this interview and follow the
instructions in your Students' Book.

INTERVIEWER:
Lisa, how exactly would you describe your job?
LISA:
I work for, um, TV-am which is a breakfast
television station and I'm the main daily
newscaster. And every day I read seven bulletins.
(And) we start at six o'clock in the morning and I
finish at nine o'clock but the whole programme
finishes at nine twenty-five.
INTERVIEWER:
So that's an early start for you. What is your
typical day? What time do you get up, for
instance?
LISA:
Well, it's a very early start for me, um, I start, I
get up at three thirty in the morning and a car
comes to pick me up at about four and I get into
the building at about four fifteen, four twenty. I
have to, er, read the papers and then I have to
spend about one hour having my make-up done
and my hair done. And then we have a very very
quick rehearsal of about ten minutes at ten to six.

PART 2
INTERVIEWER:
Did you always want to be this? I mean, how did
you get into it?
LISA:
I never ever wanted to be a newsreader. Um, I
started thinking about what I was going to do as a
career when I was in my last year at university,
which was in London.
INTERVIEWER:
Yes, and you read art history and religion, wasn't
it?
LISA:
That's right. Yes. And in my third year I decided
I want to go, wanted to go into journalism which
was actually my favourite thing – writing was my
thing – and, um, journalism was the, the course to
take.
INTERVIEWER:
When was this?
LISA:
Not too long ago. Just six years ago I started and
I went straight into local radio in the north of
England. After about nine months I decided I
wanted to, to go into television.
INTERVIEWER:
What sort of childhood did you have? Where
were you born?
LISA:
Um, I was born in South Devon, which is where
my mother is from because she's English and my
father is from Bangladesh.

INTERVIEWER:
What do you really like about the job?
LISA:
I like it because it is challenging. For a start getting up is challenging. It's not very nice but it's a challenge.
INTERVIEWER:
What do you think is a test of a good presenter?
LISA:
I think it's keeping calm when you're hearing about six, seven people shouting down your ear.

Exercise 8 WRITING

Make sure that all the students have got an accurate account of Lisa's biography before they start the writing activity. Remind them to use the linkers *Then, And then, After ... ing.* Begin the composition on the board and then go round and monitor as students write. With weaker students, you might like to prepare a model composition about another personality for students to follow, before they write about Lisa Aziz.

SUGGESTED COMPOSITION
Lisa Aziz is ... years old. She is a television newscaster for an early morning breakfast television programme. She was born in South Devon. Her mother is English but her father is from Bangladesh.
After leaving school, she went to London University and studied art history and religion. She was very interested in journalism and took a course in journalism. She then got a job in local radio in the north of England. She worked there for about six years and then she got a job in television. She likes her job very much because it is very challenging and exciting.

Suggest one or two people that the students might like to research and help them with sources for their information. Alternatively, some students may prefer to write about themselves. In this case they should start by completing Extra activity 2, below.

EXTRA ACTIVITIES

1 Who were you?

Ask students to choose a year two, five, ten, fifteen or twenty years ago and to ask and answer questions about their lifestyle at that time. Dictate the following questions.
Where did you live? Where did you work?
How much did you earn? What car did you have?
What did you look like?
What sort of clothes did you wear?
What sort of music did you like?
What sort of food did you eat?
Who were your friends?
What did you spend your money on?

2 Autobiography

Students use the framework and headings in Part 2 of Exercise 7 to plan and write their own Curriculum Vitae. This can be expanded into a composition later, similar to the one suggested in Exercise 8 Writing.

FINALE

The photographs, dialogue and exercise

Ask students questions about the photographs to establish the context for each one:
Who is Adam talking to in Picture 1 and where are they? (He's talking to his brother Michael. They're in their shared flat.)
How does Adam feel? (Angry and upset)
Where is Adam in Picture 2 and who is he talking to? (He's in a bicycle shed, perhaps at the university. He's talking to Laura's friend Sarah.)
Where are Adam and Laura in Picture 3? (They're in the university library in the catalogue department.)
Do you think they are talking loudly or quietly? Why?
How do you think Adam feels in Picture 4? (Perhaps he feels surprised.)
Where is Laura going in Picture 5? What sort of room is it? (She's going into a lecture theatre at the university.)

Ask students to read the bubble dialogue in pairs and to answer the questions. Check these with the whole class.

▣ The tape

Play the tape of the dialogue.

TAPESCRIPT
ADAM: What am I going to do?
MICHAEL: Why don't you go and talk to her?

SARAH: I think she's in the library.
ADAM: O.K. I'll go and find her.

ADAM: How was the ball?
LAURA: Fine.
ADAM: And how is David?
LAURA: Adam, David's married!
ADAM: When did you discover that?
LAURA: Oh, ages ago. He invited me to the ball because his wife was ill.

LAURA: Anyway, it's my leaving party next week. I hope you're going to come.
ADAM: Maybe ... OK, I'll come.

Exercise 1

Ask students to mask as much of the text as they can, and explain that you want them just to look at the two photographs and to use their imaginations. First ask them who the people are in the small picture and ask them what the people are doing in both pictures. Teach the vocabulary *to say goodbye, to kiss somebody goodbye* and *to see somebody off.* Then ask them to suggest what the people are saying in both pictures. Write the suggestions on the board.

COMMUNICATION FOCUS

Ask students to look at the Focus box and to compare the sentences with the suggested list of expressions you have made on the board. Go through all the expressions in the Focus box, practising them chorally and individually. Point out the idea of making a promise in the expressions, *I'll send you a postcard!* and *I'll phone you on Monday.*

 Exercise 2

Play the tape once for students to listen and shadow the speakers, before they read the dialogue in threes. Ask them to change parts, thus reading the dialogue three times. Then ask several good threes to perform the conversation for the class.

Exercise 3 ROLEPLAY

Go through each situation. Invite students to suggest possible sentences. Then ask students to prepare and practise the conversations in pairs. Ask one or two pairs to act out their situations for the whole class.

 Exercise 4 LISTENING

Ask students to complete the dialogue and then read it in pairs. When they have changed parts, play the tape for them to see if they were right. Finish by asking the following questions:
Where is Laura going? (To Paris)
What's Adam going to do? (He's going to leave the travel agent's and travel abroad.)
What places is he thinking of visiting? (Poland or Czechoslovakia)
Where does Laura want him to visit? (California)
How is Laura travelling to London? (She's going by train.)

TAPESCRIPT AND KEY
ADAM: I'm going to miss you, Laura. Can't you stay? Just a few more weeks?
LAURA: I can't, Adam. I've got to go to Paris, remember? Anyway, you've got your job.
ADAM: I think I'm going to leave the travel agent's.
LAURA: What are you going to do?
ADAM: See the world. Travel abroad for a bit.
LAURA: Where to?
ADAM: I don't know. Eastern Europe. Maybe Poland or Czechoslovakia.
LAURA: Or maybe California?
ADAM: Maybe.
LAURA: Please do. I'd really like that.
ADAM: Are you sure?

LAURA: Sure.
ADAM: The train's coming. Phone me when you get to Paris.
LAURA: O.K.! Bye, Adam. Thanks for everything.
ADAM: Take care!

Exercise 5

Explain *farewell* (goodbye). Ask students to move round the class and choose someone to act their conversation with. Choose one pair to act a farewell conversation in front of the class.

To finish, ask if any of the students know of any famous farewell scenes from films, literature or opera, e.g the balcony scene in Shakespeare's play *Romeo and Juliet* or the death scene in Verdi's opera *La Traviata.*

EXTRA ACTIVITIES
1 Make a quiz

Students think of a person, alive or dead, real or imaginary and write eight sentences about them, grading the sentences, so that information is gradually revealed. The other students guess who the person is, e.g.
1 I am quite young.
2 I am American.
3 I am not living at home at the moment.
4 I don't come from a large family.
5 I've got dark hair.
6 I often ride a bicycle.
7 I am reading a play by Oliver Goldsmith.
8 I come from San Diego.
(Laura Martinelli)

2 Farewell song

If you have a farewell party with your class or if the class is finishing completely, you may like to teach the students the 'farewell' song, *Auld Lang Syne,* which is based on a poem by the Scottish poet, Robert Burns, and is traditionally sung in Scotland and the rest of Britain at midnight on New Year's Eve. Don't worry about the words, most British people have no idea what the words mean.

Auld Lang Syne
(Note that for this song, people join crossed hands in a circle. They move their arms up and down in time to the rhythm as they sing.)

Verse
Should auld acquaintance be forgot,
And never brought to min'?
Should auld acquaintance be forgot,
For auld lang syne.

Chorus
For auld lang syne, my dear,
For auld lang syne;
We'll tak' a cup o' kindness yet
For the sake of auld lang syne.

CHECK Units 36–40

(For advice on handling this section, see the notes for Check Units 1–5.)

Ex. 1 1 very well   2 very good   3 nervously
4 quietly   5 quiet   6 quickly   7 carefully
8 hard   9 late   10 comfortably (10 marks)

Ex. 2 1b   2c   3a   4c   5c (5 marks)

Ex. 3 1 I'm looking for a jacket.   2 one
3 are   you   4 try it on   5 doesn't suit me
6 Have you got it in black?   7 too small
8 a larger size   9 here's   10 I'll leave it
(10 marks)

Ex. 4 1 MONey   2 ADdress   3 INteresting
4 HOtel   5 JApan   6 TElephone   7 BEAUtiful
8 CHInese   9 INterview   10 COMfortable
(10 marks)

Ex. 5 1b   2b   3b   4a   5a   6a   7a   8b   9b
10a (10 marks)

Ex. 6 1 is   2 is studying   3 left   4 went
5 to study   6 is working   7 is having
8 looking after   9 has got to
10 is going/is going to go   11 to do
12 have only been   13 is going to be/will be
14 lived   15 is sharing/shares   16 has got
17 does not want   18 am going to miss/will miss
19 want   20 am looking forward (20 marks)

CHECK YOUR PROGRESS
(See notes for Units 1–5.)

LEARNING TO LEARN 8
Without reference to the Students' Book, conduct a general discussion on the best way to practise English outside the classroom and list the students' ideas on the board as they suggest them. Then ask them to look at the 'Learning to learn' section in their Students' Book and see if their ideas are the same. If this is the last lesson of the term or year, encourage students to continue their English by reading simplified readers such as those provided in the *Longman Structural Readers* series. Tell them to keep a notebook to record any language queries they may have either as a result of reading, or from the English they come into contact with.

If this is the end of the year, try to counsel students individually or in pairs and discuss their progress with them. You can suggest some language work that they might usefully do before you meet again in class.

Grammar index

Grammatical item	Example sentence	Unit
ADJECTIVES		
Common adjectives and their opposites	*a big/small town*	10
Comparative and superlative:		
longer adjectives	*Milan is more fashionable than Bologna.*	29
	Helsinki is the most beautiful.	29
shorter adjectives	*She's younger than you.*	28
	Who is the tallest student in your class?	28
irregular adjectives	*The weather is better abroad.*	28
spelling changes with *-er, -est*	*He's thinner than her.*	28
Demonstrative adjectives: *this, that, these those*	*Could I have that box of chocolates, please?*	16
Position of adjectives	*a boring town*	10
Possessive adjectives: *my, your, his, her, its, our, their*	*Her name's Christine.*	1, 21
Too + adjective	*It's too modern.*	(9), 36
ADVERBS		
Adverbs of degree:		
well, not at all, a little	*Can you speak French? No, not at all.*	6
very much, not much	*I like it very much.*	9
Adverbs of frequency	*She always gets up at seven thirty.*	12
Formation of adverbs with *-ly*	*Please drive slowly.*	37
Future time adverbials: *next . . .*	*What are you doing next weekend?*	26
Irregular adverbs of manner: *well, fast, early, late, hard*	*He speaks German very well.*	37
Past time adverbials: *yesterday, last . . .*	*They went to Disneyworld last week.*	20
Position of adverbs of manner	*Close the door quietly.*	37
Position of adverbs of degree	*I can swim very well.*	6
Position of adverbs of frequency	*She usually goes to the library in the morning.*	12
Present time adverbials: *at the moment*	*Keith is learning to windsurf at the moment.*	15
probably	*I think my brother Alex is probably (sleeping).*	15
Regular adverbs of manner	*Please drive slowly.*	37
ARTICLES		
Definite and indefinite articles: *a, an, the*	*a desk, an apple, the pen*	4
Definite article (*the*) with buildings	*Where's the Eiffel Tower?*	3
Definite article (*the*) with rivers, seas, oceans	*the Pacific Ocean, the North Sea, the River Ouse*	10
Zero article:		
with certain places after *go to*	*I go to school*	12
with meals	*Lunch is at one.*	12
with *home*	*I go home at five.*	12
Zero article plural	*They're keys.*	4
CLAUSES		
Time clause *when* (= *whenever*) + present tense	*When I wake up on a rainy day I feel depressed.*	39
CONJUNCTIONS		
and, but	*My English is quite good but my Russian is very bad.*	3
because	*I like summer because I like swimming.*	19
Sentence linkers: *after . . . -ing*	*After leaving school she went to university.*	40
Sequence of time: *then, after that, after*	*After supper I go out with friends.*	12, 25
DETERMINERS		
no, some, any with countable and uncountable nouns	*We need some eggs.*	(14), 17
a little	*I can play the piano a little.*	6
ENUMERATIVES		
a cup/glass/packet/bottle of . . .	*a bottle of mineral water*	16

Grammatical item	Example sentence	Unit

GERUNDS (VERBAL NOUNS)

after	*After leaving school she went to university.*	40
enjoy	*I enjoyed meeting you.*	Fin
like/hate/love	*I hate cooking.*	9
No	*No fishing.*	38
What about (suggestions)	*What about asking that woman?*	23

INTENSIFIERS

too + adjective	*It's too big.*	(9), 36
quite, very	*I can type quite well.*	6

MODAL VERBS

can (ability)	*I can speak English.*	6
can (permission/prohibition)	*You can/can't smoke in here.*	38
can, could (request)	*Could I have a T-shirt, please?*	16
have got to	*I've got to go to the bank.*	35
must (obligation)	*You must fasten your seatbelts.*	38
will (decisions)	*I'll have the chicken.*	31
will (promise)	*I'll send you a postcard.*	Fin
Would you like (offers)	*Would you like a glass of water?*	(31), 34
	Would you like to lie down?	
Would you like to (invitation)	*Would you like to come?/Yes, I'd love to.*	26, (31)
would like (requests)	*I'd like a box of tissues.*	16, 31

NOUNS

Countable and uncountable nouns	*an egg/some bread*	17
Genitive *'s/s'* for singular and plural	*my mother's name/my parents' names*	1
Regular plural with *s*	*They're pencils.*	4

PREPOSITIONS

by with means of transport	*I never travel by plane.*	13
from, to with place and distance	*I always walk to school.*	3
Genitive *of* with inanimate nouns	*What's the name of your school?*	1
on with days of the week	*See you on Friday.*	2
Place:		
in, from with cities	*I'm from Turin.*	3
in, on	*They're on the desk.*	4
for, with, in, at, near	*We live near Leeds.*	8
in the . . . of, not far from	*York is in the north-east of England.*	10
next to, opposite, on the corner of, in front of, between, behind, outside, on the left/right of, over, under, inside	*There's a taxi outside the supermarket.*	18
Time:		
at, on, in, from . . . to	*The library opens at nine a.m.*	11
on with dates	*Are you doing anything on 8th July?*	26
ago, for	*The story began nearly 100 years ago.*	40
with (description)	*He's tall with black hair.*	24

PRONOUNS

Demonstrative pronouns:		
that,	*Who's that?*	1
this, these, those	*What are these?*	4
this, this is with person	*Claudia, this is Tony.*	2
Indefinite pronouns: *one, ones*	*Could I have the big one?*	16
Object pronouns: *me, you, her, him, it, us, you, them*	*I hate him.*	9
Personal (subject) pronouns:		
I, you, he, she, it,	*He's called George.*	1
we, they	*We're Italian.*	3
Possessive pronouns: *mine, yours, his, hers, its, ours, theirs*	*Whose car is this? It's mine.*	21
some, any, no	*Can you get some?*	17
that, it with sums of money	*How much is it? It's £7.99.*	16

QUESTION WORDS

How?	*How are you?*	2
How long?, How far?	*How long does the journey take?*	13
How many?	*How many brothers has she got?*	7
How many times?	*How many times have you seen this film?*	33
How much?	*How much is this one?*	16

Grammatical item	Example sentence	Unit
How old?	*How old are you?*	5
What?, Who?	*What's your name? Who's that?*	1
What time?	*What time is the party?*	11
When?	*When does summer start in Britain?*	19
Where?	*Where are you from?*	3
Whose?	*Whose car is this?*	21
Why?	*Why doesn't he move to London?*	13
VERBS		
be:		
present – *am, are, is*	*I'm Maria.*	1
present – all forms	*She's English.*	3
past – *was, were*	*My grandmother was Irish.*	7
past – all forms	*It was hot.*	19
be called	*She's called Chris for short.*	1
be like	*What's it like?*	10
	What was the weather like?	19
	What's she like?	24
feel	*I don't feel very well.*	34
feel with adjectives of physical discomfort	*I feel sick.*	34
Gerund – spelling rules:		
verbs ending in *-e*	*I'm writing a letter.*	15
verbs ending in *-ie*	*He's lying on the beach.*	15
one-syllable verbs ending in one consonant	*I'm getting quite fit.*	15
going to future: all forms	*I'm going to have a party.*	23
have got (availability)	*Have you got any money?*	17
have got (family relations): all forms	*I've got two brothers.*	7
have got with nouns of physical discomfort	*I've got a headache.*	34
have got with physical characteristics	*She's got long hair.*	24
Imperative	*Drive slowly.*	37
Infinitive of purpose	*She's going to Britain to learn English.*	35
Let's (suggestions)	*Let's ask that woman.*	23
Past simple:		
regular	*Bobby liked Space Mountain.*	20
irregular	*We went to Florida.*	20
narrative	*They got up at four in the morning and . . .*	25
with *ago, for*	*He worked there for three months.*	40
Present continuous: all forms	*He's writing a letter.*	15
Present continuous future: all forms	*What are you doing next weekend?*	26
Present continuous/present simple contrast	*Julian lives in Bordeaux. At the moment he is living on a farm in Australia.*	30
Present perfect:		
with *just*	*She has just passed an exam.*	32
with *ever*	*Have you ever been to Africa?*	33
Present simple:		
personal information	*She lives in Lisbon.*	8, (30)
likes and dislikes	*Do you like cooking?*	9
fixed times	*What time do the banks open?*	11
routine	*Carlos gets up at six thirty.*	12
frequency	*She sometimes goes to the theatre.*	12
with time clause *when*	*When I wake up on a rainy day, I feel depressed.*	39
there is/are	*There's a chair.*	14, 18
want + infinitive with *to*	*I want to buy a guidebook.*	18

Vocabulary and expressions

Pronunciation is shown in the system used in the *Longman Dictionary of Contemporary English*. The number indicates the unit where the word first occurs. The symbol /ɪ̥/ as in /ˈæksɪ̥dənt/ indicates that there are two alternative pronunciations, e.g. /ˈæksɪdənt/ or /ˈæksədənt/.

PV = Preview, LL = Learning to learn, FL = Fluency, CH = Check, WB = Workbook, FN = Finale

A

about /əˈbaʊt/ 5
abroad /əˈbrɔːd/ 30
accident /ˈæksɪ̥dənt/ **PV31-35**
accountant /əˈkaʊntənt/ 13
across /əˈkrɒs/ 18
act (v) /ækt/ 6
actor /ˈæktər/ 25
address /əˈdres/ 5
address book /əˈdres ˌbʊk/ 4
advice /ədˈvaɪs/ 36
aeroplane /ˈeərəpleɪn/ 30
afraid (I'm . . .) /əˈfreɪd (aɪm . . .)/ 26
after that /ˌɑːftə ˈðæt/ 12
afternoon /ˌɑːftəˈnuːn/ 2
again /əˈgen/ **LL1-5**
age /eɪdʒ/ 5
ago /əˈgəʊ/ **PV36-40**
agree /əˈgriː/ 9
airport /ˈeəpɔːt/ 8
alarm clock /əˈlɑːm ˌklɒk/ 21
album /ˈælbəm/ 9
alive /əˈlaɪv/ 7
all /ɔːl/ **PV21-25**
all (at . . .) /ɔːl (ət . . .)/ 6
allergic /əˈlɜːdʒɪk/ 22
all right /ɔːl raɪt/ 15
alone /əˈləʊn/ 8
a lot of /əˈlɒt əv/ 22
alphabet /ˈælfəbet/ 4
also /ˈɔːlsəʊ/ 3
altogether /ˌɔːltəˈgeðər/ 14
always /ˈɔːlwɪ̥z/ 12
amusing /əˈmjuːzɪŋ/ 25
ancestor /ˈænsestər/ 7
and /ænd/ 1
angry /ˈæŋgri/ 21, **PV36-40**
ankle /ˈæŋkəl/ 34
anorak /ˈænəræk/ 22
another /əˈnʌðər/ 27
answer /ˈɑːnsər/ 7
answerphone /ˈɑːnsəfəʊn/ 27
any /ˈeni/ 7
anything /ˈeniθɪŋ/ 26
anything else? /ˌeniθɪŋ ˈels/ 16
anyway /ˈeniweɪ/ 33
apple /ˈæpəl/ 4
April /ˈeɪprəl/ 19
arm /ɑːm/ 34
armchair /ˈɑːmtʃeər/ 14
arrange /əˈreɪndʒ/ **PV36-40**

arrive /əˈraɪv/ 11
art gallery /ˈɑːt gæləri/ 10
artist /ˈɑːtɪ̥st/ 18
ask /ɑːsk/ 6
asleep /əˈsliːp/ 12
at all /ət ˈɔːl/ 6
at home /ət ˈhəʊm/ 8
atlas /ˈætləs/ 21
at the moment /ət ðə ˈməʊmənt/ 15
August /ˈɔːgəst/ 19
aunt /ɑːnt/ 7
autumn /ˈɔːtəm/ 19
away /əˈweɪ/ 13
awful /ˈɔːfəl/ 20

B

baby /ˈbeɪbi/ 7
back (n) /bæk/ 34
back (at the . . .) /bæk (ət ðə . . .)/ 14
back (call . . .) /bæk (kɔːl . . .)/ 27
bacon /ˈbeɪkən/ 17
bad /bæd/ 3
bag /bæg/ 4
ball /bɔːl/ 6
ball (= dance) /bɔːl/ **PV36-40**
banana /bəˈnɑːnə/ 17
bang (v) /bæŋ/ 25
bank /bæŋk/ 1
bar /bɑːr/ 15
bargain (n) /ˈbɑːgɪ̥n/ 36
bath /bɑːθ/ 14
bathroom /ˈbɑːθrʊm/ 14
battery /ˈbætəri/ 17
be /bi/ 1
beach /biːtʃ/ 10
beard /bɪəd/ 24
beautiful /ˈbjuːtɪ̥fəl/ 10
because /bɪˈkɒz/ 13
become /bɪˈkʌm/ 36
bed /bed/ 12
bedroom /ˈbedrʊm/ 14
beer /bɪər/ 31
before /bɪˈfɔːr/ 12
begin /bɪˈgɪn/ 40
behind /bɪˈhaɪnd/ 18
beige /beɪʒ/ 22
believe /bɪ̥ˈliːv/ 36
belong to /bɪˈlɒŋ tuː/ 21
best /best/ 10, 28
best-dressed /ˈbest-drest/ 22

better /ˈbetər/ 28
between /bɪˈtwiːn/ 18
bible /ˈbaɪbəl/ 21
bicycle /ˈbaɪsɪkəl/ 13
big /bɪg/ 7
bill /bɪl/ 31
biscuit /ˈbɪskɪ̥t/ 17
bit (a . . .) /bɪt (ə . . .)/ **PV31-35**
black /blæk/ 4
blazer /ˈbleɪzər/ 22
blonde (adj) /blɒnd/ 24
blouse /blaʊz/ 22
blue /bluː/ 4
boat /bəʊt/ 13
bomb /bɒm/ 29
book (n) /bʊk/ 1
book (v) /bʊk/ 35
bookcase /ˈbʊk-keɪs/ 14
bookshop /ˈbʊkʃɒp/ 18
boots /buːts/ 22
bored /bɔːd/ 39
boring /ˈbɔːrɪŋ/ 10
born (to be . . .) /bɔːn (tə bi . . .)/ 40
both /bəʊθ/ 12
bottle /ˈbɒtl/ 16
boutique /buːˈtiːk/ 37
bowl /bəʊl/ **WB4**
box /bɒks/ 16
boy /bɔɪ/ 1
bracelet /ˈbreɪslɪ̥t/ 21
bread /bred/ 17
break (v) /breɪk/ 32
breakfast /ˈbrekfəst/ 12
bring /brɪŋ/ 23
brother /ˈbrʌðər/ 1
brown /braʊn/ 4
building /ˈbɪldɪŋ/ 9
bump (v) /bʌmp/ 24
bunch (. . . of flowers) /ˌbʌntʃ (. . . əv ˈflaʊəs)/ 25
bungalow /ˈbʌŋgələʊ/ 30
bus /bʌs/ 8, 13
bus driver /ˈbʌs ˌdraɪvər/ 8
businessman /ˈbɪznɪ̥smən/ 29
bus station /ˈbʌs ˌsteɪʃən/ 18
busy /ˈbɪzi/ **PV21-25**
but /bət/ 1
butter /ˈbʌtər/ 17
buy /baɪ/ 17
by /baɪ/ 13
Bye! /baɪ/ **PV1-5**
by the way /ˌbaɪ ðə ˈweɪ/ 30

C

café /ˈkæfeɪ/ 1
cafeteria /ˌkæfɪ̥ˈtɪəriə/ 12
cake /keɪk/ 37
call (phone . . .) /kɔːl (ˈfəʊn . . .)/ **PV21-25**
call back /kɔːl ˈbæk/ 27
called (to be . . .) /kɔːld (tə bi . . .)/ 1
camera /ˈkæmərə/ 16
can (n) /kæn/ 16
can (v) /kæn/ 6
capital /ˈkæpɪ̥tl/ 3
captain /ˈkæptɪ̥n/ 32
car /kɒːr/ 13
card (playing) /kɑːd (ˈpleɪŋ . . .)/ 9
card (= postcard) /kɑːd/ 15
cardigan /ˈkɑːdɪgən/ 22
careful(ly) /ˈkeəfəl(li)/ 37
carnival /ˈkɑːnɪ̥vəl/ 19
car park /ˈkɑː pɑːk/ 18
carpet /ˈkɑːpɪ̥t/ 14
carton /ˈkɑːtn/ **PV16-20**
cash (v) /kæʃ/ 35
cassette recorder /kəˈset rɪˌkɔːdər/ 4
casual /ˈkæʒuəl/ 22
cat /kæt/ 15
catch /kætʃ/ 24
catch a train /ˌkætʃ ə ˈtreɪn/ 13
cathedral /kəˈθiːdrəl/ 10
ceiling /ˈsiːlɪŋ/ 14
central heating /ˌsentrəl ˈhiːtɪŋ/ 14
centre /ˈsentər/ 8
century /ˈsentʃəri/ 11
cereal /ˈsɪəriəl/ 17
certainly /ˈsɜːtnli/ 16
chair /tʃeər/ 4
chambermaid /ˈtʃeɪmbəmeɪd/ 30
change (v) (money) /tʃeɪndʒ/ 18, 35
change (v) (of weather) /tʃeɪndʒ/ 19
changing room /ˈtʃeɪndʒɪŋ ˌruːm/ 36
cheap /tʃiːp/ 16
checked (pattern) /tʃekt/ 22
check-in (n) /ˈtʃekɪn/ 8
check in (v) /ˌtʃek ˈɪn/ 35
cheerful(ly) /ˈtʃɪəfəl(li)/ 37
cheese /tʃiːz/ 17

117

chemist /'kem$\frac{1}{2}$st/ **16**
cheque /tʃek/ **35**
chicken /'tʃɪk$\frac{1}{2}$n/ **17, 31**
child /tʃaɪld/ **7**
children /'tʃɪldrən/ **7**
chips /tʃɪps/ **16**
chocolate /'tʃɒkl$\frac{1}{2}$t/ **16**
choose /tʃu:z/ **9**
church /tʃɜ:tʃ/ **10, 12**
cigarette /ˌsɪgə'ret/ **FL6-10**
cinema /'sɪn$\frac{1}{2}$mə/ **9**
city /'sɪti/ **3**
class /klɑ:s/ **2**
classical (music) /'klæsɪkəl/ **9**
clean (adj) /kli:n/ **28**
clean (v) /kli:n/ **9**
clear(ly) /'klɪə^r(li)/ **37**
clerk /klɑ:k/ **18**
climb (v) /klaɪm/ **33**
clock /klɒk/ **11**
close (v) /kləʊz/ **11**
clothes /kləʊðz/ **FL6-10, 22**
cloud(y) /'klaʊd(i)/ **19**
coast /kəʊst/ **PV6-10**
coat /kəʊt/ **22**
cocktail /'kɒkteɪl/ **31**
coffee /'kɒfi/ **17**
cold (adj) /kəʊld/ **16**
cold (n) /kəʊld/ **34**
collect /kə'lekt/ **13**
college /'kɒlɪdʒ/ **1**
colour /'kʌlə^r/ **4**
come /kʌm/ **PV31-35**
comedy (film) /'kɒm$\frac{1}{2}$di/ **9**
comfortable /'kʌmftəbəl/ **37**
come from /'kʌm frɒm/ **PV6-10**
compact disc player (CD) /ˌkɒmpækt 'dɪsk ˌpleɪə^r (ˌsi: 'di:)/ **4**
company /'kʌmpəni/ **1**
compare /kəm'peə^r/ **28**
compartment /kəm'pɑ:tmənt/ **25**
competition /ˌkɒmp$\frac{1}{2}$'tɪʃən/ **32**
computer /kəm'pju:tə^r/ **6**
concert /'kɒnsət/ **11**
conductor /kən'dʌktə^r/ **25**
confident(ly) /'kɒnf$\frac{1}{2}$dənt(li)/ **37**
conversation /ˌkɒnvə'seɪʃən/ **6**
cook (v) /kʊk/ **6**
cooker /'kʊkə^r/ **14**
cool /ku:l/ **19**
cordless /'kɔ:dləs/ **27**
corner /'kɔ:nə^r/ **PV16-20**
cost (v) /kɒst/ **16**
cough (n) /kɒf/ **34**
cough (v) /kɒf/ **24**
Could I have . . .? /'kʊd aɪ ˌhæv . . ./ **16**
country /'kʌntri/ **3**
country (opp. town) /'kʌntri/ **8**
countryside /'kʌntrisaɪd/ **28**
couple /'kʌpəl/ **3**
course (of study) /kɔ:s/ **20**
course (of . . .) /kɔ:s (əv . . .)/ **36**
cousin /'kʌzən/ **7**
crash (v) /'kræʃ/ **25**
credit card /'kred$\frac{1}{2}$t ˌkɑ:d/ **36**
crisps /krɪsps/ **16**
cross (v) /krɒs/ **24**

cry /kraɪ/ **39**
cup /kʌp/ **17**
cupboard /'kʌbəd/ **14**
curly /'kɜ:li/ **24**
curtain /'kɜ:tn/ **14**
cycle /'saɪkəl/ **9**

D

dad (= father) /dæd/ **24**
dance /'dɑ:ns/ **6**
dangerous /'deɪndʒərəs/ **29**
dark (of colour) /dɑ:k/ **PV12-25, 22**
date /deɪt/ **26**
daughter /'dɔ:tə^r/ **7**
day /deɪ/ **2**
dead /ded/ **7**
death /deθ/ **18**
December /dɪ'sembə^r/ **19**
deliver /dɪ'lɪvə^r/ **13**
department store /dɪ'pɑ:tmənt ˌstɔ:^{r}/ **36**
depend (it depends) /dɪ'pend (ˌɪt dɪ'pendz)/ **13**
depressed /dɪ'prest/ **39**
desk /desk/ **4**
dessert /dɪ'zɜ:t/ **17**
diary /'daɪəri/ **4**
dictionary /'dɪkʃənəri/ **4**
die /daɪ/ **15**
different /'dɪfərənt/ **17**
difficult /'dɪfɪkəlt/ **CH1-5, 27**
dining room /'daɪnɪŋ ˌru:m/ **14**
dinner /'dɪnə^r/ **20**
dirty /'dɜ:ti/ **28**
disappear /ˌdɪsə'pɪə^r/ **17**
disco /'dɪskəʊ/ **12**
discover /dɪs'kʌvə^r/ **FN**
dish (food) /dɪʃ/ **17**
divorced /d$\frac{1}{2}$'vɔ:st/ **5**
dizzy /'dɪzi/ **PV31-35**
do /du:/ **2**
doctor /'dɒktə^r/ **9**
dog /dɒg/ **15**
doll /dɒl/ **39**
dolphin /'dɒlf$\frac{1}{2}$n/ **32**
door /dɔ:^{r}/ **14**
double /'dʌbəl/ **5**
downstairs /ˌdaʊn'steəz/ **14**
draw /drɔ:/ **6**
drawer /drɔ:^{r}/ **4**
dress /dres/ **22**
dressing table /'dresɪŋ ˌteɪbəl/ **14**
drill (n) /drɪl/ **21**
drink /drɪŋk/ **15**
drive (v) /draɪv/ **6**
drop (v) /drɒp/ **32**
dry /draɪ/ **19, 24**

E

ear /ɪə^r/ **34**
early /'ɜ:li/ **FL11-15, 37**
earn /ɜ:n/ **30**
earthquake /'ɜ:θkweɪk/ **40**
east /i:st/ **10**
easy /'i:zi/ **CH1-5**
eat /i:t/ **2**
economy /ɪ'kɒnəmi/ **29**
egg /eg/ **17**
elbow /'elbəʊ/ **34**

electric (drill) /ɪ'lektrɪk (drɪl)/ **21**
else (anything . . .?) /els (ˌeniθɪŋ . . .)/ **16**
emigrate /'em$\frac{1}{2}$greɪt/ **40**
end /end/ **40**
engineer /ˌendʒ$\frac{1}{2}$'nɪə^r/ **13**
enjoy /ɪn'dʒɔɪ/ **9**
envelope /'envələʊp/ **4**
escape (v) /ɪ'skeɪp/ **40**
even /'i:vən/ **27**
evening /'i:vnɪŋ/ **2**
ever /'evə^r/ **33**
every (day) /ˌevri ('deɪ)/ **12**
everything /'evriθɪŋ/ **33**
everywhere /'evriweə^r/ **27**
exactly /ɪg'zæktli/ **10**
exam(ination) /ɪg,zæm($\frac{1}{2}$'neɪʃən)/ **32**
except /ɪk'sept/ **11**
excited /ɪk'saɪt$\frac{1}{2}$d/ **39**
Excuse me. /ɪk'skju:z mi/ **18**
expensive /ɪk'spensɪv/ **16**
extra /'ekstrə/ **40**
eye /aɪ/ **24, 34**

F

factory /'fæktəri/ **8**
fair (appearance) /feə^r/ **24**
fall (v) /fɔ:l/ **24**
fall off /ˌfɔ:l 'ɒf/ **PV31-35**
family /'fæməli/ **7**
famous /'feɪməs/ **10**
far /fɑ:^{r}/ **10**
farm /fɑ:m/ **8**
fashionable /'fæʃənəbəl/ **29**
fast (adv) /fɑ:st/ **37**
fat /fæt/ **24, 28**
father /'fɑ:ðə^r/ **1**
favourite /'feɪvər$\frac{1}{2}$t/ **1**
February /'februəri/ **19**
feel /fi:l/ **PV31-35, 34**
few (a . . .) /fju: (ə . . .)/ **11**
film /fɪlm/ **9**
find /faɪnd/ **21**
Fine, thanks. /ˌfaɪn ˌθæŋks/ **2**
finger /'fɪŋgə^r/ **34**
finish /'fɪnɪʃ/ **11**
firm(ly) /'fɜ:m(li)/ **37**
first (name) /fɜ:st (neɪm)/ **5**
fish (n) /fɪʃ/ **17**
fish (v) /fɪʃ/ **38**
flag /flæg/ **WB4**
flat (n) /flæt/ **5**
flight /flaɪt/ **11**
floor /flɔ:^{r}/ **14**
flower /'flaʊə^r/ **15**
flowery /'flaʊəri/ **22**
fluent(ly) /'flu:ənt(li)/ **6**
fly (n) /flaɪ/ **30**
fly (v) /flaɪ/ **29**
fog /fɒg/ **19**
foggy /'fɒgi/ **19**
folk song /'fəʊk ˌsɒŋ/ **23**
food /fu:d/ **17**
foot /fʊt/ **34**
forest /'fɒr$\frac{1}{2}$st/ **38**
forget /fə'get/ **30**
fortnight /'fɔ:tnaɪt/ **11**
for short /fə 'ʃɔ:t/ **1**
free (opp. busy) /fri:/ **26**
freezer /'fri:zə^r/ **14**
fresh /freʃ/ **31**

Friday /'fraɪdi/ **2**
fridge /frɪdʒ/ **14**
friend /frend/ **1**
friendly /'frendli/ **24**
from /frəm/ **PV1-5**
front (n) /frʌnt/ **14**
front (in . . . of) /frʌnt (ɪn . . . əv)/ **18**
fun /fʌn/ **30**
funny /'fʌni/ **37**
furniture /'fɜ:nɪtʃə^r/ **14**

G

garage /'gærɑ:ʒ, -ɪdʒ/ **14**
garden (n) /'gɑ:dn/ **14**
garden (v) /'gɑ:dn/ **9**
gently /'dʒentli/ **PV36-40**
get (= buy) /get/ **17**
get home/to work /get 'həʊm/tə 'wɜ:k/ **13**
get undressed /get ˌʌn'drest/ **25**
get up (v) /get 'ʌp/ **PV11-15**
girl /gɜ:l/ **1**
give /gɪv/ **36**
give (me a ring) /ˌgɪv (mi ə 'rɪŋ)/ **PV6-10**
glass (n) /glɑ:s/ **16**
glasses (= spectacles) /'glɑ:s$\frac{1}{2}$z/ **24**
go /gəʊ/ **PV1-5**
go home /gəʊ 'həʊm/ **12**
gold /gəʊld/ **21**
good /gʊd/ **3**
Good afternoon. /gʊd ˌɑ:ftə'nu:n/ **2**
Goodbye. /gʊd'baɪ/ **2**
Good evening. /gʊd 'i:vnɪŋ/ **2**
good looking /gʊd 'lʊkɪŋ/ **24**
Good morning. /gʊd 'mɔ:nɪŋ/ **2**
Goodnight /gʊd'naɪt/ **2**
go to bed /ˌgəʊ tə 'bed/ **PV11-15**
government /'gʌvəmənt/ **8**
grandfather /'græn,fɑ:ðə^r/ **7**
grandmother /'græn,mʌðə^r/ **7**
grandparents /'græn,peərənts/ **7**
great (= big) /greɪt/ **33**
great (= good) /greɪt/ **15**
green /gri:n/ **4**
group /gru:p/ **PV26-30**
grown-up (adj) /grəʊn 'ʌp/ **8**
guide book /'gaɪd bʊk/ **18**
guitar /gɪ'tɑ:^{r}/ **6**

H

hair /heə^r/ **PV21-25**
half /hɑ:f/ **11**
hall /hɔ:l/ **14**
hamburger /'hæmbɜ:gə^r/ **17**
hand /hænd/ **34**
handsome /'hænsəm/ **24**
happen /'hæpən/ **25**
happy /'hæpi/ **32**
Happy birthday! /ˌhæpi 'bɜ:θdeɪ/ **WB2**
hard (adv) /hɑ:d/ **37**
hard (= difficult) /hɑ:d/ **30**
hat /hæt/ **15**
harbour /'hɑ:bə^r/ **10**
hate /heɪt/ **9**

have /hæv/ 2
have got /hæv gɒt/ 7
Have a nice evening! /ˌhæv ə
 naɪs 'iːvnɪŋ/ 2
have lunch /hæv 'lʌntʃ/ 12
head /hed/ 34
headache /'hedeɪk/ 34
hear /hɪəʳ/ 6
heavy /'hevi/ 28
Hello /hə'ləʊ/ 1
help (Can I . . . you?) /help
 (kən aɪ . . . ju)/ PV1-5
here /hɪəʳ/ PV1-5
Hi! /haɪ/ 2
high /haɪ/ 28
historical /hɪ'stɒrɪkəl/ 10
hit /hɪt/ PV31-35
hobby /'hɒbi/ 3
holiday /'hɒlᵻdi/ 15
home /həʊm/ 14
homesick /'həʊmˌsɪk/ 39
honest(ly) /'ɒnᵻst(li)/ 37
honey /'hʌni/ 17
hope /həʊp/ 15
horror (film) 'hɒrəʳ/ 9
horse /hɔːs/ 6
horseriding /'hɔːsˌraɪdɪŋ/ 30
hospital /'hɒspɪtl/ 12
hostel /'hɒstl/ 8
hot /hɒt/ 19
hotel /həʊ'tel/ 16
hour /aʊəʳ/ 11
house /haʊs/ 8
How? /haʊ/ 4
How are you? /ˌhaʊ əʳ 'ju/ 2
How do you do? /ˌhaʊ də ju
 'duː/ 2
How far? /haʊ 'fɑːʳ/ 13
How many? /haʊ 'meni/ 7
How much? /haʊ 'mʌtʃ/ 16
How often? /haʊ 'ɒfən/ 12
How old? /haʊ 'əʊld/ 5
hungry /'hʌŋgri/ 25
hurt (v) /hɜːt/ PV31-35
husband /'hʌzbənd/ 7

I

ice cream /aɪs 'kriːm/ 31
identity card /aɪ'dentᵻti
 ˌkɑːd/ 27
I don't know /aɪ ˌdəʊnt 'nəʊ/ 1
ill /ɪl/ 34
I'm afraid /aɪm ə'freɪd/ 26
immediately /ɪ'miːdiətli/ 37
important /ɪm'pɔːtənt/ 5, 23
in /ɪn/ 1
industrial /ɪn'dʌstriəl/ 10
inside /ɪn'saɪd/ 18
interesting /'ɪntrᵻstɪŋ/ 10
international
 /ˌɪntə'næʃənəl/ 30
interview /'ɪntəvjuː/ 37
into /'ɪntʊ/ 25
invite /ɪn'vaɪt/ PV26-30

J

jacket /'dʒækᵻt/ 22
January /'dʒænjuəri/ 19
jeans /dʒiːnz/ 16, 22
jewellery /'dʒuːəlri/ 22
job /dʒɒb/ 8
jog (v) /dʒɒg/ 9
journey /'dʒɜːni/ 13

juice /dʒuːs/ PV16-20
July /dʒʊ'laɪ/ 19
June /dʒuːn/ 19
just (adv) /dʒʌst/ 10

K

keep fit /kiːp 'fɪt/ 9
key /kiː/ 4
kilometre /kɪ'lɒmɪtəʳ/ 13
kitchen /'kɪtʃᵻn/ 14
knee /niː/ 34
know (fact) /nəʊ/ 1
know (a city/a person)
 /nəʊ/ 10

L

lager /'lɑːgəʳ/ 31
lake /leɪk/ 38
lamb /læm/ 31
lamp /læmp/ 4
land (n) /lænd/ 32
land (v) /lænd/ 32
language /'læŋgwɪdʒ/ 3
large /lɑːdʒ/ 16
last (week) /lɑːst (wiːk)/ 20
late /leɪt/ 23
later /'leɪtəʳ/ 27
laugh (v) /lɑːf/ 25
lazy /'leɪzi/ 17
leaf /liːf/ 19
learn /lɜːn/ 15
least /liːst/ 28
leave /liːv/ 11
leave a message /ˌliːv ə
 'mesɪdʒ/ 27
left (on the . . .) /left (ɒn ðə
 . . .)/ 18
leg /leg/ 32, 34
lemonade /ˌlemə'neɪd/ 16
less /les/ 28
let's /lets/ PV21-25
letter /'letəʳ/ 4
library /'laɪbrəri/ PV11-15
lie down /laɪ (daʊn)/ 15
life /laɪf/ 13
lift (v) /lɪft/ 24
light (of colour) /laɪt/ 22
like (v) /laɪk/ PV6-10
like (to be . . .)
 /laɪk (tə bi . . .)/ 10
lion /'laɪən/ 33
listen to /'lɪsən tuː/ 15
litre /'liːtəʳ/ 16
little (a . . .) (adj)
 /'lɪtl (ə . . .)/ 3
little (a . . .) (adv)
 /'lɪtl (ə . . .)/ 6
live (v) /lɪv/ PV6-10
lively /'laɪvli/ 28
loaf /ləʊf/ 16
lock (v) /lɒk/ 25
lonely /'ləʊnli/ 30
long (hair) /lɒŋ/ 24
long (time) /lɒŋ/ 13
look after /lʊk 'ɑːftəʳ/ 8
look at /'lʊk æt/ PV21-25
look for /'lʊk fɔːʳ/ 9
look like /'lʊk laɪk/ 24
lose /luːz/ 21
lottery /'lɒtəri/ 32
loud(ly) /'laʊd(li)/ 37
love (v) /lʌv/ 9

love (from) /lʌv (frəm)/ 15
lovely /'lʌvli/ PV6-10
low /ləʊ/ 28, 38
lunch /lʌntʃ/ 12

M

machine /mə'ʃiːn/ 27
magazine /ˌmægə'ziːn/ 16
main (meal) /meɪn (miːl)/ 17
mainland /'meɪnlənd/ 30
make a cake /meɪk ə 'keɪk/ 37
make coffee /meɪk 'kɒfi/ 15
make a journey /meɪk ə
 'dʒɜːni/ 25
make money /meɪk 'mʌni/ 40
make a noise /meɪk ə 'nɔɪz/ 37
make-up (n) /'meɪkʌp/ 37
man /mæn/ 3
mansion /'mænʃən/ 14
many /'meni/ 10
map /mæp/ 3, 18
March /mɑːtʃ/ 19
market /'mɑːkᵻt/ 33
marmalade /'mɑːməleɪd/ 17
married /'mærid/ 5
marvellous /'mɑːvələs/ 20
matter (What's the . . .?)
 /'mætəʳ (wɒts ðə . . .)/ 6
May /meɪ/ 19
maybe /'meɪbi/ 15
meal /miːl/ 17
mean (v) /miːn/ LL1-5
meat /miːt/ 17
medicine /'medsən/ 34
medium (height) /'miːdɪəm
 (ˌhaɪt)/ 24
meet /miːt/ 8
menu /'menjuː/ 6
message /'mesɪdʒ/ 27
midday /ˌmid'deɪ/ 11
middle (name) /'mɪdl
 (neɪm)/ 5
midnight /'mɪdnaɪt/ 11
mile /maɪl/ 13
milk /mɪlk/ 17
mineral water /'mɪnərəl
 ˌwɔːtəʳ/ 16
minute /'mɪnᵻt/ PV11-15
mirror /'mɪrəʳ/ 14
Miss /mɪs/ 5
miss (a turn) /mɪs (ə 'tɜːn)/ 32
modern /'mɒdn/ 9
Monday /'mʌndi/ 2
money /'mʌni/ 17
month /mʌnθ/ 11, 19
more /mɔːʳ/ 13, 28
morning /'mɔːnɪŋ/ 2
most /məʊst/ 28
mother /'mʌðəʳ/ 1
mountain /'maʊntᵻn/ 20
moustache /mə'stɑːʃ/ 24
mouth /maʊθ/ 34
move /muːv/ 32
Mr /'mɪstəʳ/ 1
Mrs /'mɪsᵻz/ 1
Ms /mɪz, məz/ 1, 5
much /mʌtʃ/ PV6-10
mug /mʌg/ 16
museum /mju'zɪəm/ 10
mushroom /'mʌʃruːm/ 31
music /'mjuːzɪk/ 6
musician /mju'zɪʃən/ 8
must /məst/ 2

N

name /neɪm/ PV1-5
nationality /ˌnæʃə'nælᵻti/ 3
near /nɪəʳ/ PV6-10
nearly /'nɪəli/ 40
neck /nek/ 34
need (v) /niːd/ 17
neighbour /'neɪbəʳ/ 29
nephew /'nefjuː/ 7
nervous(ly) /'nɜːvəs(li)/ 37
never /'nevəʳ/ 12
new /njuː/ 10
news /njuːz/ 6
newsagent /'njuːzˌeɪdʒənt/ 16
newspaper /'njuːsˌpeɪpəʳ/ 6
next week /nekst wiːk/ 23
next to /'nekst tuː/ 18
nice /naɪs/ 2
niece /niːs/ 7
night /naɪt/ 2
nightlife /'naɪtlaɪf/ 10
no /nəʊ/ 3
noisy /'nɔɪzi/ 28
noon /nuːn/ 11
north /nɔːθ/ 10
nose /nəʊz/ 34
note (money) /nəʊt/ 17
notepad /'nəʊtpæd/ 4
nothing /'nʌθɪŋ/ 24
November /nəʊ'vembəʳ/ 19
now /naʊ/ 3
nuisance /'njuːsəns/ 27
number /'nʌmbəʳ/ 5
Numbers 1-100 5
nurse /nɜːs/ 12

O

ocean /'əʊʃən/ 10
o'clock /ə'klɒk/ 11
October /ɒk'təʊbəʳ/ 19
of course /əv 'kɔːs/ 36
office /'ɒfᵻs/ 13
often /'ɒfən, 'ɒftən/ 12
oil /ɔɪl/ 17
O.K. /əʊ'keɪ/ 2
old /əʊld/ 10
on /ɒn/ 2
on (It's . . . at) /ɒn
 (ɪts . . . ət)/ 26
once /wʌns/ 19
onion /'ʌnjən/ 31
only /'əʊnli/ PV11-15
only (an . . . child) /'əʊnli (ən
 . . . tʃaɪld)/ 7
open (v) /'əʊpən/ PV11-15
open-air /ˌəʊpən'eəʳ/ 38
operator (telephone)
 /'ɒpəreɪtəʳ/ 8
opposite /'ɒpəzᵻt/ 18
or /ɔːʳ/ 6
orange (colour) /'ɒrᵻndʒ/ 4
orange (fruit) /'ɒrᵻndʒ/ 4
order (v) /'ɔːdəʳ/ 31
outside /aʊt'saɪd/ 18
over /'əʊvəʳ/ 18
over there /ˌəʊvə 'ðeəʳ/ 36
own (adj) /əʊn/ 14
own (on my . . .) /əʊn
 (ɒn maɪ . . .)/ 24

P

packet /'pækᵻt/ 16

119

painting /'peɪntɪŋ/ **39**
paper (= newspaper)
　/'peɪpə^r/ **6**
parcel /'pɑ:səl/ **18**
parent /'peərənt/ **1**
park (n) /pɑ:k/ **33**
parking ticket /'pɑ:kɪŋ
　ˌtɪkɪ̥t/ **21**
particularly /pə'tɪkjə̥ləli/ **36**
party /'pɑ:ti/ **11, 23**
pass (v) (. . . an exam)
　/pɑ:s (. . . ən ɪg'zæm)/ **32**
passer-by /ˌpɑ:sə'baɪ/ **23**
passport /'pɑ:spɔ:t/ **32**
patio /'pætɪəʊ/ **14**
patterned /'pætənd/ **22**
pay (for) /peɪ (fə^r)/ **36**
pen /pen/ **4**
pence /pens/ **16**
pencil /'pensəl/ **4**
penfriend /'penfrend/ **9**
people /'pi:pəl/ **3**
pepper /'pepə^r/ **17**
percentage /pə'sentɪdʒ/ **38**
perfectly /'pɜ:fɪktli/ **36**
perfume /'pɜ:fju:m/ **37**
permanent /'pɜ:mənənt/ **30**
person /'pɜ:sən/ **22**
pet /pet/ **21**
petrol /'petrəl/ **16**
phone call /'fəʊn ˌkɔ:l/
　PV21-25
photograph /'fəʊtəgrɑ:f/ **7**
photography /fə'tɒgrəfi/ **9**
piano /pi'ænəʊ/ **6**
pink /pɪŋk/ **4**
pizza /'pi:tsə/ **1**
place (n) /pleɪs/ **10**
plain (adj) /pleɪn/ **22**
plane /pleɪn/ **13**
play (n) /pleɪ/ **PV26-30**
play (. . . the piano) /pleɪ
　(. . . ðə pi'ænəʊ)/ **6**
play (. . . volleyball) /pleɪ
　(. . . 'vɒlibɔ:l)/ **6**
please /pli:z/ **PV1-5**
pleasure /'pleʒə^r/ **FN**
plenty /'plenti/ **24**
plug (n) /plʌg/ **6**
poet /'pəʊɪ̥t/ **12**
policeman /pə'li:smən/ **23**
polite /pə'laɪt/ **28**
polluted /pə'lu:tɪd/ **29**
poor /pʊə^r/ **40**
population /ˌpɒpjʊ̥'leɪʃən/ **14**
pork /pɔ:k/ **17**
portion /'pɔ:ʃən/ **16**
postcard /'pəʊstkɑ:d/ **15**
postcode /'pəʊstkəʊd/ **5**
poster /'pəʊstə^r/ **23**
post office /'pəʊst ˌɒfɪ̥s/
　PV16-20
potato /pə'teɪtəʊ/ **17**
pound (money) /paʊnd/ **16**
prawn /prɔ:n/ **31**
prefer /prɪ'fɜ:^r/ **17**
present (n) /'prezənt/ **PV1-5**
pretty /'prɪti/ **24**
probably /'prɒbəbli/ **9**
problem /'prɒbləm/ **CH15, 36**
programme /'prəʊgræm/ **6**
pronounce /prə'naʊns/ **LL1-5**
proud /praʊd/ **29**
pub (= public house) /pʌb/**18**

public place /ˌpʌblɪk 'pleɪs/ **38**
punctual(ly) /'pʌŋktʃʊəl(li)/ **37**
puncture /'pʌŋktʃə^r/ **6**
purple /'pɜ:pəl/ **4**
purse /pɜ:s/ **4**
put /pʊt/ **37**
pyramid /'pɪrəmɪd/ **9**

Q

quarter /'kwɔ:tə^r/ **11**
quick(ly) /'kwɪk(li)/ **37**
quiety(ly) /'kwaɪət(li)/ **37**
quite well /ˌkwaɪt 'wel/ **6**

R

radio /'reɪdiəʊ/ **15**
railway /'reɪlweɪ/ **13**
rain (n) /reɪn/ **19**
rain (v) /reɪn/ **PV16-20**
rainy /'reɪni/ **19**
razor /'reɪzə^r/ **21**
read /ri:d/ **6**
Really? /'rɪəli/ **PV6-10**
really (= very) /'rɪəli/
　PV21-25
receive /rɪ'si:v/ **32**
recently /'ri:səntli/ **27**
recipe /'resɪ̥pi/ **40**
record (n) /rɪ'kɔ:d/ **7**
red /red/ **4**
relax /rɪ'læks/ **20**
repair (v) /rɪ'peə^r/ **6**
restaurant /'restərɒnt/ **9**
return (a book) /rɪ'tɜ:n (ə
　bʊk)/ **35**
return (a call) /rɪ'tɜ:n (ə
　kɔ:l)/ **PV21-25**
rice /raɪs/ **31**
rich /rɪtʃ/ **14**
ride (v) /raɪd/ **6**
right (on the . . .) /raɪt
　(ɒn ðə . . .)/ **18**
right (all . . .) /raɪt (ɔ:l . . .)/
　PV31-35
ring (n) (jewellery) /rɪŋ/ **21**
ring (n) (phone call) /rɪŋ/
　PV6-10
ring (v) (make a phone call)
　/rɪŋ/ **6**
river /'rɪvə^r/ **10**
road /rəʊd/ **5**
roll (n) (bread) /rəʊl/ **16**
romantic /rəʊ'mæntɪk/ **9**
roof /ru:f/ **14**
room /ru:m/ **PV11-15**
round (prep) /raʊnd/ **37**
rude(ly) /ru:d(li)/ **37**
ruin (n) /'ru:ɪ̥n/ **18**
run (v) /rʌn/ **15**

S

sad /sæd/ **39**
salad /'sæləd/ **31**
salt /sɔ:lt/ **17**
same (The . . . to you!)
　/seɪm (ðə . . . tə ju:)/ **2**
sandwich /'sænwɪdʒ/ **16**
Saturday /'sætədi/ **2**
sauce /sɔ:s/ **40**
sausage /'sɒsɪdʒ/ **17**
say /seɪ/ **LL1-5, 25**

scarf /skɑ:f/ **22**
school /sku:l/ **1**
science fiction /ˌsaɪəns
　'fɪkʃən/**9**
sea /si:/ **10**
season /'si:zən/ **19**
second (of time) /'sekənd/ **11**
secretary /'sekrɪ̥təri/ **WB13**
see /si:/ **6**
See you (on . . . day.) /ˌsi:
　ju: (ɒn '. . . deɪ)/ **2**
sell /sel/ **FL6-10, 40**
send /send/ **15**
September /sep'tembə^r/ **19**
serious /'sɪəriəs/ **36**
serve /sɜ:v/ **30**
settle down /'setl daʊn/ **30**
several /'sevərəl/ **40**
sewing machine /'səʊɪŋ
　məˌʃi:n/ **21**
shampoo /ʃæm'pu:/ **35**
sheep /ʃi:p/ **30**
ship /ʃɪp/ **20**
shirt /ʃɜ:t/ **22**
shoe(s) /ʃu:(z)/ **22**
shop (n) /ʃɒp/ **10**
shop (v) /ʃɒp/ **9**
shopping (go . . .) /'ʃɒpɪŋ
　(gəʊ . . .)/ **9, FL11-15**
short (adj) /ʃɔ:t/ **24**
shorts /ʃɔ:ts/ **22**
shoulder /'ʃəʊldə^r/ **34**
shout (v) /ʃaʊt/ **25**
show (n) /ʃəʊ/ **26**
show (v) /ʃəʊ/ **23**
shower /'ʃaʊə^r/ **12**
shut /ʃʌt/ **PV36-40**
sick /sɪk/ **34**
sightseeing /'saɪtˌsi:ɪŋ/ **20**
sign (v) /saɪn/ **5**
signature /'sɪgnətʃə^r/ **5**
silver /'sɪlvə^r/ **25**
simple /'sɪmpəl/ **6**
since /sɪns/ **38**
sing /sɪŋ/ **6**
single /'sɪŋgəl/ **5**
sink /sɪŋk/ **14**
sister /'sɪstə^r/ **1**
sit /sɪt/ **15**
sitting room /'sɪtɪŋ ˌru:m/ **14**
size /saɪz/ **PV36-40**
ski /ski:/ **6**
skirt /skɜ:t/ **PV21-25, 22**
slam /slæm/ **PV36-40**
sleep /sli:p/ **25**
sleeping bag /'sli:pɪŋ
　ˌbæg/ **33**
slide (n) /slaɪd/ **23**
slim /slɪm/ **24**
slow(ly) /'sləʊ(li)/ **37**
small /smɔ:l/ **7**
smart /smɑ:t/ **22**
smile (v) /smaɪl/ **13**
smoke (v) /sməʊk/ **23**
sniff /snɪf/ **39**
snow (n) /snəʊ/ **19**
snow (v) /snəʊ/ **19**
so (= therefore) /səʊ/ **22**
so (= very) /səʊ/ **37**
sock /sɒk/ **22**
sofa /'səʊfə/ **14**
solicitor /sə'lɪsɪ̥tə^r/ **13**
some /sʌm/ **17**
sometimes /'sʌmtaɪmz/ **12**

son /sʌn/ **7**
soon /su:n/ **26**
sore (adj) /sɔ:^r/ **34**
sorry /'sɒri/ **PV21-25**
soup /su:p/ **17**
sour /saʊə^r/ **17**
south /saʊθ/ **10**
speak /spi:k/ **3**
speaking /'spi:kɪŋ/ **PV26-30**
spell /spel/ **PV1-5**
spend (money) /spend/ **22**
spend (time) /spend/ **20**
spoon(ful) /'spu:n(fʊl)/ **34**
sport /spɔ:t/ **6**
sports centre /'spɔ:ts
　ˌsentə^r/**21**
spotted /'spɒtɪd/ **22**
spring /sprɪŋ/ **19**
square /skweə^r/ **32**
stairs /steəz/ **14**
stamp /stæmp/ **4**
stand /stænd/ **15**
start (v) /stɑ:t/ **11**
station /'steɪʃən/ **13**
stay (v) /steɪ/ **PV11-15**
steak /steɪk/ **31**
stereo system /'steriəʊ
　ˌsɪstɪ̥m/ **21**
still /stɪl/ **33**
stocking /'stɒkɪŋ/ **22**
stomach /'stʌmək/ **34**
stomachache /'stʌmək-eɪk/ **34**
stop (v) /stɒp/ **25**
story /'stɔ:ri/ **25**
straight (adj) /streɪt/ **24**
straight /streɪt/ **40**
strange /streɪndʒ/ **25**
stranger /'streɪndʒə^r/ **25**
strap /stræp/ **21**
street /stri:t/ **5**
striped /straɪpt/ **22**
student /'stju:dənt/ **PV6-10**
study /'stʌdi/ **8**
successful /sək'sesfəl/ **40**
sudden(ly) /'sʌdn(li)/ **25**
sugar /'ʃʊgə^r/ **17**
suit (n) /su:t/ **22**
suit (v) /su:t/ **36**
suitcase /'su:tkeɪs/ **25**
summer /'sʌmə^r/ **19**
sun /sʌn/ **19**
sunbathe /'sʌnbeɪð/ **20**
Sunday /'sʌndi/ **2**
sunny /'sʌni/ **19**
suntan /'sʌntæn/ **15**
surname /'sɜ:neɪm/ **5**
surprising /sə'praɪzɪŋ/ **29**
sweater /'swetə^r/ **22**
sweet (adj) /swi:t/ **17**
sweets /swi:ts/ **FL6-10**
swim /swɪm/ **6**
swimming pool /'swɪmɪŋ
　ˌpu:l/ **14**
swimsuit /'swɪmsu:t/ **22**

T

table /'teɪbəl/ **WB4, 14**
take a message /teɪk ə
　'mesɪdʒ/ **27**
take (opp. bring) /teɪk/ **23**
take (time) /teɪk/ **PV11-15**
take (somebody somewhere)
　/teɪk/ **PV31-35**

take-away (food)
  /ˈteɪkəweɪ/ 31
take off (v) /ˌteɪk ˈɒf/ 39
talk (v) /tɔːk/ 20
tall /tɔːl/ 24
taxi /ˈtæksi/ 13
taxi rank /ˈtæksi ˌræŋk/ 18
tea /tiː/ 17
teach /tiːtʃ/ 30
teacher /ˈtiːtʃəʳ/ 8
technology /tekˈnɒlədʒi/ 29
telephone /ˈtelɪ̩fəʊn/ 4
telephone number /ˈtelɪ̩fəʊn
  ̩nʌmbəʳ/ 5
television (TV)
  /ˈtelɪ̩vɪʒən (̩tiː ˈviː)/ 12
tell /tel/ 9
temple /ˈtempəl/ 33
tennis /ˈtenɪs/ 6
temperature /ˈtemprətʃəʳ/ 19
temporary /ˈtempərəri/ 30
textbook /ˈtekstbʊk/ 1
thanks /ˈθæŋks/ PV1-5
thank you /ˈθæŋk juː/ PV1-5
that /ðæt/ 4
theatre /ˈθɪətəʳ/ 18
then /ðen/ 12
there (adv) /ðeəʳ/ 8
these /ðiːz/ 4
thin /θɪn/ 24
think /θɪŋk/ 3
thirsty /ˈθɜːsti/ PV16-20
this /ðɪs/ 2
those /ðəʊz/ 4
thousands /ˈθaʊzəndz/ 39
throat /θrəʊt/ 34
throughout (prep) /θruːˈaʊt/
  40
throw (v) /θrəʊ/ 24
thumb /θʌm/ 34
Thursday /ˈθɜːzdi/ 2
ticket /ˈtɪkɪt/ PV1-5
tie (n) /taɪ/ 22
tight /taɪt/ PV36-40
tights /taɪts/ 22
time /taɪm/ 11
timetable /ˈtaɪmˌteɪbəl/ 11
tired /taɪəd/ 25
tissues /ˈtɪʃuːz/ 16
Titles (Ms, Mrs, Miss, Mr)
  1, 5
toast /təʊst/ 17
today /təˈdeɪ/ 2
toe /təʊ/ 34
together /təˈgeðəʳ/ 7
toilet /ˈtɔɪlɪt/ 14
tomorrow /təˈmɒrəʊ/ 2
too (= also) /tuː/ 3
too (+ adj) /tuː/ 9
too much /ˌtuː ˈmʌtʃ/ 23
toothbrush /ˈtuːθbrʌʃ/ 35
toothpaste /ˈtuːθpeɪst/ 16
tough (= difficult) /tʌf/ 30
tourist (adj) /ˈtʊərɪst/ 10
town /taʊn/ 3
traffic /ˈtræfɪk/ 13
train /treɪn/ 13
trainers /ˈtreɪnəz/ 22
travel (v) /ˈtrævəl/ 9
travel agents /ˈtrævəl
  ̩eɪdʒənts/ PV6-10
traveller's cheque /ˈtrævələz
  ̩tʃek/ 18
trip (= travel) /trɪp/ 23

trousers /ˈtraʊzəz/ 22
try (= attempted) /traɪ/ 22
try (= experience) /traɪ/ 33
try on /traɪ ˈɒn/ 36
T-shirt /ˈtiːʃɜːt/ 16
tube (of toothpaste) /tjuːb əv
  ˈtuːθpeɪst/ 16
Tuesday /ˈtjuːzdi/ 2
turn (n) (your . . .) /tɜːn
  (jɔː . . .)/ 32
turn (v) /tɜːn/ 25
twice /twaɪs/ 33
type (n) /taɪp/ 9
type (v) /taɪp/ 6
typical /ˈtɪpɪkəl/ 12

U

ugly /ˈʌgli/ 10
umbrella /ʌmˈbrelə/ 4
uncle /ˈʌŋkəl/ 7
under /ˈʌndəʳ/ 18
underground (train)
  /ˈʌndəgraʊnd (treɪn)/ 13
understand /ˌʌndəˈstænd/ 6
unfortunately /ʌnˈfɔːtʃənɪ̩tli/
  18, 25
university /ˌjuːnɪ̩ˈvɜːsɪ̩ti/ 10
unlock /ʌnˈlɒk/ 25
until /ʌnˈtɪl/ 11
unusual /ʌnˈjuːʒuəl/ 33
up /ʌp/ 24
upset /ʌpˈset/ 39
upstairs /ˌʌpˈsteəz/ 14
use (v) /juːz/ 6
usually /ˈjuːʒuəli/ 12

V

valuable (adj) /ˈvæljuəbəl/ 21
vegetable /ˈvedʒtəbəl/ 17
very much /ˌveri ˈmʌtʃ/
  PV6-10
very well /ˌveri ˈwel/ 6
vest /vest/ 22
village /ˈvɪlɪdʒ/ 13
vinegar /ˈvɪnɪgəʳ/ 17
visit /ˈvɪzɪt/ 20
visitor /ˈvɪzɪtəʳ/ 18
volleyball /ˈvɒlibɔːl/ 6

W

wait (v) /weɪt/ 25
waiter /ˈweɪtəʳ/ 15
wake (v) /weɪk/ 25
walk (n) /wɔːk/ 9
walk (v) /wɔːk/ 13
wall /wɔːl/ 14
wallet /ˈwɒlɪt/ 4
want /wɒnt/ 11
wardrobe /ˈwɔːdrəʊb/ 14
war film /ˈwɔː ̩fɪlm/ 9
warm /wɔːm/ 19
wash (v) /wɒʃ/ 25
washbasin /ˈwɒʃˌbeɪsən/ 14
washing machine /ˈwɒʃɪŋ
  mə̩ʃiːn/ 14
wash up /wɒʃ ˈʌp/ 9
watch (n) /wɒtʃ/ 21
watch (v) /wɒtʃ/ 12
water /ˈwɔːtəʳ/ 16
waterfall /ˈwɔːtəfɔːl/ 18
wave /weɪv/ 39

wavy /ˈweɪvi/ 24
wear /weəʳ/ 15
weather /ˈweðəʳ/ PV16-20
wedding /ˈwedɪŋ/ 35
Wednesday /ˈwenzdi/ 2
week /wiːk/ 2
weekday /ˈwiːkdeɪ/ PV11-15
weekend /ˌwiːkˈend/ 2
well (adv) /wel/ 6
west /west/ PV6-10,10
wet /wet/ 19
What? /wɒt/ PV1-5
What about? /wɒt əˈbaʊt/ 8
What's the matter? /wɒts ðə
  ˈmætəʳ/ 6
What time? /wɒt ˈtaɪm/ 11
wheel (n) /wiːl/ 6
When? /wen/ 19
when (conj) /wen/ 39
Where? /weəʳ/ 3
Which? /wɪtʃ/ 16
while /waɪl/ 24
white /waɪt/ 4
Who? /huː/ 1
whole /həʊl/ 40
Whose? /huːz/ 21
Why? /waɪ/ 13
wife /waɪf/ 7
win (v) /wɪn/ 32
wind (n) /wɪnd/ 19
window /ˈwɪndəʊ/ PV11-15
windsurf (v) /ˈwɪndsɜːf/ 6
windy(y) /ˈwɪnd(i)/ 19
wine /waɪn/ 31
winter /ˈwɪntəʳ/ 19
with /wɪð/ PV1-5
woman /ˈwʊmən/ 3
wonderful /ˈwʌndəfəl/ 15
work (n) /wɜːk/ 13
work (v) /wɜːk/ PV6-10
world /wɜːld/ 3
worse /wɜːs/ 28
worst /wɜːst/ 28
wrist /rɪst/ 34
write /raɪt/ 6, 15
writer /ˈraɪtəʳ/ 18
writing /ˈraɪtɪŋ/ 6
wrong /rɒŋ/ 25

Y

years old /ˌjɪəs ˈəʊld/ 5
yellow /ˈjeləʊ/ 4
yes /jes/ PV1-5
yesterday /ˈjestədi/ 2
yoghurt /ˈjɒgət/ 17
young /jʌŋ/ 28
yourself /jəˈself/ 17

Z

zoo /zuː/ 10

Workbook tapescript

Units 1 – 5

Exercise 1

Listen to the doctor's interview with Anna and complete the information on the medical card in your Workbook.
DOCTOR: Good morning.
ANNA: Good morning.
DOCTOR: Do take a seat. Now I just need a few details. What's your name, please?
ANNA: Anna Ternberg.
DOCTOR: Can you say that again, please?
ANNA: Anna Ternberg.
DOCTOR: How do you spell Ternberg?
ANNA: T.E.R.N.B.E.R.G.
DOCTOR: Thank you. What's your address?
ANNA: 25, Hull Road – that's H.U. double L Road, York, YO1 5JS.
DOCTOR: What's your telephone number?
ANNA: Two eight two, one double oh five.
DOCTOR: Double oh nine?
ANNA: No, double oh five.
DOCTOR: Thank you. And now . . .

Exercise 2

Look at your Workbook. Listen and circle the letters Anna gets wrong in her eye test.
DOCTOR: Please read the letters.
ANNA: O R, I Y, Q U W, A H J K, er, E L, M N S X Z, B, C, er, O, er, sorry!
DOCTOR: That's fine. Thank you.

Exercise 3

Do the hearing test. Circle the word or number you hear.
1 brother 2 Sunday 3 thirty 4 grey
5 double three nine

Exercise 4

Answer the doctor's questions and read the eye test letters.
Good morning. [bleep]
Just a few details. What's your name? [bleep]
How do you spell your surname? [bleep]
Thank you. Now please read the letters. [bleep]

Exercise 5

Respond to the introductions. Listen to the example first.
T: My name's Adam.
S: *How do you do, Adam.*

Now you do it.
1 My name's Adam. [bleep]
   How do you do, Adam.
2 My name's Chris. [bleep]
   How do you do, Chris.
3 This is my sister, Anna. [bleep]
   How do you do, Anna.
4 This is my brother, John. [bleep]
   How do you do, John.
5 This is Mr Burton. [bleep]
   How do you do, Mr Burton.

Exercise 6

Correct the numbers. Listen to the example first.
T: Is that oh eight double oh four?
S: *No, it isn't, it's oh eight double oh FIVE.*

Now you do it.
1 Is that oh eight double oh four? [bleep]
   No, it isn't, it's oh eight double oh FIVE.
2 Is that five two six, – three seven nine four? [bleep]
   No, it isn't, it's five two six three seven nine ONE.
3 Is that five nine two, four seven double one? [bleep]
   No, it isn't, it's NINE nine two four seven double one.
4 Is that oh seven double nine? [bleep]
   No, it isn't, it's oh seven double FIVE.
5 Is that number thirty? [bleep]
   No, it isn't, it's number THIRTEEN.

Exercise 7

Listen to a word and ask how to spell it. Then write it in the space in your Workbook. Listen to the example first.
T: Mother.
S: *How do you spell that?*
T: M.O.T.H.E.R.

Now you do it.
1 Mother. [bleep]
   How do you spell that?
   M.O.T.H.E.R.
2 Father. [bleep]
   How do you spell that?
   F.A.T.H.E.R.
3 Aunt. [bleep]
   How do you spell that?
   A.U.N.T.
4 Uncle. [bleep]
   How do you spell that?
   U.N.C.L.E.
5 Cousin. [bleep]
   How do you spell that?
   C.O.U.S.I.N.

Exercise 8

Listen to a word, ask the speaker to repeat it and underline the stressed syllable in your Workbook. Listen to the example first.
T: Yesterday.
S: *Can you say that again, please?*
T: Yesterday.

Now you ask and underline the stressed syllable.
1 Yesterday. [bleep]
   Can you say that again, please?
   Yesterday.
2 Tomorrow. [bleep]
   Can you say that again, please?
   Tomorrow.
3 Morning. [bleep]
   Can you say that again, please?
   Morning.
4 Afternoon [bleep]
   Can you say that again, please?
   Afternoon.
5 Italy. [bleep]
   Can you say that again, please?
   Italy.
6 Italian [bleep]
   Can you say that again, please?
   Italian.
7 Japan. [bleep]
   Can you say that again, please?
   Japan.

8 Japanese. [bleep]
Can you say that again, please?
Japanese.

Vowel sounds
/ɪ/ It's English. /iː/ He's Japanese.

Exercise 9

Listen and tick the sound you hear.
1 she   2 its   3 he's   4 week   5 his   6 Chris

Exercise 10

Listen and repeat some words and phrases with the /ɪ/ sound.
It's English. [bleep]   This is Chris. [bleep]   Chris is his name. [bleep]   Chris is English. [bleep]   This is Mrs Gibson. [bleep]   What's this in English? [bleep]

Now listen and repeat some words and phrases with the /iː/ sound.
he [bleep   we [bleep]   she [bleep]   He's Japanese. [bleep]   She's fourteen. [bleep]   We speak Chinese. [bleep]   She's Teresa Green. [bleep]

Consonant sound
/dʒ/ Japan   German

Exercise 11

Listen and repeat some words and phrases with the /dʒ/ sound.
George [bleep]   John [bleep]   Jan [bleep]   German [bleep]   Germany [bleep]   Japan [bleep]   Japanese [bleep]   Algiers [bleep]   Algerian [bleep]

Units 6 – 10

Exercise 1

Listen to some of the interviews about the Sports Centre and complete the opinion poll questionnaire in your Workbook.

Interview with Mr Ben Ross:
INTERVIEWER: What do you do, Mr Ross?
BEN: I'm a teacher at Woodstock Primary School.
INTERVIEWER: Have you got any children?
BEN: No, I haven't. Not yet.
INTERVIEWER: Do you like sport?
BEN: Yes, I do, very much.
INTERVIEWER: Can you swim?
BEN: Yes, I can.
INTERVIEWER: Can you play tennis?
BEN: Yes, I can but not very well.
INTERVIEWER: Do you like the new sports centre idea?
BEN: Yes. It's good for the children, good for the family, good for the community and good for me. You need to keep fit in my job.

Interview with Mrs Betty Jones:
INTERVIEWER: What do you do, Mrs Jones?
BETTY: I'm a singer, I sing opera for television and radio.
INTERVIEWER: Have you got any children?
BETTY: Yes, I've got two children and four grandchildren.
INTERVIEWER: Can you swim?
BETTY: Yes, but not very well.
INTERVIEWER: Can you play tennis?
BETTY: No, not really. I did a bit years ago but I don't like sports very much. I like reading, the cinema, gardening. Things like that.

INTERVIEWER: Do you like the plan for the new sports centre?
BETTY: No, I don't, not at all. This is a beautiful old town and all those big modern buildings are spoiling it.

Interview with Mary Bordas:
INTERVIEWER: What do you do, Ms Bordas?
MARY: I'm a student.
INTERVIEWER: Have you got any children?
MARY: No, I haven't.
INTERVIEWER: Do you like sport?
MARY: Yes, I do. I love it.
INTERVIEWER: Can you swim?
MARY: Yes, I can. I love swimming.
INTERVIEWER: Can you play tennis?
MARY: Yes, I can but there's nowhere to play round here.
INTERVIEWER: What do you think of the new sports centre plan?
MARY: I think it's a great idea.

Exercise 2

Answer questions about children. Listen to the example first.
T: Have Mr and Mrs Smith got any children?
S: *Yes, they have.*

Now you do it.
1 Have Mr and Mrs Smith got any children? [bleep]
   Yes, they have.
2 Has Bill got any children? [bleep]
   Yes, he has.
3 Has Ben got any children? [bleep]
   No, he hasn't.
4 Has Betty got any children? [bleep]
   Yes, she has.
5 Has Mary got any children? [bleep]
   No, she hasn't.

Exercise 3

Answer questions about people's opinion of the sports centre plan. Listen to the example first.
Do Mr and Mrs Smith like the sports centre plan?
Yes, they do.

Now, you do it.
1 Do Mr and Mrs Smith like the sports centre plan? [bleep]
   Yes, they do.
2 Does Ben like the sports centre plan? [bleep]
   Yes, he does.
3 Does Mary like the sports centre plan? [bleep]
   Yes, she does.
4 Do Bill and Betty like the sports centre plan? [bleep]
   No, they don't.

Exercise 4

Use your completed opinion poll questionnaire to say what people can and can't do. Listen to the examples first.
T: What can Mr and Mrs Smith do?
S: *They can swim but they can't play tennis.*
T: What can Bill do?
S: *He can't swim or play tennis.*
T: What can Ben do?
S: *He can swim and play tennis.*

Now you do it.
1 What can Mr and Mrs Smith do? [bleep]
   They can swim but they can't play tennis.
2 What can Bill do? [bleep]
   He can't swim or play tennis.

3 What can Ben do? [bleep]
   He can swim and play tennis.
4 What can Betty do? [bleep]
   She can swim but she can't play tennis.
5 What can Mary do? [bleep]
   She can swim and play tennis.

Exercise 5

Listen and underline the stressed syllable.
doctor   housewife   farmer   teacher   singer   student

Exercise 6

Use the questionnaire to answer questions about people's jobs. Imagine you are the people. Listen to the example first.
T: What do you do, Mr Smith?
S: *I'm a doctor. What do you do?*

Now you do it.
1 What do you do, Mr Smith? [bleep]
   I'm a doctor. What do you do?
2 What do you do, Mrs Smith? [bleep]
   I'm a housewife. What do you do?
3 What do you do, Mr Brown? [bleep]
   I'm a farmer. What do you do?
4 What do you do, Mr Ross? [bleep]
   I'm a teacher. What do you do?
5 What do you do, Mrs Jones? [bleep]
   I'm a singer. What do you do?
6 What do you do, Ms Bordas? [bleep]
   I'm a student. What do you do?

Vowel sounds
/æ/ Yes, I can.   /ɑ:/ No, I can't.

Exercise 7

Listen to the sentences and tick the sound you hear.
1 Who's that man?   2 He's my father. 3 Who's that?
4 She's my aunt.   5 Yes, I can.   6 No, I can't.

Consonant sounds
/θ/ Thank you.   /ð/ This is for you.

Exercise 8

Listen and repeat the words and sentences.
thanks [bleep]   thank you [bleep] this [bleep]
these [bleep]   that [bleep] those [bleep]   This is my
mother. [bleep]   This is my brother. [bleep]   My brother
is thirty-three. [bleep]

Units 11 – 15

Exercise 1

Listen and circle the correct answers in your Workbook.
SUE: Hello, Harry.
HARRY: Oh, hello Sue. Are you jogging?
SUE: Yes, I go jogging every morning. Where are you
       going?
HARRY: I'm going to work.
SUE: To work! It's only seven o'clock in the morning.
HARRY: I know. I'm walking to work.
SUE: Goodness! How far is it?
HARRY: It's about five miles.
SUE: Do you always walk to work?
HARRY: No, I don't. I usually go by train.
SUE: So why are you walking today?
HARRY: Because there aren't any trains or buses today.
       They're all on strike. This is Britain, remember?
SUE: Don't you like walking?
HARRY: No, I hate it!

SUE: Well I hope you get there O.K! Bye.
HARRY: Bye.

Exercise 2

Listen and look at the plans of two flats in your Workbook.
Put a tick next to the correct flat.
MUM: Hello 27149.
JULIE: Hello, Mum. It's Julie.
MUM: Hello, Julie.
JULIE: Listen, we've got a flat.
MUM: Oh, good. Where is it?
JULIE: It's near the station.
MUM: Oh, that's good. What's it like?
JULIE: Well, it's quite big. There's a large hall, a sitting
       room and a kitchen . . .
MUM: Is there a dining room?
JULIE: No, there isn't but the kitchen's quite big.
MUM: How many bedrooms are there?
JULIE: There are two bedrooms and there's a bathroom
       with a shower and a toilet in it.
MUM: Mmm. How much is it?

Exercise 3

Ask how often people drive to work.
Listen to the example first.
T: you/always?
S: *Do you always drive to work?*

Now you ask the questions.
1 you/always? [bleep]
   Do you always drive to work?
2 he/usually? [bleep]
   Does he usually drive to work?
3 she/often? [bleep]
   Does she often drive to work?
4 they/sometimes? [bleep]
   Do they sometimes drive to work?
5 you/never? [bleep]
   Do you never drive to work?

Exercise 4

Ask questions about time. Listen to the example first.
T1: The concert starts at six o'clock.
T2: Finish.
S: *What time does it finish?*

Now you ask the questions.
1 The concert starts at six o'clock.
   Finish. [bleep]
   What time does it finish?
2 The library opens at half past nine.
   Close. [bleep]
   What time does it close?
3 The class begins at quarter to ten.
   End. [bleep]
   What time does it end?
4 The plane leaves at twenty past twelve.
   Arrive. [bleep]
   What time does it arrive?

Exercise 5

Ask questions about what people are doing now. Listen to the example first.
T: John plays football every day.
S: *Is he playing football now?*

Now you ask the questions.
1 John plays football every day. [bleep]
   Is he playing football now?
2 Sue plays tennis every week. [bleep]
   Is she playing tennis now?
3 My father cleans the car every Sunday. [bleep]
   Is he cleaning the car now?

4 My mother likes writing letters. [bleep]
  Is she writing letters now?
5 My brother watches TV all the time. [bleep]
  Is he watching TV now?
6 My sister telephones her boyfriend every hour. [bleep]
  Is she telephoning her boyfriend now?

Exercise 6

Listen and underline the stressed words in each question.
1 What time is it?   4 How old is it?
2 How far is it?   5 What are you doing?
3 How long is it?   6 Where are they going?

Vowel sound

/ɜ:/ He works in Germany.

Exercise 7

Listen and repeat the words and phrases.
word [bleep]   work [bleep]   world [bleep]   her [bleep]
German [bleep]   girl [bleep]   learn [bleep]   thirty
German girls [bleep]   His girlfriend works in Germany.
[bleep]   She's learning German at work. [bleep]

Consonant sound

/h/ How are you?

Exercise 8

Listen to the sentences and write the number of times you
hear the sound /h/ in each sentence.
1 Harry is here.
2 How are you?
3 Who are you talking to?
4 How old is Helen?
5 Have you got a hall in your house?
6 Can you hear who's speaking?

Exercise 9

Ask questions. Listen to the example first.
T: I can see Harry.
s: *Who's Harry?*

Now you ask the questions.
1 I can see Harry.
  Who's Harry?
2 I can see Helen.
  Who's Helen?
3 I can see Henry.
  Who's Henry?
4 I can see Hilary.
  Who's Hilary?

Units 16 – 20

Exercise 1

Listen and correct the statements in your Workbook.
SARAH: Brr! It's very cold today!
DEREK: And it's starting to rain. Is there a café near here?
SARAH: Yes, there's one on the corner, opposite the
        newsagent's.
DEREK: Ah, there it is.
SARAH: Let's go in and have a coffee.
DEREK: Yes, and something to eat. I'm quite hungry.
SARAH: Can we have two cups of coffee, please?
WOMAN: Large or small?
SARAH: How much is a large cup?
WOMAN: 70p.
SARAH: O.K. Two large coffees, please.
WOMAN: Anything else?
SARAH: Yes, er, I'd like a sandwich.
DEREK: Me too. How much are the sandwiches?
WOMAN: They're all £1.25.

DEREK: What sort have you got?
WOMAN: We've got cheese and tomato, ham, egg or roast
        beef.
SARAH: Cheese and tomato, please.
DEREK: And a ham sandwich for me.
SARAH: O.K. I've got some money. I'll pay.
WOMAN: That's £3.90 altogether, please. Thank you. And
        here's 10p change.
DEREK: Thanks, Sarah. Oh, here's a table. Now tell me,
        how was your holiday in Spain?
SARAH: Oh, it was wonderful. We had a marvellous time.
        I sunbathed every day!

Exercise 2

Now listen again. Tick what Sarah and Derek order and fill
in the prices.

Exercise 3

Ask for things in shops. Listen to the example first.
T: Can I help you?
s: *Yes, I'd like an evening newspaper, please.*

Now you speak.
1 Can I help you? [bleep]
  Yes, I'd like an evening newspaper, please.
2 Can I help you? [bleep]
  Yes, I'd like a box of matches, please.
3 Can I help you? [bleep]
  Yes, I'd like a tube of toothpaste, please.
4 Can I help you? [bleep]
  Yes, I'd like a litre of oil, please.
5 Can I help you? [bleep]
  *Yes, I'd like two tickets for the seven o'clock
  performance, please.*

Exercise 4

Ask how much things cost. Listen to the example first.
T: Yes, next please.
s: *How much is a ham sandwich?*
T: It's £1.25.

Now you ask the questions.
1 Yes, next please. [bleep]
  How much is a ham sandwich?
  It's £1.25.
2 Yes, next please. [bleep]
  How much is a packet of crisps?
  It's 23p.
3 Yes, next please. [bleep]
  How much is a portion of chips?
  It's 65p.
4 Yes, next please. [bleep]
  How much is a large cup of coffee?
  It's 70p.
5 Yes, next please. [bleep]
  How much is a small glass of orange juice?
  It's 45p.

Exercise 5

Ask people to get things for you. Listen to the example
first.
T: Do you want anything at the shops?
s: *Yes, can you get me some tomatoes, please?*

Now you speak.
1 Do you want anything at the shops? [bleep]
  Yes, can you get me some tomatoes, please?
2 Do you want anything at the shops? [bleep]
  Yes, can you get me a newspaper, please?
3 Do you want anything at the shops? [bleep]
  Yes, can you get me some potatoes, please?
4 Do you want anything at the shops? [bleep]
  Yes, can you get me a battery, please?

5 Do you want anything at the shops? [bleep]
   Yes, can you get me some cigarettes, please?

Exercise 6

Say what the weather is like. Listen to the example first.
T: What's the weather like in January?
S: *It's usually cold.*
T: What's the weather like in February?
S: *It usually snows.*

Now you speak.
1 What's the weather like in January? [bleep]
   It's usually cold.
2 What's the weather like in February? [bleep]
   It usually snows.
3 What's the weather like in March? [bleep]
   It's usually cold and windy.
4 What's the weather like in April? [bleep]
   It usually rains.
5 What's the weather like in July? [bleep]
   It's usually quite hot.

Exercise 7

Use the pictures in your Workbook to say where places are. Listen to the example first.
T: Is there a bank near here?
S: *Yes, there's one opposite the post office.*

Now you speak.
1 Is there a bank near here? [bleep]
   Yes, there's one opposite the post office.
2 Is there a supermarket near here? [bleep]
   Yes, there's one next to the newsagent's.
3 Is there a hairdresser's near here? [bleep]
   Yes, there's one over the newsagent's.
4 Is there a flower shop near here? [bleep]
   Yes, there's one between the café and the restaurant.
5 Is there a video shop near here? [bleep]
   Yes, there's one on the corner.
6 Is there a car park near here? [bleep]
   Yes, there's one behind the cinema.

Exercise 8

Listen to the patterns.
1 lots of milk   2 lots of butter

Listen and say which pattern (1 or 2) these phrases follow.
1 fog in June   2 buy some pepper   3 rain in August
4 went to Spain   5 get some bread   6 stayed in London

Vowel sounds
/ɒ/ It's very hot.   /əʊ/ I'm going home.

Exercise 9

Listen and tick the sound you hear.
1 dog   2 lots   3 no   4 not   5 snow   6 phone

Exercise 10

Listen and repeat the words and phrases.
Oh no. [bleep]   lots of snow [bleep]
It snowed in October. [bleep]   Oh no, not Joe. [bleep]
Tom knows Joe. [bleep]

Consonant sounds
/r/ That's wrong.   /l/ That's long.

Exercise 11

Listen and circle the word you hear.
1 red   2 right   3 long   4 road   5 low   6 late

Exercise 12

Listen and repeat the phrases.

I like Laura. [bleep]   The lights are red. [bleep]
A letter for Laura. [bleep]   Richard likes Laura. [bleep]
A red one, please. [bleep]

Units 21 – 25

Exercise 1

Martin and Bob are at a conference. Bob wants to know who people are. Listen to the conversation and complete the chart in your Workbook.
BOB: Who's that woman?
MARTIN: Which one?
BOB: The one in the red dress.
MARTIN: Oh, you mean the tall woman with the dark hair?
BOB: Mm, that's right.
MARTIN: That's Sally Howden. She's the staff training officer.
BOB: Who's she talking to?
MARTIN: I can't see.
BOB: He's quite short and he's got red hair. And he's wearing a grey suit.
MARTIN: Oh, that's Angus. He's from Accounts. Poor Sally. He's very boring!
BOB: By the way, who's the organiser of the conference?
MARTIN: Sandra Carrigan. She's over there by the door.
BOB: I need to speak to her. Which one is she?
MARTIN: She's got blonde hair.
BOB: Short blonde hair and medium height?
MARTIN: Yes. She's wearing black trousers and a black jacket.
BOB: O.K. I can see her. Thanks!

Exercise 2

Identify belongings. Listen to the example first.
T: Which is your jacket?
S: *That's mine.*

Now you speak.
1 Which is your jacket? [bleep]
   That's mine.
2 Which is Adam's desk? [bleep]
   That's his.
3 Which is Laura's room? [bleep]
   That's hers.
4 Which is the Gibsons' house? [bleep]
   That's theirs.
5 Which is our classroom? [bleep]
   That's ours.

Exercise 3

Say what people look like. Listen to the example first.
T: What's Simon like?
S: *He's tall and he's got blond hair.*

Now you answer the questions.
1 What's Simon like? [bleep]
   He's tall and he's got blond hair.
2 What's Tessa like? [bleep]
   She's medium height and she's got short brown hair.
3 What's Tony like? [bleep]
   He's quite short and he's got red hair and a beard.
4 What's your father like? [bleep]
   He's quite tall and he's got grey hair and glasses.
5 What's your sister like? [bleep]
   She's quite small and she's got short curly hair.

Exercise 4

Talk about future plans. Listen to the example first.
T: What are your plans for next year?
S: *I'm going to work in Germany.*

Now you speak.
1 What are your plans for next year? [bleep]
I'm going to work in Germany.
2 Oh, what are you going to do? [bleep]
I'm going to work in a restaurant in Hamburg.
3 Where are you going to live? [bleep]
I'm going to live in a hostel.
4 When are you going to leave for Germany? [bleep]
I'm going to leave in October.
5 When are you going to start learning German? [bleep]
I'm going to start learning German next week.

Exercise 5

Ask about past events. Listen to the example first.
T: Ask Adam if he had a good weekend.
s: *Did you have a good weekend, Adam?*

Now you ask the questions.
1 Ask Adam if he had a good weekend. [bleep]
Did you have a good weekend, Adam?
2 Ask Laura if she went to the library this morning.
[bleep]
Did you go to the library this morning, Laura?
3 Ask Chris if she enjoyed her holiday in Barbados.
[bleep]
Did you enjoy your holiday in Barbados, Chris?
4 Ask her how long she spent there. [bleep]
How long did you spend there, Chris?
5 Ask Michael if he saw his girlfriend last night. [bleep]
Did you see your girlfriend last night, Michael?

Exercise 6

Listen to the two patterns.
1 a blue jacket   2 an orange tie

Listen and say which pattern (1 or 2) these phrases follow.
1 a red sweater   2 a yellow shirt   3 an orange hat
4 a green jacket   5 a purple tie   6 a blue blazer

Vowel sounds
/æ/ the black cat   /ʌ/ He cut his finger.

Exercise 7

Listen and say if the sounds you hear are the same or different.
1 cat   cut   4 ran   run
2 sun   sun   5 fat   fat
3 had   had   6 sang   sung

Exercise 8

Listen and repeat the words and phrases.
a sunny month [bleep]   Can you come to lunch?
[bleep]   Sally can but her mum can't. [bleep]
Sam has the money. [bleep]

Consonant sounds
/tʃ/ Do you like cheese?
/ʃ/ He likes sugar in his tea.

Exercise 9

Listen and tick the sound you hear.
1 cheap   2 cheese   3 she   4 sugar   5 short   6 chip

Exercise 10

Listen and repeat the shopping list.
a Chinese shirt [bleep]   a pair of cheap summer shoes
[bleep]   a chicken [bleep]   a cheese sandwich [bleep]
a bar of chocolate [bleep]   sugar [bleep]

Units 26 – 30

Exercise 1

Listen to a radio programme and complete the information on the poster in your workbook.

ANNOUNCER: And don't forget all you jazz lovers, there are still plenty of tickets going for the London Jazz Festival at the London Arena in Docklands on July 30th. Tickets are on sale at all ticket agencies at fifteen, ten and eight pounds. Or phone the Credit Card Hotline on 01-931 3311. That's 01-931 3311. So don't forget the London Jazz Festival, July 30th at the London Arena.

Exercise 2

Invite people to do things. Listen to the example first.
[bleep]
s: *Would you like to come to lunch?*
T: Yes, I'd love to.

Now this time you give the invitations when you hear [bleep]. Are you ready?
1 [bleep]
Would you like to come to lunch?
Yes, I'd love to.
2 [bleep]
Would you like to sit next to the window?
Oh, thank you.
3 [bleep]
Would you like to look at this magazine?
Thanks. That's kind of you.
4 [bleep]
Would you like to see my holiday photographs?
Yes, I would. Where did you go?
5 [bleep]
Would you like to meet my family?
Yes, that would be nice.
6 [bleep]
Would you like to see something of the city?
Yes, lovely – if you've got the time.

Exercise 3

Arrange dates. Listen to the example first.
T: What about meeting on January 4th?
s: *Well, January 5th is better for me.*

Now you speak.
1 What about meeting on January 4th? [bleep]
Well, January 5th is better for me.
2 Let's make a date for February 1st. [bleep]
Well, February 2nd is better for me.
3 Is August 2nd any good for you? [bleep]
Well, August 3rd is better for me.
4 What about September 15th? [bleep]
Well, September 16th is better for me.
5 I'm free on May 29th. How about you? [bleep]
Well, May 30th is better for me.
6 Is June 30th a good day to meet? [bleep]
Well, July 1st is better for me.

Exercise 4

Compare things. Listen to the example first.
T: I'm afraid the bill for your car is £120.
s: *Oh, it's more expensive than I thought.*

Now you compare things.
1 I'm afraid the bill for your car is £120. [bleep]
Oh, it's more expensive than I thought.
2 This watch is only £4.99. [bleep]
Oh, it's cheaper than I thought.
3 John Cleese is nearly 1 metre 95 tall. [bleep]
Oh, he's taller than I thought.

4 You know, their house is over a hundred years old.
[bleep]
Oh, it's older than I thought.
5 Do you know the temperature is already 35°C? [bleep]
Oh, it's hotter than I thought.
6 Kylie Minogue is only 1m 62 tall. [bleep]
Oh, she's shorter than I thought.

Exercise 5

Talk on the telephone. Look at the note in your
Workbook, then give Martin Page the message.

Hello. 654755. LMS Services. Can I help you? [bleep]
Yes, who's speaking, please? [bleep]
One moment. I'm sorry, he's not here. [bleep]
Yes, of course. Hold on, I'll get a pen. Right, what is the
message? [bleep]
Sorry, can you say that again, please? [bleep]
O.K. I'll give him the message. [bleep]
You're welcome. Goodbye. [bleep]

Now listen to someone giving the same message and check
your answer.
MAN: Hello. 654755. LMS Services. Can I help you?
GIRL: Yes, can I speak to Martin Page?
MAN: Yes, who's speaking, please?
GIRL: This is Gill Fowler here, from Cable and Wireless.
MAN: One moment. I'm sorry he's not here.
GIRL: Oh, that's a nuisance. Can I leave a message?
MAN: Yes, of course. Hold on, I'll get a pen. Right, what is
the message?
GIRL: Can you tell him that Sue Winters is now arriving on
Monday 23rd, not on Sunday 22nd.
MAN: Sorry, can you say that again, please?
GIRL: Yes. Sue Winters is now arriving on Monday 23rd,
not Sunday 22nd.
MAN: O.K. I'll give him the message.
GIRL: Thanks very much.
MAN: You're welcome. Goodbye.
GIRL: Goodbye.

Exercise 6

The weak form /ə/ (*schwa*) has many spellings in English.
Listen and circle the weak syllables in the phrases and
sentences in your Workbook.
1 Older than me. 2 Cheaper and better. 3 Britain and
France. 4 The police are here. 5. John's parents are at
home. 6 An apple and a banana.

Vowel sounds
/e/ Let's go. /eɪ/ It's late.

Exercise 7

Listen and write how many times you hear the sound /eɪ/ in
each sentence.
1 He went to bed at eight.
2 Eight o'clock is late.
3 Let's have some cake.
4 Eggs and bacon for breakfast.
5 On Wednesday at eight.
6 What date is Christmas Day?

Exercise 8

Now listen and repeat the words and phrases.
Let's go to bed. [bleep] Henry is late. [bleep] They
went to bed at eight. [bleep] She ate some bacon and
eggs for breakfast. [bleep] Wednesday 8th May. [bleep]

Consonant sound
The linking *r*: bigger and better

Exercise 9

Listen and repeat the phrases. Try to link the *r* with *and*
each time.
cheaper and better [bleep]   bigger and taller [bleep]
cleaner and nicer [bleep]   father and mother [bleep]
mother and daughter [bleep]   sugar and milk [bleep]
more and more [bleep]

Units 31 – 35

Exercise 1

Listen to the conversation and circle the correct answer in
your Workbook.
SAM: What time does the film start?
GINA: Eight thirty.
SAM: That's good. We've got plenty of time to have
something to eat. Let's go to that new Spanish
restaurant in King Street.
GINA: O.K.
SAM: What would you like?
GINA: I don't know.
SAM: Have you ever tried tapas?
GINA: No, I've never been to a Spanish restaurant
before. What is it?
SAM: It's a lot of small dishes, um, olives, sardines,
things like that.
GINA: O.K. It sounds nice.
WAITER: Si señor?
SAM: Can we have some tapas and a jug of sangria?
WAITER: Certainly, señor. Rodriguez, tapas and a jug of
sangria . . .
GINA: I don't feel very well.
SAM: What's the matter?
GINA: I feel sick and dizzy.
SAM: I hope it's not the food.
GINA: No, it's not the food. You see, I've just stopped
smoking and I get terrible stomachaches
sometimes!
SAM: Oh, I'm sorry. Would you like to go home?
GINA: No, we've got to go to the cinema.
SAM: It doesn't matter. We haven't got any tickets yet.
Waiter. Can you ring for a taxi, please?
WAITER: Si señor.

Exercise 2

Offer things to eat and drink. Look at the pictures in your
Workbook. Listen to the example first.
[bleep] s: *Would you like a cup of tea?*

Now you offer things to eat and drink when you hear the
bleep.
1 [bleep] *Would you like a cup of tea?*
2 [bleep] *Would you like an ice cream?*
3 [bleep] *Would you like a glass of wine?*
4 [bleep] *Would you like a sandwich?*
5 [bleep] *Would you like a piece of cake?*
6 [bleep] *Would you like a cup of coffee?*

Exercise 3

Look at the pictures in Exercise 2 again and decide what to
have. Listen to the example first.
T: *Would you like something to drink?*
s: *Yes, please. I think I'll have a cup of tea.*

Now say what you want to have.
1 Would you like something to drink? [bleep]
Yes, please. I think I'll have a cup of tea.
2 Would you like something to eat? [bleep]
Yes, please. I think I'll have an ice cream.
3 Would you like something to drink? [bleep]
Yes, please. I think I'll have a glass of wine.

4 Would you like something to eat? [bleep]
  Yes, please. I think I'll have a sandwich.
5 Would you like something to eat? [bleep]
  Yes, please. I think I'll have a piece of cake.
6 Would you like something to drink? [bleep]
  Yes, please. I think I'll have a cup of coffee.

Exercise 4

Talk about experiences. Listen to the example first.
T: Have you ever been to Paris?
s: *No, I've never been to France.*

Now you answer the questions.
1 Have you ever been to Paris? [bleep]
  No, I've never been to France.
2 Have you ever been to Buenos Aires? [bleep]
  No, I've never been to Argentina.
3 Have you ever been to Sydney? [bleep]
  No, I've never been to Australia.
4 Have you ever been to Lisbon? [bleep]
  No, I've never been to Portugal.
5 Have you ever been to Budapest? [bleep]
  No, I've never been to Hungary.
6 Have you ever been to Kyoto? [bleep]
  No, I've never been to Japan.

Exercise 5

Ask what the matter is. Listen to the example first.
T: Oh! My head!
s: *What's the matter? Have you got a headache?*

Now you ask what the matter is.
1 Oh! My head! [bleep]
  What's the matter? Have you got a headache?
2 Atishoo! Atishoo! [bleep]
  What's the matter? Have you got a cold?
3 Oh! My tooth! [bleep]
  What's the matter? Have you got toothache?
4 Have you got any throat pastilles? [bleep]
  What's the matter? Have you got a sore throat?
5 (Sound of coughing) [bleep]
  What's the matter? Have you got a cough?
6 I feel terribly hot. [bleep]
  What's the matter? Have you got a temperature?

Exercise 6

Say where you've got to go. Listen to the example first.
T: I need to get some money.
s: *Yes, I've got to go to the bank too.*

Now you speak.
1 I need to get some money. [bleep]
  Yes, I've got to go to the bank too.
2 I need to get some stamps. [bleep]
  Yes, I've got to go to the post office too.
3 I'd like to get a new video. [bleep]
  Yes, I've got to go to the video shop too.
4 I want to change my library books. [bleep]
  Yes, I've got to go to the library too.
5 I must get some more film for my camera. [bleep]
  Yes, I've got to go to the chemist's too.
6 I want to get a magazine. [bleep]
  Yes, I've got to go to the newsagent's too.

Exercise 7

Listen to the stress pattern.
I've got to buy some bread.

Now underline the words in the sentences in your
Workbook which carry the main stress.
1 I want to go to bed.
2 She's got to go to school.
3 He came to buy the fridge.

4 He's got to leave at nine.
5 She's got a nasty cold.
6 I'd like some bread and cheese.
7 I've bought a loaf of bread.

Vowel sounds
The silent *r*: /ɑː/ card   /ɜː/ heard

Exercise 8

Sometimes you can hear the *r* and sometimes you can't.
Look at your Workbook and circle the *r*s which you think
are silent. Be careful of the longer phrases.
1 train 2 hair 3 there 4 are 5 hearing 6 learning to
read 7 four 8 mother and father

Exercise 9

Now listen and repeat these words and phrases.
are [bleep]   part [bleep]   card [bleep]   car park [bleep]
or [bleep]   port [bleep]   four [bleep]   learn [bleep]
work [bleep]   heard [bleep]   fair [bleep]   hair [bleep]
wear [bleep]   near [bleep]   here [bleep]   dear [bleep]
It's quite near here. [bleep]   The car's in the car park.
[bleep]   He's working hard. [bleep]

Consonant sounds
/s/ sink   /θ/ think   /ð/ this

Exercise 10

Listen and repeat the phrases.
Sam thinks you're right. [bleep]
I thought so. [bleep]
This is very thick. [bleep]
Thank you so much. [bleep]
He's so thin. [bleep]
That's the third time. [bleep]
There's the bus. [bleep]

Units 36 – 40

Exercise 1

Listen and choose the best adjective from your Workbook
to describe how each person feels.
1
BOY: Oh no! There's someone standing behind the shower
  curtain.
GIRL: It's the nurse.
BOY: I'm not going to look.

2
ANNOUNCER: Calm down everybody. Here's the moment
you've all been waiting for. And here he is . . . that star of
stars . . . Jason Donovan!

3
MAN: What's the matter, darling?
WOMAN: I don't know. Maybe it's the weather. It's just
     . . . I feel so . . . I don't know . . . low!
MAN: Would you like to go out?
WOMAN: No, I don't really want to do anything.

4
MAN: La donna e mobile . . . cheaper than yesterday . . .
   da da da da de da.

5
MAN: I don't care if it's early closing. I've telephoned you
   three times today! Either you want my business or
   you don't!

Exercise 2

Listen to a radio interview with a paragliding champion and complete the information about her past life in your Workbook.

DAVID: And now we have an interview with paragliding champion, Lucy MacSwiney. Lucy, who is only twenty-six years old, has had fantastic success in a very short time. She started paragliding only eighteen months ago. And today she has just won the women's world paragliding title in Austria. She flew for a record fifteen miles.

DAVID: When did this all start, Lucy?

LUCY: It started on my twenty-fifth birthday but before that I was a model. I modelled ski clothes. It was my first job.

DAVID: How long were you a model for?

LUCY: I started in 1983 and I modelled for four years.

DAVID: So how did you start paragliding?

LUCY: Well, as a surprise on my twenty-fifth birthday, a friend gave me a paragliding lesson. I went to the top of a mountain with a Swiss instructor. He put me in a harness and said 'Hold on'.

DAVID: And then what?

LUCY: Well, we skied down the mountain and suddenly we were flying. It was fantastic.

DAVID: Weren't you frightened?

LUCY: I was a bit, at the beginning. But it was so exciting!

Exercise 3

Say what's wrong with the clothes. Listen to the example first.

T: Is it too large?

S: *Yes, it is. Have you got a smaller one?*

Now you say what's wrong.
1 Is it too large? [bleep]
   Yes, it is. Have you got a smaller one?
2 Is it to short? [bleep]
   Yes, it is. Have you got a longer one?
3 Is it too tight? [bleep]
   Yes, it is. Have you got a larger one?
4 Is it too expensive? [bleep]
   Yes, it is. Have you got a cheaper one?
5 Is it too small? [bleep]
   Yes, it is, Have you got a larger one?

Exercise 4

Give rules. Look at the notices in your Workbook and say the rules. Listen to the example first.

T: Let's park here.

S: *No, we mustn't park here. Look!*

Now you give the rules.
1 Let's park here. [bleep]
   No, we mustn't park here. Look!
2 Oh, let's have our lunch at this table. [bleep]
   No, we mustn't eat or drink here. Look!
3 Oh look, aren't they sweet? Give them some of your sandwiches. [bleep]
   No, we mustn't feed the birds here. Look!
4 Oh what lovely flowers! Let's pick some to take home. [bleep]
   No, we mustn't pick the flowers here. Look!
5 Let's have our picnic under the tree over there. [bleep]
   No, we mustn't walk on the grass here. Look!
6 Here. Have a cigarette. [bleep]
   No, we mustn't smoke here. Look!

Exercise 5

Give instructions in different places. Listen to the example first.

T: Look I'm going at 120.

S: *Don't drive so fast.*

Now you give the instructions.
1 Look I'm going at 120. [bleep]
   Don't drive so fast.
2 Ithinkoneofthethingsthatpeopleoftendowrongat interviewsisweartoomuchjewellery. [bleep]
   Don't speak so quickly.
3 Come on! We want to get home! [bleep]
   Don't walk so fast.
4 All things bright and beautiful. [bleep]
   Don't sing so loudly.
5 Anyway, this girl comes into the restaurant, looks around, and then comes up to me and asks: 'Is this table free?' So then I say. . . [bleep]
   Don't speak so loudly.

Exercise 6

Listen and underline the words which carry the main stress in the sentences. Listen to the example first.

T1: Did you say five o'clock?

T2: No, I said six o'clock.

Now underline the words or syllables which carry the main stress.
1 Did you say five o'clock?
   No, I said six o'clock.
2 Did you say Wednesday?
   No, I said Thursday.
3 Is John coming?
   No, not John. Martha.
4 Are we having the party in Tom's house?
   No, we're having it in your house.
5 Hi! How are you?
   I'm fine. How are you?
6 Don't put it there. Put it here.

Vowel sounds
/ʊ/ book   /u:/ boot

Exercise 7

Listen and tick the sound you hear.
1 look   2 June   3 who   4 could   5 noon
6 rude   7 foot   8 cook

Exercise 8

Repeat the phrases.
I'm cooking some food. [bleep]
Could you come at noon? [bleep]
It's a very good book. [bleep]
Could you put your boots here? [bleep]

Consonant sound
/b/ bet   /v/ vet   /w/ wet

Exercise 9

Listen and tick which sound you hear.
1 bed   2 very   3 wet   4 vote   5 boat   6 but   7 want
8 win   9 be   10 week

Exercise 10

Now listen and repeat the phrases.
It's better and better. [bleep]
It's wetter and wetter. [bleep]
He went back to bed. [bleep]
It was very wet and windy. [bleep]
The weather was very bad. [bleep]
I'm playing volleyball tomorrow. [bleep]

Workbook key

Unit 1

1 2 What's her name ?
Her name's Laura.
3 What's her name?
Her name's Chris.
4 What's his name?
His name's Jorge.
5 What's her name?
Her name's Sarah.

2 2 What's her sister's name?
3 What's his mother's name?
4 What's her brother's name?
5 What's your friend's name?

3 I – my
you – your
he – his
she – her
it – its

4 2 He is my brother.
3 She is my sister.
4 It is your ticket.
5 What is your book called?

Unit 2

1 2 Thursday   4 on Saturday
3 George's   5 birthday on Sunday

2 2 I'm fine   5 Thanks
3 this is   6 Goodbye
4 How do you do   7 on Monday

3 2 On Wednesday morning he meets Juliet
Jackson and her father.
3 It is Juliet's birthday on Sunday.

4 Monday   morning   yesterday
Tuesday   afternoon   today
Wednesday   evening   tomorrow
Thursday   night
Friday
Saturday
Sunday

Unit 3

1 3 Yes, it is.   5 Yes, it is.
4 No, it isn't.   6 No, it isn't.

2 2 It's Turkish.   5 It's Greek.
3 It's Italian.   6 It's Russian.
4 It's Chinese.

3

-an	-ian	-ish	-ese
American	Russian	Swedish	Portuguese
German	Italian	Spanish	Japanese
	Argentinian	British	Chinese
		Turkish	

4 DAVID: My name's David Walker.
YOU: Are you American?
DAVID: No, I'm not.
YOU: Where are you from?
DAVID: I'm from Toronto.
YOU: Where's Toronto?
DAVID: It's in Canada.
YOU: Oh, you're Canadian!

5 His name's *David Walker*. He's *Canadian*.
He's from *Toronto* in *Canada*. He speaks
English and *French*.

Example paragraph
Her name's Ann. She's Welsh. She's from
Cardiff in Wales. She speaks English and
Welsh.

Unit 4

1 4 What are those in English?
They're pens.
5 What's that in English?
It's a chair.
6 What's that in English
It's an envelope.
7 What are those in English?
They're books.

2 3 Where's the umbrella?
It's on the chair.
4 Where are the pens?
They're in the mug.
5 Where are the books?
They're on the chair.
6 Where's the envelope?
It's on the table.

3 3 The apples and the oranges are in the bowl.
4 The Italian flag is red, white and green.
5 The dictionary and the notebook are
Laura's.
6 John, Karen and Michael are from Leeds.

4

Colours	Furniture	Fruit
blue	chair	apples
green	desk	oranges
white	drawer	
yellow	lamp	

5 3 It's red.   5 They're pink.
4 It's yellow.   6 They're black.

Unit 5

1 2 How old are you?
   3 Where are you from?
   4 Are you married?
   5 What's your telephone number?

2 Example paragraph
Hannelore Beck is a Danish teacher from Copenhagen. She is thirty-one years old. She is divorced. Her address in Britain is: c/o Barnes, 34 Clevedon Road, Richmond, TW1 2FX, England.

3 Mrs H. Beck,
   c/o Barnes,
   34, Clevedon Road,
   Richmond,
   TW1 2FX
   England

4
2	two	13	thirteen
3	three	30	thirty
4	four	58	fifty eight
10	ten	60	sixty
11	eleven	75	seventy-five

Listening and speechwork 1–5

1 Address: 25, Hull Road, York, YO1 5JS
Telephone: 282-1005

2 F D

3 2 Sunday 3 thirty 4 grey 5 339

7 2 father 3 aunt 4 uncle 5 cousin

8 1 <u>y</u>esterday 2 t<u>o</u>morrow 3 <u>mo</u>rning
   4 after<u>noo</u>n 5 <u>I</u>taly 6 <u>I</u>tali<u>a</u>n 7 Ja<u>pan</u>
   8 Japa<u>ne</u>se

9 2 /ɪ/ 3 /iː/ 4 /iː/ 5 /ɪ/ 6 /ɪ/

Unit 6

1 3 Kate can but Richard can't
   4 Yes, they can.
   5 Richard can but Kate can't
   6 Yes, they can.

2 Open exercise

Unit 7

1 *See Workbook page 12.*

2 2 Mr and Mrs Singh at number 3 have got three children.

   3 Mr and Mrs Woodhead at number 5 have got two children.
   4 Mr and Mrs Kildare at number 7 haven't got any children.

3 3 She's got two. 5 They've got two.
   4 He's got one. 6 They haven't got any.

4 3 Norman has got a son and a daughter.
   4 Jenny has got a brother called Mark.
   5 Surinder is Shadi's wife.
   6 Who is Gina's husband?

5
Female	Male	Male and female
grandmother	grandfather	grandparent
wife	husband	–
mother	father	parent
daughter	son	child
sister	brother	–
aunt	uncle	–
niece	nephew	–
–	–	cousin
		baby

6
Singular	Plural
wife	wives
uncle	uncles
baby	babies
cousin	cousins
aunt	aunts
child	children

Unit 8

1 2 Where do you live?
   3 What does your girlfriend do?
   4 Where does she live?
   5 Where do your parents live?

2 2 Yes, I do. 4 Yes, they do.
   3 No, he doesn't. 5 Yes, she does.

3 2 at/for/with 4 for
   3 on .... in 5 at ... with

4 2 He's Argentinian.
   3 (He plays for) Sheffield United.
   4 She's a teacher.
   5 (They live) near Buenos Aires.
   6 He's a farmer.

5 Example paragraph
Dolena Suarez is a nurse. She is Portuguese but she works in a hospital in Birmingham in England. She is married and lives in Birmingham with her husband, Jose-Luis. Her husband is a waiter in a hotel. Her family live near Oporto. Her father sells newspapers and magazines and her mother is a housewife.

Unit 9

1 CLARE: No, not very much.
ANDY: Really? Why not?
CLARE: I don't like parties.
ANDY: Why don't you like them?
CLARE: I don't drink, I can't dance and I don't like talking to strangers.
ANDY: Oh! Sorry! Goodbye!

2 **Example conversation**
2 My name's/I'm [OPEN]. Where are you from?
3 I'm from [OPEN]. Where do you live?
4 I'm from/I live in [OPEN]. What do you do?
5 I'm a [OPEN]. Do you like the music?
6 [OPEN]. I like [OPEN].
7 Do you like dancing?
8 No, not very much. I can't dance.
9 Oh! Sorry! I must go. Goodbye.
10 Goodbye.

3 4 No, she doesn't like it at all.
5 Yes, they like it very much.
6 No, she doesn't. (She thinks they're boring.)
7 Yes, they do.

4
Ostermalmsgatan-68A,
11145 Stockholm,
Sweden
(*Today's date*)

Dear Mr and Mrs Cross,
I am a twenty-year-old male student from Sweden. I'm studying English and French. I like travelling and I am interested in music, literature, keep fit and politics.

I can do most household jobs. I can cook and I like gardening. I can drive a car very well and I enjoy cycling. I can swim quite well and I like walking very much. I love children. Have you got many children?

Last summer I was an 'au pair' for Mrs J. Cooper at 42, Old Street, Cambridge. Please write to her. She can tell you all about me.
Yours sincerely,
Mats Olsson

Unit 10

1 3 It's on the north-west coast of the island.
4 It's in the east of the island.
5 It's in the south of the island.
6 It's on the south-west coast of the island.

2 2 The 3 the 4 The ... the ... the ... the
5 a 6 a ... the

3 2 Where is it/St Lucia?
3 Where exactly are the Windward Islands?
4 What's St Lucia like?
5 What's it/St Lucia famous for?
6 What language do people/St Lucians speak?

4 2 f 3 e 4 a 5 d 6 c

5 2 Munich is a big industrial city in the south of Germany.
It is famous for its football team.
3 Rio de Janeiro is a big tourist port on the east coast of Brazil. It is famous for its beaches and for Sugarloaf Mountain.
4 Cambridge is a beautiful old city in the east of England. It is famous for its university.
5 San Francisco is a beautiful and interesting city on the west coast of the USA. It is famous for its bridge and cable cars.

Listening and speechwork 6–10

Name	Job	Children	Swim	Tennis	Opinion
Ben Ross	Teacher	X	✓	✓	✓
Betty Jones	(Opera) singer	✓	✓	X	X
Mary Bordas	Student	X	✓	✓	✓

5 2 housewife 3 farmer 4 teacher
5 singer 6 student

7 2 /ɑ:/ 3 /æ/ 4 /ɑ:/ 5 /æ/ 6 /ɑ:/

Unit 11

1 2 It's half past six/six thirty in the evening.
3 It's eleven o'clock in the morning.
4 It's quarter past three/three fifteen in the afternoon.
5 It's quarter to eight/seven forty-five in the morning.

2 2 do 3 do 4 does 5 do

3 2 at ... at 3 to ... in 4 on 5 at 6 to

4 2 On Mondays and Wednesdays.
3 'Countdown'.
4 At eleven o'clock.
5 A comedy.

5 **Example note**
(*Partner's name*)
Please record 'Time to travel'.
It starts at 8.30 p.m. and finishes at 9 p.m.
Thanks, (*Your name*)

Unit 12

1 8 a.m. – get up 3 p.m. – play tennis
9.30 a.m. – arrive at club 7.30 p.m. – go home
12 p.m. – lunch 10 p.m. – go to bed

2 2 She starts to play tennis at half past nine/
nine thirty.
3 She has lunch at twelve o'clock/from twelve
(o'clock) to two (o'clock).
4 She does her keep-fit exercises at 6 o'clock/
from six o'clock to half past seven.
5 She goes home at half past seven/seven
thirty.

3 2 do you arrive
3 do you do
4 's your coach's name?
5 do you have lunch?
6 do you do
7 do you go home?

4 Open exercise

5 2 and 3 but 4 and 5 but

Unit 13

1 2 half an hour 4 forty minutes
3 a quarter of an hour 5 three quarters of an
hour

2 2 Jenny is a secretary. She goes to work by
train. It takes her an hour.
3 William is a teacher. He goes to work by
bicycle. It takes him twenty minutes.
4 Helen is a solicitor. She goes to work by car.
It takes her half an hour.
5 Harry is an accountant. He goes to work by
taxi. It takes him twenty minutes.

3 2 bus 3 takes 4 walk 5 river 6 boat

4 2 How far is it?
3 How do you get
4 How long does it take?
5 How do you get
6 How long does the journey/it take altogether?

Unit 14

1 2 Are there any pictures on the walls?
No, there aren't.
3 Is there a bag on the wardrobe?
Yes, there is.
4 Are there any books on the desk?
Yes, there are.
5 Is there a lamp on the desk?
No, there isn't.

2 2 No, she doesn't. 5 No, there isn't.
3 No, it isn't. 6 No, there aren't.
4 Yes, it is.

3 Example letter
Dear Ruth,
I like the college hostel very much. It's very
near the college and it's very modern. My
room is very big. There's an armchair and
there are some pictures on the walls. There's a
bed, a wardrobe, a table and a chair and
there's a bookcase for my books.
I like the college, the students and the work!
See you in December.
Love,
Jenny

Unit 15

1 2 reading 4 opening ... doing 5 'm helping

2

+ *ing*	- *e* + *ing*	Double consonant + *ing*
ending	driving	running
watching	cycling	swimming
going	using	stopping
reading	closing	putting
finishing	writing	
learning	leaving	
doing	having	
walking	arriving	
starting		
cleaning		
listening		
skiing		
playing		

3 Example letter
This is a photo of my family camping in
France. My father is making dinner.
My grandfather is reading the/a paper. My
mother and sister are cleaning the car and my
brother is playing with the dog.

4 **Across** 1 carpet 4 eat 6 reading
8 do 9 E.M. 11 a.m. 13 roof 16 at
17 mirror
Down 2 Road 3 It 5 age 7 door
10 My 11 Are 12 to 14 our 15 far

Listening and speechwork 11–15

1 2 b 3 c 4 b 5 a 6 c

2 B

6 Stressed words: 2 How far 3 How long
4 How old 5 doing 6 going

8 2 1 3 1 4 2 5 3 6 2

Unit 16

1 2 I'd like the green ones, please.
3 I'd like a large one, please.
4 I'd like a Japanese one, please.
5 I'd like the Swiss one, please.

2 2 Large 3 How much is 3 Can I

3 b g d f a e h c

Unit 17

1 2 Have they got any oranges?
No, they haven't.
3 Have they got any eggs?
Yes, they have.
4 Have they got any bread?
No, they haven't.
5 Have they got any coffee?
No, they haven't.

2 2 They've got some eggs but they haven't got any cheese.
3 They've got some lager but they haven't got any wine.
4 They've got some salt but they haven't got any sugar.
5 They've got some biscuits but they haven't got any bread.
6 They've got some tea but they haven't got any coffee.

3 **Across** 1 drink 5 vegetables 8 Cheese
9 Oil 10 Bread
Down 2 kitchen 3 Milk 4 Fish
6 pepper 7 Tea 8 Chips

Unit 18

1 2 It's (in Davygate,) in York.
3 It's fifty metres.
4 There are fifty.
5 Yes, they have.
6 Yes, there is.
7 It's behind the hotel.
8 No, there isn't.

2 How far
Is there a car park near the hotel?
there's one

3 2 on the right 3 next to 4 between
5 behind 6 in front of 7 under

Unit 19

1 2 sunny 3 cloudy 4 snowing 5 windy
6 foggy 7 hot 8 cold

2 2 December 3 March 4 April 5 August
6 April

3 Open exercise

Unit 20

1 2 got up 3 went 4 was 5 didn't arrive
6 went 7 arrived 8 walked 9 weren't
10 had 11 wasn't 12 started 13 went
14 were 15 didn't see 16 had 17 went
18 was 19 got 20 didn't enjoy

2 2 No, they weren't.   5 Yes, they were.
3 No, it wasn't.   6 No, he didn't.
4 Yes, it did.

3 2 What time did she go to the airport?
3 What time did she check in?
4 What time did the plane leave (London)?
5 What time did the plane/it/she arrive (in Budapest)?
6 What time did she have lunch?
7 What time did she go to a/the Museum?

4 **Example paragraph**
Karen got up at 6.30 a.m. and went to the airport at 8 a.m. She checked in at 8.30 a.m. and the plane left at 10 a.m. She arrived in Budapest at 1.35 p.m. and had lunch at 2.30 p.m. She went to a museum at 4 p.m.

Listening and speechwork 16–20

1 2 No, they want to find a café.
3 No, they find one opposite the newsagent's.
4 No, they have coffee and sandwiches.
5 No, she went to Spain.
6 No, she sunbathed everyday.

2 2 large coffees: 70p each
2 sandwiches (cheese and tomato and ham):
£1.25 each

8 2 2 3 2 4 1 5 1 6 2

9 2 /ɒ/   3 /əʊ/   4 /ɒ/   5 /əʊ/   6 /əʊ/

11 2 right 3 long 4 road 5 low 6 late

Unit 21

1 3 Whose is the sewing machine?
It's Mrs Gibson's.
4 Whose is the computer?
It's Adam's.
5 Whose is the watch?
It's Michael's.
6 Whose are the cats?
They're Mr and Mrs Gibson's.

2 3 The atlas is mine.
4 The compact discs are hers.
5 The razor is his.
6 The dogs are ours.
7 The piano is yours.
8 The TV set is theirs.

3 2 It's a T-shirt with a black cat on it.
3 It's a sports bag with some tennis balls in it.
4 It's an address book with gold letters on it.
5 It's a handbag with some car keys in it.

Unit 22

1 Top: blouse, cardigan, jacket, vest, shirt, sweater
Bottom: stockings, jeans, shorts, skirt, trousers
Top and bottom: coat, suit
Feet: socks, trainers, boots

2 2 Alison is wearing a (black) suit, a (white) blouse and a coat
3 George is wearing a spotted shirt, a sweater and trousers.
4 Jeff and Lisa are wearing (sandals,) striped T-shirts and shorts.

Unit 23

1 2 Where are you going to go?
3 How are you going to get there?
4 Where are you going to stay?
5 How long are you going to stay?
6 Who are you going to go with?

2 2 A: What are we going to eat?
B: What about having a Chinese meal?
A: No, not a Chinese meal. Let's have fish and chips instead.
B: O.K. That's a good idea.
3 A: What are we going to give Laura for her birthday?
B: What about giving her a book about York Minster?
A: No, not a book about York Minster. Let's give her a book about the Brontës instead.
B: O.K. That's a good idea.

Unit 24

1 2 beard 3 big 4 curly 5 slim

2 2 Is she tall?
3 What colour are her eyes?
4 What colour hair has she got?
5 Is it long?
6 Is she slim?

3 slim   wavy   small moustache and glasses

4 Sally is quite short and she's got long, brown hair and glasses.
Ted is big and tall and he's got short, dark hair and a thin moustache.
Andrew is tall and he's got curly, red hair and a beard.

Unit 25

1 2 Did Robert buy a CD album?
No, he didn't. He bought a video cassette/ video tape.
3 Did you and your friends play tennis?
No, we didn't. We played football.
4 Did you wear a suit?
No, I didn't. I wore jeans and a sweater.
5 Did Mr and Mrs Abbott watch a quiz show?
No, they didn't. They watched the news.

2 2 drove 3 did 4 took 5 was 6 decided
7 changed 8 left 9 spent 10 got
11 could 12 had 13 bought 14 told
15 found 16 were 17 said 18 liked

3 2 I finished breakfast and then I read the paper. After that I went back to bed.
3 I wrote some notes and then I made a plan. After that I wrote the essay.
4 I went to the bank and then I met some friends. After that I went home to lunch.

4 2 (It cost) £10.
3 (He) telephoned immediately.
4 (It was) beautiful – large shiny and silver.
5 The woman's husband's./Her husband's.
6 He left her/his wife.
7 He needed money.
8 (He asked her) to sell the car/the Jaguar.

Listening and speechwork 21–25

1 Sally red dress – tall – dark hair
Angus grey suit – quite short – red hair
Sandra black trousers + black jacket – medium height – short, blonde hair

6 1 1 2 2 3 2 4 1 5 2 6 1

7 2 same   3 same   4 different   5 same
6 different

9 2 /tʃ/   3 /ʃ/   4 /ʃ/   5 /ʃ/   6 /tʃ/

Unit 26

1 2 Would you like to play tennis on Tuesday afternoon?
I'm sorry, I can't. I'm going to the dentist.
What about Wednesday?
Yes, I'd love to.
3 Would you like to have dinner on Thursday evening?
I'm sorry, I can't. I'm babysitting at the Henleys'.
What about Friday?
Yes, I'd love to.
4 Would you like to spend the day with us on Saturday?
I'm sorry. I can't. I'm going to Stratford.
What about Sunday?
Yes, I'd love to.

2 Open exercise

Unit 27

1 2 I'm afraid   6 call me back
3 Can you   7 the car phone
4 Who's speaking?   8 Thanks.
5 his wife

2 2 Can I leave a message (, please)?
3 Can you ask her to meet me after work tomorrow?
4 Thanks. Goodbye.

3 Hello. This is a message for Ann and Julian. It's Sandy here. I'd like to invite you both to lunch on Sunday 23rd June. Can you call me back? My number is 574 9985. Thanks. Bye!

Unit 28

1 2 longer   longest   long
3 big   bigger   biggest
4 colder   coldest   cold
5 hottest   hotter   hot

2 2 The Mississippi is longer than the Yangtze but the Nile is the longest.
3 Canada is bigger than China but the USSR is the biggest.
4 Copenhagen is colder than Berlin but Moscow is the coldest.
5 Istanbul is hotter than Athens but Cairo is the hottest.

3 dirtier   lower   shorter
wetter   colder   fatter
earlier   longer   older
worse

4 1 (It consists of) about 3,000 (islands).
2 (It's) 54,680 km (long).
3 (It's) 273,400 km (long).
4 Fourteen (nations are larger).

Unit 29

1 2 A bunch of flowers is more expensive than a bunch of grapes.
3 A packet of biscuits is less expensive than a box of chocolates.
4 A music cassette is more expensive than a story cassette.
5 A magazine is less expensive than a book.

2 **Example answers**
2 most interesting   5 most difficult
3 most dangerous   6 most polluted
4 most fashionable

3 PARIS
I think Paris is one of the most beautiful cities in the world. I think it is the best city for a holiday. Perhaps the French are not so friendly but I think they are friendlier than the English. The best time to visit Paris is in the spring. I go there every year but it is harder now to find a cheap hotel.

Unit 30

1 2 am living   3 working   4 am enjoying
5 is   6 go out   7 am   8 started
9 is getting   10 don't know

2

Marian	**Mathieu**	**Sandra**
Scotland	France	Wales
Aberdeen	London	York
Russian	German	French
at home	at work	at evening classes

3 2 Mathieu is from France. At the moment he is working in London. He wants to work in Austria and is learning German at work.
3 Sandra is from Wales. At the moment she is working in York. She wants to work in France and is learning French at evening classes.

4 Julio is a journalist from Mexico City. At the moment he is working for the American magazine *Newsweek* in New York. He is planning to visit/go to/work in Europe and is learning English and French at a private language school in New York.

Listening and speechwork 26–30

1 **Date:** July 30th
Tickets: £15   £10   £8
Credit cards: 01-931-3311

5 2 (*Student's name*)
3 Can I leave/you take
4 Can you tell him that Sue Winters is now arriving on Monday 23rd, not Sunday 22nd.
5 Yes, Sue Winters is now arriving on Monday 23rd, not Sunday 22nd.
6 Thanks very much.
7 Goodbye.

6 1 Older than ...   2 cheaper and better.
3 Britain and ...   4 The ... are
5 ... parents are at ...
6 An ... and a banana.

7 2 2   3 1   4 1   5 1   6 2

Unit 31

1 2 Would you like something to eat?
Yes, please. I think I'll have a sandwich.
3 Would you like something to drink?
Yes, please. I think I'll have a beer.
4 Would you like something to eat?
Yes, please. I think I'll have a hamburger.
5 Would you like something to drink?
Yes, please. I think I'll have a cup of/pot of tea.

2 would you   I'd   would you like   think I'll

3 2 I'd   3 I'll   4 I'd   5 I'll   6 I'll

4 2 potatoes   3 chicken   4 mushrooms
5 cheese   6 prawns

Unit 32

1

Past	Past participle
passed	passed
happened	happened
looked	looked
won	won
found	found
lost	lost
saw	seen
hurt	hurt

2 2 Have you looked   4 haven't looked
3 've looked   5 've just dropped

3 2 passed   3 win   4 broke   5 arriving
6 received

4 2 water   3 house   4 factory

Unit 33

1 2 Have you ever played Monopoly?
3 Have you ever eaten paella?
4 Have you ever slept in a sleeping bag?
5 Have you ever seen the Statue of Liberty?
6 Have you ever been to New Zealand?

2 2 a   3 c   4 b   5 c

3 Joe and Cindy have just had a baby.
Jack Hayward has just got a new job.
Sarah Jones has gone to Sweden and Jeremy Saunders has just come back from Australia.

Unit 34

1 2 his   3 her   4 your   5 its

2 1 hand   2 head   3 ankle   4 knee   5 eye
6 ear   7 arm   8 mouth   9 finger
10 thumb   11 toe   12 back/body   13 nose
14 leg   15 wrist

3 2 it is.   7 matter?
3 speaking?   8 sore throat
4 It's   9 I've got
5 Would you like   10 what
6 don't feel

4 **Example dialogue**
JOHN: Hello. Is that Richard?
RICHARD: Yes, it is. Who's speaking?
JOHN: It's John here. Would you like to play tennis tomorrow morning?
RICHARD: I'm afraid I can't. I don't feel very well
JOHN: Oh, what's the matter?
RICHARD: I've got a temperature and I'm in bed.
JOHN: Oh, what a nuisance! I hope you're better soon.

5 2 B   3 A   4 E   5 C

Unit 35

1 2 I'm afraid I've got to go to the dentist.
3 I'm afraid I've got to meet my mother for lunch.
4 I'm afraid I've got to see the/my bank manager at 2.30 p.m.
5 I'm afraid I've got to go to work at 3 p.m.

2 2 She's got to go to the post office to collect a parcel.
   3 You've got to go to the passport office to get a visa.
   4 He's got to go to the shoe shop to return some shoes.
   5 We've got to go to the travel agent's to book some tickets to Madrid.

3 C F B A D E

Listening and speechwork 31–35

1 2 a 3 c 4 b 5 a 6 c

7 1 I <u>want</u> to <u>go</u> to <u>bed</u>.
   2 She's <u>got</u> to <u>go</u> to <u>school</u>.
   3 He <u>came</u> to <u>buy</u> the <u>fridge</u>.
   4 He's <u>got</u> to <u>leave</u> at <u>nine</u>.
   5 She's <u>got</u> a <u>nasty</u> <u>cold</u>.
   6 I'd <u>like</u> some <u>bread</u> and <u>cheese</u>.
   7 I've <u>bought</u> a <u>loaf</u> of <u>bread</u>.

8 2 hair 3 there 4 are 6 learning 7 four
   8 father

Unit 36

1 2 It's too small. Have you got it in a larger size?
   3 Can I try this on?
   4 Do you take credit cards?
   5 I think I'll leave it.

2 2 I'm afraid it's too long. Have you got a shorter one?
   3 I'm afraid it's too big. Have you got a smaller one?
   4 I'm afraid it's too expensive. Have you got a cheaper one?
   5 I'm afraid it's too short. Have you got a longer one?

3 **Across** 1 Swiss   5 smaller   6 we   7 tea
   8 cards   10 too   11 one   12 large
   13 red
   Down 1 size   2 some   3 colour   4 try
   5 sweater   7 took   8 cold   9 dog

Unit 37

1 2 Adv   3 Adv   4 Adj   5 Adj   6 Adv   7 Adv

2 quietly   slowly   happily
   well   politely   nervously
   early

3 2 Please don't use the telephone so often.
   3 Please don't eat your food so quickly.
   4 Please don't drive your motorbike so fast.
   5 Please don't speak to your sister so rudely.
   6 Please don't slam the front door so noisily.

Unit 38

1 2 You must have a shower before you swim.
   3 You mustn't eat or drink in the pool area.
   4 You mustn't shout or scream.
   5 You mustn't run.
   6 You must look after small children.

2 2 can ... must   3 can ... can't   4 can't
   5 mustn't

3 2 can 3 can't 4 can 5 can't 6 can

Unit 39

1 **Positive:** happy, cheerful, pleased, excited
   Negative: frightened, depressed, lonely, worried, bored, nervous, upset

2 2 happy/cheerful/pleased/excited
   3 worried/upset/nervous
   4 frightened/upset
   5 bored/depressed
   6 sad/depressed/upset

3 **Example sentences**
   2 When I think about our trip to the USA, I feel excited.
   3 When I travel by plane, I feel nervous.
   4 When I lose something valuable, I feel upset.
   5 When I am away from home for a long time, I feel homesick.
   6 When I watch a horror film late at night, I feel frightened.

4 2 My purse, three cheque books, my toothbrush and a banana.
   3 My husband, Geoff, and my daughter, Gracie.
   4 Hitting somebody in my car.
   5 I get upset when things go wrong in the house.
   6 I don't hate anyone.
   7 At the Rochdale Youth Theatre Workshop, in the summer of 1968.
   8 I feel quite pleased with life, actually.

Unit 40

1 2 ago 3 in 4 for 5 for 6 ago 7 on
8 ago 9 on 10 for

2 2 (She went) in 1970.
3 She worked as a language teacher.
4 For five years.
5 (She learned) in 1975.
6 (She sailed around the world) in 1977.
7 (She was) twenty-eight.
8 (It took) just under 272 days.
9 She was the first woman to sail around the world.

3 Cole Porter
Cole Porter was born in Indiana, USA, in 1891. When he was young, his mother taught him to play the piano and the violin. After leaving high school, he studied law at Harvard University and music at Yale, where he wrote football songs. In 1917 he went to Europe and joined the French Foreign Legion. After the war he got married and lived in Paris and Venice. He worked very hard for ten years writing songs but he was not successful. Then he wrote a song called 'Let's Do It'. It was a big hit and he became one of the greatest song writers of all time. Cole Porter died in 1964 but his songs will live for ever.

4 2 After finishing his studies, he went to Europe.
3 After leaving the Foreign Legion, he got married.
4 After living for some time in Paris and Venice, he returned to the USA.
5 After writing songs for ten years, he was still unsuccessful.
6 After writing *Let's Do It*, he became very famous.

Listening and speechwork 36–40

1 2 excited 3 depressed 4 happy 5 angry

2 Age: 26 Started paragliding: 18 months ago
First job: A model (from 1983 to 1987)
First paragliding lesson: On her 25th birthday.

6 1 <u>Did</u> you say <u>five</u> o'clock?
<u>No</u>, I said <u>six</u> o'clock.
2 <u>Did</u> you say <u>Wednes</u>day?
<u>No</u>, I said <u>Thurs</u>day.
3 Is <u>John</u> coming ?
<u>No</u>, not <u>John</u>, <u>Martha</u>.
4 Are we having the party in <u>Tom's</u> house.
No, we're having it in <u>your</u> house.

5 <u>Hi</u>! How are <u>you</u>?
I'm <u>fine</u>. How are <u>you</u>?
6 <u>Don't</u> put it <u>there</u>. Put it <u>here</u>.

7 2 /uː/ 3 /uː/ 4 /ʊ/ 5 /uː/ 6 /uː/ 7 /ʊ/
8 /ʊ/

9 2 /v/ 3 /w/ 4 /v/ 5 /b/ 6 /b/ 7 /w/
8 /w/ 9 /b/ 10 /w/

Finale

1 1 b 2 c 3 b 4 c 5 a

2 2 swimming 7 to see
3 to see 8 to come
4 to learn 9 inviting
5 shopping 10 to answer
6 to do

Blueprint Quiz
1 George
2 Saturday and Sunday
3 Portuguese
4 22, York Road
5 Dear Mr Birch
6 Lisbon
7 the Atlantic Ocean
8 9.30 a.m.
9 James Dean
10 Charlotte, Emily and Anne
11 Florida
12 sunny
13 striped or checked
14 He's tall and dark.
15 1st May
16 better – best
17 fish and chips
18 Australia/the Pacific Ocean
19 toes
20 No (you can't)